SOME PRESIDENTIAL INTERPRETATIONS
OF THE PRESIDENCY

SOME
PRESIDENTIAL INTERPRETATIONS
OF THE PRESIDENCY

BY NORMAN J. SMALL

DA CAPO PRESS · NEW YORK · 1970

99208

A Da Capo Press Reprint Edition

This Da Capo Press edition of *Some Presidential Interpretations of the Presidency* is an unabridged republication of the first edition published in Baltimore in 1932 as Series L, Number 2 in the *Johns Hopkins University Studies in Historical and Political Science.*

Library of Congress Catalog Card Number 71-87353

SBN 306-71663-1

Published by Da Capo Press
A Division of Plenum Publishing Corporation
227 West 17th Street
New York, N.Y. 10011

Manufactured in the United States of America

SOME PRESIDENTIAL INTERPRETATIONS
OF THE PRESIDENCY

SOME PRESIDENTIAL INTERPRETATIONS OF THE PRESIDENCY

BY

NORMAN J. SMALL

A DISSERTATION

Submitted to the Board of University Studies of the Johns
Hopkins University in Conformity with the Requirements
for the Degree of Doctor of Philosophy

1930

BALTIMORE
1932

COMPOSED AND PRINTED IN THE U. S. A. BY
THE J. H. FURST CO., BALTIMORE, MARYLAND

PREFACE

The writer wishes to acknowledge his indebtedness to the following members of the faculty of The Johns Hopkins University, under whose guidance this work was completed. To Dr. James Hart, at whose suggestion this work was begun, and to Dr. W. W. Willoughby, the writer is especially grateful, both for their helpful instruction and generous supervision. For profitable suggestions and information pertaining to American History, to which this work is relevant, the writer is indebted to the late Dr. John H. Latané.

N. J. S.

June, 1930.

CONTENTS

INTRODUCTION

A survey of the history of the Presidency reveals the notable fact that, while the development of the office ot the Chief Executive has been cumulative, its growth has, in its larger aspects, been intermittent, rather than gradual. Though the American Chief Magistracy is recognized today as one of the most powerful executive offices in the world, its present position of distinction can be attributed to advancements completed at intervals the total duration of which comprises less than one-third of the century and half of its existence. Hence, by disregarding altogether the lengthier periods in the life of the Presidency, during which it was concerned chiefly in fortifying its possession of advantages previously acquired, and by confining the present inquiry to these less frequent intervals in which appreciable expansions of executive authority were recorded, it will be possible to present an adequate survey of the principal stages in the development of the office.

To state that the advancement of the Chief Magistracy has been effected at brief intervals in its existence is merely to acknowledge the accomplishments of the Executives who presided during such intervals; for the development of that office has been determined more by the calibre of its incumbents than by attending circumstance. Since a survey of the important stages in the growth of the Presidency roughly coincides with a discussion of the contributions of the foremost occupants of that office, the writer will accordingly attempt to study the Presidency, not by offering a history of these critical stages, but by presenting the opinions of the foremost prominent Executives as to what the limits of the authority of their office ought to be, and by indicating, through a review of their official activities, the manner in which they undertook to apply their theories in practice.

Manifestly, the accuracy of this method will in a large

measure depend upon the correctness of the writer's choice of our most prominent Chief Magistrates. Although, as has been already intimated, this selection has in general been determined by the significance of their contributions to their office, the inclusion of at least one of the Executives chosen has also been influenced by the unique circumstances attending his Administration. Whether or not Washington was endowed with capacities equal to those possessed by his successors, his selection was unavoidable; for, as the first incumbent of the newly created Chief Magistracy, he presented the first forecast of what that office in practice was to be.

Though a similar importance might be attached to Jefferson's affiliation with the " founding fathers," the significance of his contribution to the Presidency will of itself warrant his inclusion. That he attained everlasting distinction as the exponent of the principles of strict construction and States' rights, two doctrines which permeated the political thought of the Nation for half a century, cannot be denied; but, since the acceptance of these theories would have militated against the expansion of the Federal Government, and, incidentally, of the Presidency, his sponsorship of them cannot be regarded as having been especially conducive to the growth of his office. One the other hand, in establishing and assuming control of the destinies of what was to be a permanent political party, Jefferson not only contributed to the Chief Magistracy the valuable asset of political leadership, but opened the way for its democratization; and it is upon the enduring merits of that achievement that his selection is founded.

Roosevelt and Wilson were also responsible for an increase in the political authority of the Presidency. Through their frank avowal of an intention to assume an ascendancy in the field of legislation, an endeavor which involved a leadership of public opinion, party, and Congress, and their success in procuring for the people the reforms which they desired, these two Executives secured for the Chief Magistracy an undisputable right to be denominated the only federal office nationally representative of the people as a whole. Indeed, their Administrations seem to permit the forecast that the subsequent development of the political aspects of the Presidency will exceed in importance the continued growth of its legal authority.

However, to discover those incumbents of the Chief Magistracy who have contributed most of the expansion of its constitutional powers, one must have recourse to a study of the more serious conflicts to which the United States has been a party; for it is under such circumstances that the Executive, as Commander-in-Chief of the Army and Navy, receives the opportunity to exercise the full measure of his authority. In making that statement, the writer does not wish to commit himself on the disputed proposition that crises make men; but it is evident that the exigencies of a war present aspects of the office not normally observable.

While the gravity of the situation created by Secession did not rouse Buchanan to action, it provided the occasion for Lincoln's acquisition of fame. The only President to be presented with an issue of such magnitude, involving as it did the future existence of the Union, he was obliged to determine whether an Executive, in undertaking to preserve that Union, was also bound under such circumstances to a religious observance of its Constitution; and although his answer to the latter question was partially erroneous, his unprecedented exercise of authority has had a permanent influence upon that office. On the other hand, with the advent of the World War, Wilson correctly demonstrated that a vigorous Executive, officiating under less imperious circumstances than those of the Civil War, could, by a perfectly legal procedure, arrogate to himself even greater dictatorial powers than those employed by Lincoln.

That the five Executives chosen, Washington, Jefferson, Lincoln, Roosevelt, and Wilson, are worthy of being termed foremost American Presidents, will probably not be disputed. Accordingly, if any criticism is to be made of the writer's selection, it will be directed, not against the merits of any one of those included, but against the wisdom of omitting other

Chief Magistrates of prominence. To those who may adhere to that view the writer concedes that reasons may be offered to warrant the selection of Jackson, and perhaps Cleveland; but, since they have perhaps not distinguished themselves throughout their respective Administrations as consistently as have the previously designated Executives, he is not disposed thoroughly to review their activities. In recognition, however, of the unquestionable significance of specific precedents established by these two Presidents, the writer will, in the appropriate chapters, consider the conduct of Jackson in the removal of the Bank Deposits, and the action of Cleveland in suppressing the Chicago strike in 1893.

SOME PRESIDENTIAL INTERPRETATIONS
OF THE PRESIDENCY

CHAPTER I

GENERAL THEORIES OF THE OFFICE

WASHINGTON

Whether Washington, like his successors, was in possession of any definite opinions as to the powers of the Presidency at the date of his entry into that office, or whether he formulated any theory as to the Chief Magistracy during his subsequent years in the service cannot be conclusively determined. Certainly the circumstances attending his inauguration would seem to preclude an affirmative answer to the first question; for, since the newly created Federal Government first began to operate in 1789, no one was competent to do more than prophesy what in practice the American Executive was to be. That the innovations introduced into the federal system were not understood even by his more learned colleagues is evidenced by their diverse expressions of opinion at the first assembly of Congress; some being unable to comprehend the Federal Executive except in terms of the English Monarch,[1] and others venturing only to suggest in negative terms the dissimilarity of our Chief Magistrate to any continental rulers.

Nor did Washington consider the moment auspicious for any determined endeavor to remove such doubts, or for the application of any preconceived opinions of his own to the execution of the duties of his office. Being essentially a man of deed and not of contemplation, a man for whom facts and not abstractions had any attraction, he was preoccupied with the problem of putting into successful operation the product of the Philadelphia Convention. To assure the future per-

---

[1] Journal of William Maclay, (1890 ed.) pp. 1-50.

manence of the Federal Union, Washington therefore urged his associates to postpone for future settlement all contentious questions of constitutional interpretation, and to cooperate with him by a rigid observance of the strict letter of the law, in order to avoid any questionable act which might stimulate rather than dispel existing distrust of the new Government. In adopting this position, he was not unmindful, however, of the inevitability of the establishment of significant precedents.   He merely expressed the fear that, in view of the present uncertainty of the public sentiment, any far-reaching decision would be inopportune.[2]

It may be preferable at this point to support these conclusions with quotations:

> In our progress toward political happiness my station is new, and if I may use the expression, I walk on untrodden ground.   There is scarcely an action, the motive of which may not be subject to a double interpretation.   There is scarcely any part of my conduct which may not hereafter be drawn into precedent.   Under such a view of the duties inherent in my arduous office, I could not but feel a diffidence in myself on the one hand, and an anxiety for the community . . .
> It was to be a government of accommodation as well as a government of laws.   Much was to be done by prudence, much by conciliation, much by firmness.[3]
> Yet in a point of such vast magnitude, as that of the preservation of the peace of the Union, particularly in this very early stage of affairs, and at a period so little removed from an exhausting war, the public welfare and safety evidently enjoin a conduct of circumspection, moderation, and forbearance.[4]

Guided by such public spirited motives as well as by unwarranted confidence in the correctness of his understanding of executive power, Washington was destined therefore very clearly to counsel against the danger of a too liberal interpretation of the Constitution.[5]   A second principle, the observ-

---

2 " Precedents are dangerous things."   Quoted by John Marshall, Life of Washington, V, 119.
3 Jared Sparks, Life and Writings of Washington, X, 69.
4 Ibid., p. 193.
5 " The powers of the executive of this country are more definite, and better understood, perhaps, than those of any other country; and my aim has been, and will continue to be, neither to stretch nor relax them in any instance whatever, unless compelled to it by imperious circumstances."   Ibid., p. 422.   For like utterances on the question of necessity, see statements by Jefferson, Lincoln, and Roosevelt.

ance of which engaged his attention, was that of the separation of powers; for while his conduct of his own department suggests an earnest effort to abide by his first admonition, he did find it necessary to defend the powers of his office against supposed aggressions by the popular branch of the Government.[6] In venturing, however, to assume full responsibility for the solution of the foreign difficulties confronting the Nation during his terms in office, he indicated rather emphatically that he was not bound by any impracticable principles of constitutional construction. Whatever errors he may have committed, either through inexperience or through a too zealous conformity to the written word of that instrument, in his conduct of our foreign relations, his decisions have remained permanent precedents.[7]

It was doubtless because of his faith in the completeness of the Constitution that he ranged himself against the introduction of political parties. Very probably construing the silence of the members of the Philadelphia Convention on this question and the absence of any provision in the Constitution concerning their operation as a manifest injunction against the furtherance of a factional spirit, Washington looked with disfavor upon its appearance, particularly at so early a date. Since he believed that the firm establishment of the new Government was a matter on which there could be no patriotic division of opinion, and that it should be the only problem occupying the attention of public officials, he could not escape the conclusion that political parties, even though their development was inevitable, could perform no beneficial service during his Administration.[8]

---

[6] "It is important, likewise, that the habits of thinking in a free country should inspire caution in those intrusted with its administration, to confine themselves within their respective constitutional spheres, avoiding, in the exercise of the powers of one department, to encroach upon another. The spirit of encroachment tends to consolidate the powers of all the departments in one, and thus to create, whatever the form of government, a real despotism." Quoted by James M. Beck, The Political Philosophy of George Washington, in 70th Cong., 2d sess., H. Doc. No. 611, p. 16.

[7] For his activities in the conduct of American foreign affairs, see ch. ii.

[8] "Differences in political opinions are as unavoidable, as, to a cer-

In his own mind, moreover, political parties always remained an evil, though an unavoidable one. Though brought to the realization that their emergence could not be delayed, he never acknowledged their existence to the extent of affiliating himself with any one of them.[9] That, despite this personal dislike, he probably would have, had he served at a later date, consented to membership in a political organization, seems fairly certain; but, in view of the peculiar responsibilities confronting him as the first incumbent of his office, he considered himself above partisan considerations.

Having been chosen, unlike his successors, on a non-partisan basis, presumably by all persons favoring the installation of the new Government, Washington was induced to believe that, whereas he represented the primary interests and aspirations of the people, the political parties fostered only their more material interests and prejudices, and hence served no purpose in common with the Executive. Consequently, when measures deemed by him essential to the national welfare were bitterly attacked by large numbers of citizens arrayed in opposing partisan groups, he refused to recognize their outbursts as expressions of the true public opinion of the Nation. In fact, his observations as to the rapidity with which the populace was aligning itself with political factions, and injecting itself into their violent yet petty disputes,

---

tain point, they may be necessary; but it is exceedingly to be regretted, that subjects cannot be discussed with temper on the one hand, or decisions submitted to without having the motives, which led to them, improperly implicated on the other; and this regret borders on chagrin, when we find that men of abilities, zealous patriots, having the same general objects in view, and the same upright intentions to prosecute them, will not exercise more charity in deciding on the opinions and actions of one another." Jared Sparks, Life of Washington (abridged ed.), II, 273. In his Farewell Address he again issued warnings as to the "baneful" influence of political parties.

[9] "Moreover, that I was no believer in the infallibility of the politics or measures of any man living. In short, that I was no party man myself, and that the first wish of my heart was, if parties did exist, to reconcile them." Marshall, V, 675. His inability to persuade existing factions to desist momentarily from their rivalry in order to assent to the adoption of measures necessary to sustain the new Government did, however, influence him to favor Hamilton's group as a means of securing that result. Jefferson, nevertheless, saw in this association only the "sinister influence" of Hamilton. See ch. v.

tended to diminish his faith in the ability of the people to discern its own good, and to confirm him in his opinion that he must henceforth endeavor to guide, rather than to reflect, opinion. Confident that the public, if uninfluenced by partisan propaganda, would approve his policies, or ultimately, at least, would recognize their merit, he refused to permit their execution to be prevented by immediate evidences of opposition.

Further expressions of his opinions on this subject are to be found in the following statements:

> But the truth is, the people must feel before they will see; consequently they are brought slowly into the measures of public utility. Past experience or the admonition of a few have but little weight. But the evils of this nature work their own cure, though the remedy comes slower than comports with the wishes of those who foresee, or think they foresee the danger.
>
> The real people, occasionally assembled in order to express their sentiments upon political subjects ought never to be confounded with the permanent self-appointed societies usurping the right to control the constituted authorities, and to dictate to the Public Opinion. While the former was entitled to respect, the latter was incompatible with all, and must sink into general disesteem, or finally overturn the established order of things.
>
> Next to a conscientious discharge of my public duties, to carry along with me the approbation of my constituents, would be the highest gratification of which my mind is susceptible. But the latter being secondary, I cannot make the former yield to it, unless some criterion more infallible than partial (if they are not party) meetings can be discovered as the touchstone of public sentiment. If any person on earth could, or the great power above would, erect the standard of infallibility in political opinions, no being that inhabits this terrestrial globe would resort to it with more eagerness than myself, so long as I remain a servant of the public. But as I have hitherto found no better guide than upright intentions and a close investigation, I shall adhere to them while I keep the watch; leaving it to those who will come after me, to explore new ways, if they like or think them better.[10]

Woodrow Wilson at one time stated that the strength or weakness of a President could largely be determined by his independence of, or reliance upon, his Cabinet for the formation of his policies. In Washington's case, however, the fact that he frequently sought the advice of his Cabinet is of less importance than that he ever established a Cabinet at all. While the several proposals for the creation of an advisory

---

[10] Ibid., pp. 79, 635.

council to the Executive, submitted at the Philadelphia Convention, had been abandoned, there remained no obstacle to the extra-legal development of a Cabinet by any one of the methods hitherto announced; and Washington, at the time of his election, was accordingly free to choose whether he would have a Cabinet, and, if so, by what means he would establish it.   As presiding officer at the Convention he was assuredly acquainted with all the plans suggested, and it might easily be expected, therefore, that he would first experiment with those with which he was best acquainted.   Since the Senate, or Upper House, in colonial and State Governments, had served both as a legislative body and as an advisory council to the Governor, and had been suggested for service in the latter capacity in the Federal Government, Washington was disposed to grant first preference to that body. The abrupt refusal of the Senate to consult orally with him as intimately as he desired not only destroyed his hopes of adding this function to its expressly granted powers (of participation in the confirmation of treaties and appointments) but deterred him from ever reentering its confines.[11] Influenced by a similar analogy, to wit, the advisory duties performed by the judiciary in the States, Washington, on occasions, sought the counsel of the Chief Justice, and, prior to his issuance of the neutrality proclamation, had also endeavored to procure the assistance of the entire Supreme Court; but its members declined to assume the irrelevant duty of advising on political questions.[12] Final resort was thereupon had to the heads of the departments; first, merely by requiring their opinions in writing in pursuance of the constitutional provision;[13] second, by dispatching a circular letter pertaining to a single issue to all, and asking for a formal reply from each; and, finally, the meeting of these department secretaries as an informal body.[14]

---

[11] Journal of William Maclay, (1890 ed.) p. 128; below, p. 69.
[12] Mary L. Hinsdale, A History of the President's Cabinet, p. 15. The author of this volume declares that this experiment was also influenced by Hamilton.
[13] Art. 2, Sec. 2.
[14] Hinsdale, pp. 1-16.

Reverting again to the statement attributed to Wilson, one might add in fairness to Washington that the frequency with which he did consult his Cabinet is indicative of no irresolution or lack of courage in the man, but rather of a zealous effort to fulfil the responsibility imposed upon him. Aware of his own inexperience in government, and fearful lest by the commission of a single error he should delay or defeat the immediate progress of the new Nation, he observed the precaution of refraining from the execution of any important decision until he had obtained the advice and opinions of his executive associates. Though inclined to attach greater importance to the views of Hamilton and Jefferson, he read with equal care the replies of each one of his counsellors, and generally elected to abide by the opinions of those which were more nearly in harmony with his own. It was probably his singular position, and not any infirmity of mind, that dissuaded him from adopting the rule attributed to Lincoln, of " one aye, nine nay, the ayes have it "; [15] for, while he never considered himself under any obligation to accede to the views expressed by his Cabinet members, a sense of precaution prevented him from balancing his own judgment against the opinions of many.

JEFFERSON

With the election of Jefferson a more normal point of departure is reached for the purpose of a discussion of the Presidency. The Government having been in operation for twelve years at the date of his assumption of office, presumably all questions pertaining to the establishment of the Union had been settled. Factions opposed to the new order of things had disbanded, and the public had become interested primarily in the benefits to be derived from the program of a presiding administration, or in disputes involving the authority of the central Government to assume control of particular problems. Similarly, officials, having had the opportunity of observing the Government functioning for a decade, acquired a confidence in the exercise of the powers of their office and

---

[15] William H. Taft, Our Chief Magistrate and His Powers, p. 35.

were no longer perturbed by a fear that by a single error of judgment they could seriously threaten the stability of the Union. In short, there remained no consideration to deter a successful candidate, such as Thomas Jefferson, from venturing to utilize the powers of his office in conformity with his preconceived ideas.

Excepting Woodrow Wilson, probably no succeeding Chief Magistrate was endowed with as complete a knowledge of Government or was the exponent of so large a number of theories as to the function of his office or of Government in general. Merely to cite such terms as State Rights and Strict Construction is to suggest the name of Jefferson. As a vigorous advocate of these doctrines during the long campaign preceding his election, he was expected, as well as in good faith obligated, to institute them in practice. But while there is to be found in the records of his Administration ample evidence of an honest intention to fulfil these expectations,[16] his conduct, in general, suggests a complete reversal of position. Thus, notwithstanding his insistence upon strict construction, he ventured to negotiate a treaty for the acquisition of the Louisiana Territory; despite his previous approval of the doctrine of State Rights,[17] he neglected to object to the adoption of legislation providing for domestic improvements; and, in apparent denial of the sanctity of the separation of powers, he exceeded even his predecessors in his leadership of Congress.[18] It is to his credit, however, that he should have had the courage, even at the risk of subjecting himself to the ridicule of his opponents, to alter his policies upon discovery that the theories evolved by him in private were not readily applicable to the unforeseen difficulties which confronted an administration.

Nevertheless, since he was unable to renounce completely his allegiance to the principles which had claimed his attention for more than a decade, no discussion of his general con-

---

[16] See ch. iii.

[17] " My general plan would be to make the states one as to everything connected with foreign nations, and several as to everything purely domestic." Writings (Ford Ed.), IV, 424. (1787).

[18] See ch. v.

ception of the Presidency can be complete which does not include a presentation of the views entertained by Jefferson both before and during his term in office. That this partial retention of his former theories would produce occasional inconsistencies is well illustrated by the utterly contradictory positions assumed by him with reference to the observance of a separation of powers. Thus, whereas he manifested no disinclination to control the passage of legislation in Congress, he denounced as an encroachment the arrogation by the Supreme Court of a power of judicial review. Hence, although the judiciary might construe the Alien and Sedition Laws to be valid, and decree fines and imprisonment for infractions thereof, he, believing the acts to be unconstitutional, could render them a nullity by pardoning all offenders.

You seemed to think that it devolved upon the Judges to decide upon the validity of the Sedition Law. But nothing in the Constitution has given them a right to decide for the executive more than the executive to decide for them. Both Magistrates are equally independent in the sphere of action assigned to them. The Judges, believing the law unconstitutional, had a right to pass a sentence of fine and imprisonment, because the power was placed in their hands by the Constitution. But the executive, believing the law to be unconstitutional, were bound to remit the execution of it, because that power had been confided in them by the Constitution. That instrument meant that its coördinate branches should be checks on each other. But the opinion which gives to the Judges the right to decide what laws are unconstitutional, and what are not, not only for themselves in their own sphere of action, would make the judiciary a despotic branch.[19]

By acting in this manner, Jefferson was virtually sanctioning nullification; for were each department to reserve the right, which he believed it to possess, of determining for itself the validity of every law and the legality of its own conduct, chaos or stagnation would result. In accordance with his construction, the principle of separation of power and checks and balances would operate not as a measure of precaution but of obstruction.[20] But, since he had employed his constitutional power of pardon to effect this nullification, his con-

[19] Writings (Ford Ed.), VIII, 311.
[20] Taft, p. 138.

duct, however reprehensible the motives which induced it, technically retained the aspect of legality.[21]

As opposed to such dangerously impractical conduct, representing the application of an equally unworkable theory of constitutional construction, there is to be considered his successful negotiation of a treaty for the acquisition of Louisiana, a measure which, it is said, involved a broader interpretation of the Constitution than had ever been contemplated by Hamilton.   But, while this precedent is a laudable example of his practical statesmanship,[22] and of his masterly skill as a party leader in mobilizing the support necessary to secure an immediate acceptance of this treaty in the Senate, this event did not, in theory at least, represent his conversion from the principle of strict construction.   It did indicate, however, that he was prepared to acknowledge that the obligation of

---

[21] While it might not be possible in a court of law to question the motives which prompted the exercise of a power clearly possessed, it is obvious, nevertheless, that the employment of the pardoning power for such purposes is an abuse of discretion.   Indeed, when exercised in that manner, that power might be said to resemble the obsolete monarchial prerogative of dispensation or suspension.   Although Jackson and Lincoln also issued statements, in which they affirmed their intention not to be bound by the rulings of the Supreme Court, their position is less difficult to justify than that of Jefferson. Notwithstanding the previous judicial approval of the validity of the older National Bank Acts, Jackson, like Jefferson, was at liberty to employ his fullest discretion in exercising his constitutional power of veto.   But whereas Jefferson was nullifying an existing law, his successor merely negatived a prospective statute.   From Lincoln is to be had a more temperate statement, in which he declared his intention to work for the modification of a judicial decision, in this instance the Dred Scott case, with which he, a political officer, was dissatisfied.

"And while it is obviously possible that such decision may be erroneous in any given case, still the evil effect following it, being limited to that particular case, with the chance that it may be overruled and never become a precedent for other cases, can better be borne than could the evils of a different practice.   At the same time, the candid citizen must confess that if the policy of the Government upon vital questions affecting the whole people is to be irrevocably fixed by decisions of the Supreme Court, the instant they are made in ordinary litigation between parties in personal actions the people will have ceased to be their own rulers, having to that extent practically resigned their government into the hands of that eminent tribunal."   Messages and Papers of the Presidents, VII, 3210; Taft, pp. 137-138; Westel W. Willoughby, On the Constitution of the United States, III, 1502-1504.

[22] John W. Foster, A Century of American Diplomacy, p. 201.

the President to promote the best interests of the people may, on occasion, justify a relaxation of his constitutional scruples in order to achieve a result indubitably necessary to the national welfare. For only the sudden prospects of withdrawal by France from its offer to sell the territory deemed by him essential to national prosperity persuaded him to abandon a desire to legalize his conduct by preceding the ratification of the treaty by an amendment to the Constitution.[23]

The gradual modification of his views during the progress of these negotiations is presented in the following statements:

> To take a single step beyond the boundaries specifically drawn (around the powers in Congress) is to take possession of a boundless field of power, no longer susceptible of any definitions.[24]
>
> I suppose they must then appeal to the nation for an additional article to the Constitution, approving and confirming an act which the nation had not previously authorized. The Constitution has made no provision for our holding foreign territory, still less for incorporating foreign nations into our Union.
>
> The executive in seizing the fugitive occurrence, which so much advances the good of their country, has done an act beyond the Constitution. The Legislature in casting behind them metaphysical subtleties, and risking themselves like faithful servants, must ratify and pay for it, and throw themselves upon their country for doing for them unauthorized, what we know they would have done for themselves had they been in a situation to do it. It is the case of the guardian, investing the money of its ward in purchasing an important adjacent territory; and saying to him when of age, I did this for your good; I pretend to no right to bind you; you may disavow me and I must get out of the scrape as I can; I thought it my duty to risk myself for you. But we shall not be disavowed by the nation, and their act of indemnity will confirm and not weaken the Constitution by more strongly marking out its lines.[25]

In likening the President to a guardian or trustee of the Nation, on whom is imposed the responsibility of furthering its well-being, Jefferson set forth a conception of his office that is similar to the belief, presented more emphatically by Roosevelt, that the Chief Magistrate is the " steward " of the people. From the records of both Executives are to be obtained examples of the beneficial as well as undesirable results [26] that may be induced by such motives of national

---

[23] Ibid., p. 200.
[24] Writings (Ford Ed.), V, 288.
[25] Ibid., VIII, 244.
[26] Taft, pp. 145-155; below, pp. 157-158.

service; but, whereas this concept of trusteeship influenced Roosevelt to adopt an exceptionally broad theory of executive power, Jefferson apparently continued to espouse principles of strict construction.

Since the competency of the Federal Government to acquire territory is no longer in doubt, Jefferson, contrary to his beliefs and utterances, did not in fact exceed his authority in attempting to dispose of what was to him an exceptional emergency. Whether, indeed, he would have transcended the law, had he been presented with a problem equal in gravity to that which confronted Lincoln, is a question for speculation. Judged on the basis of his reputation as a strict constructionist, it cannot be presumed that he would have approved the conduct of his successor; but if any importance can safely be attributed to his following statement, the writer is tempted to answer the question in the affirmative.

> The question you propose, whether circumstances do not sometimes occur, which make it a duty in officers of high trust, to assume authorities beyond the law, is easy of solution in principle, but sometimes embarrassing in practice. A strict observance of the written laws doubtless is one of the high duties of a good citizen, but it is not the highest. The laws of necessity, of self-preservation, of saving our country when in danger, are of a higher obligation. To lose our country by a scrupulous adherence to written law, would be to lose the law itself, with life, liberty, property, and all those who are enjoying them with us; thus absurdly sacrificing the end to the means. . . . The public advantage offered, in this supposed case, was indeed immense, but a reverence for law and the probability that the advantage might still be legally accomplished by a delay of three weeks, were powerful reasons against hazarding the act. But suppose it foreseen that a John Randolph would find means to protract the proceeding on it by Congress, until the ensuing spring, by which time new circumstances would change the mind of the other party. Ought the Executive, in that case, and with that foreknowledge, to have secured the good to his country, and to have trusted to their justice for the transgression of the law? I think he ought and the act would have been approved. . . . The officer who is called to act on this superior ground, does indeed risk himself on the justice of the controlling powers of the Constitution, and his station makes it his duty to incur that risk. But those controlling powers, and his fellow citizens generally, are bound to judge according to the circumstances under which he acted.[27]

As the first Executive succeeding Washington to whom an opportunity to serve a third term was presented, it was also

---

[27] Writings (Ford Ed.), IX, 279.

incumbent upon Jefferson to determine whether, by his own observance, he should raise to the rank of custom the decision of our first Chief Magistrate not to occupy the Presidency for more than eight years. In announcing to the country at large his long cherished resolution to retire at the expiration of his second term, Washington, it will be recalled, assigned only personal reasons for this decision.[28] There is contained in his Farewell Address no statement that would indicate, either that he considered the acceptance of three or more terms as dangerous on principle, or that he advocated a future limitation of the tenure of the Executive. Unsupported by averment as to the inexpediency of a protracted tenure, his retirement, in itself, could have acquired no significance, nor could there have been any inducement, other than reverence for the first Chief Magistrate, to future Presidents to conform their conduct to that of Washington. But when Jefferson, an almost immediate successor, not only adopted the same resolution, but justified his action on grounds of policy, the foundation of the tradition against a third term was started upon the road of firm establishment.

Prior to arriving at this decision, as the following quotation will indicate, Jefferson had favored a long single term of seven years, with a stipulation as to ineligibility for reelection thereafter; but he finally concluded that a total period of eight years of service, consisting of two four-year terms with an opportunity of defeat in the interim, was more desirable. That he also would have been opposed to a third, but not consecutive term, seems fairly certain; but it should be noted that, in his subsequent advocacy of a two-term limitation, he failed to add any statement as to reeligibility.

My opinion originally was that the President of the United States should have been elected for seven years, and forever ineligible afterwards. I have since become sensible that seven years is too long to be irremovable, and that there should be a peaceable way of withdrawing a man in midway who is doing wrong. The service for

---

[28] " Satisfied that, if any circumstances have given peculiar value to my services, they were temporary, I have the consolation to believe, that while choice and prudence invite me to quit the political scene, patriotism does not forbid it." Farewell Address.

26 PRESIDENTIAL INTERPRETATIONS OF THE PRESIDENCY

eight years, with a power to remove at the end of the first four, comes nearly to my principle as corrected by experience; and it is in adherence to that, that I determined to withdraw at the end of my second term. The danger is that the indulgence and attachments of the people will keep a man in the chair after he becomes a dotard, that reelection through life shall become habitual, and election for life follow that. General Washington set the example of voluntary retirement after eight years. I shall follow it. And a few more precedents will oppose the obstacle of habit to any one after awhile who shall endeavor to extend his term. . . . There is, however, but one circumstance which could engage my acquiescence in another election; to wit, such a division about a successor as might bring in a monarchist. But that circumstance is impossible.[29]

---

[29] Writings (Ford Ed.), VIII, 339.

Although, by good fortune or otherwise, no breach of the tradition fostered by Jefferson had been recorded, the willingness of several later Presidents, two of them (Roosevelt and Coolidge) having had dangerously fine prospects of success, may well give rise to doubts as to whether there exists any inalterable popular aversion to a relaxation of this custom. Excepting Jackson, however, whose advancing age readily induced the abandonment of his inclination to extend his stay in office, and Grant and Coolidge, whose willingness to be drafted was not heeded by their party, Roosevelt was the only aspirant to succeed in having his name placed upon the ballot. In fact, had he received the united support of the Republican Party in 1912, he probably would have been returned to office.

Unlike Grant, who, having had ambitions for a third consecutive term, could defend his position only by declaring that the Constitution expressed no limitation concerning reelection, and by frankly condemning as injudicious a blind adherence to custom under all circumstances, Roosevelt sought reelection after a retirement of four years, and was accordingly enabled to employ this distinction as an argument for denying the application of this tradition to his situation. Questionable as may have been any defense founded upon such a technicality, its value, if any, was in this instance considerably diminished by a previous resolution adopted by Roosevelt at the date of his election in 1904. Acknowledging that he had served in the capacity of Chief Magistrate for almost the complete term of his late predecessor, McKinley, and that he had been selected to serve an additional period of four years, he graciously, and with finality, announced at that time that he would not quibble over the question as to whether or not he had received two full terms, but would conform his conduct to established practice and not be a candidate for reelection. "The wise custom which limits the President to two terms regards the substance and not the form, and under no circumstances will I be a candidate for or accept another nomination."

In the light of this clear and definite statement, his ingenious argument concerning a third non-consecutive term was indeed necessary to save him from the charge of inconsistency or lack of good faith. Explaining that the finality of his earlier statement was induced by an inability to foresee that a party or public demand might persuade him to reenter the contest in 1912, and affirming his approval of the merits of the third term tradition, he submitted the following brief as his defense: "The American people have wisely

To have been able to depart so radically from his preelection policies without suffering a political annihilation for his inconsistency is undeniably a convincing testimonial of Jefferson's ability to retain the support of the electorate. Guided by the belief that "the energy of the government depends mainly upon the confidence of the people in the Chief Magistrate," [30] he deliberately set forth to ingratiate himself with the large masses of the people, which at that date comprised the agricultural class: [31] first, by observing in office a simplicity of demeanor which appealed to their anti-monarchial prejudices; and second, by furnishing them with a political organization which would more accurately reflect their opinions. To Washington and the partisans upon whom he bestowed his favor,[32] this procedure may have appeared undignified, but to Jefferson it offered a most effective means of keeping himself in harmony with the sentiments of the people; for one of the charges preferred by him against the Federalists was that they were too contemptuous of expressions of hostile opinion.[33] But, while he professed to have greater faith in the people than his Federalist precursors, and, in fact, excelled the latter in his ability to originate policies which commanded instant popular approval, it must be acknowledged that he guided public opinion no less aggressively than did his predecessor.[34]

---

established a custom against allowing any man to hold that office for more than two consecutive terms. But every shred of power which a President exercises while in office vanishes absolutely when he has once left office. An ex-President stands precisely in the position of any other private citizen, and has not one particle more power to secure a nomination or election than if he had never held office at all—indeed, he probably has less because of the very fact that he has held the office. Therefore the reasoning on which the anti-third term custom is based has no application whatever to an ex-President. and no application whatever to anything except consecutive terms." Autobiography, pp. 422-423.

[30] Writings, V, 90 (1807).

[31] Frank R. Kent, The Democratic Party: A History, p. 22.

[32] See ch. v.

[33] "There are certainly persons in all the departments who are driving too fast. Government being founded on opinion, the opinion of the public, even when it is wrong, ought to be respected to a certain degree." Writings (Ford Ed.), V, 282.

[34] Kent, pp. 16-19.

Were it not for the success which attended his efforts to create a second political party, Jefferson's election to the Presidency and his subsequent retention of popular support, might not have been possible. Having been, since the inception of the Government, an advocate of principles which were distasteful to those with whom he had been associated in office, Jefferson instinctively turned to the party as the instrument by which he could most effectively secure official recognition for his policies. Although aware that the establishment of a party of opposition would stimulate the factional strife which Washington had constantly deplored, he did not share the latter's belief that parties, for that reason alone, should, or indeed could, be avoided. On the contrary, he contended that provision of opportunity for rival popular groups to obtain a representation of their divergent principles in the policy-forming organs of government was a necessity, and that, since parties satisfactorily supplied that result, this service more than compensated the evils which accompanied their existence.[35]

Even the procedure adopted by Jefferson for consulting members of his Cabinet represented a departure from theories which he had originally entertained. From his observations as a member of Washington's Cabinet, he had previously concluded that the most preferable method of communication with his Cabinet Secretaries was by their submission of opinions in writing; not only because that method, in his opinion, was more strictly in accord with the letter of the Constitution, but also because it was better calculated to preserve harmony among his colleagues by preventing the personal encounter of two opposing subordinates. But when called

---

[35] " I am no believer in the amalgamation of parties, nor do I consider it as either desirable or useful for the public. . . . " Writings (Ford Ed.), X, 317. " That each party endeavors to get into the administration of the government and exclude the other from power is true, and may be stated as a motive of action; but this is only secondary, the primary motive being a real and radical difference of political principles." Ibid., IX, 374. Moreover, he was not adverse to indulging in practical politics when by the use of less commendable methods he could further the principles of his party. Henry J. Ford, The Rise and Growth of American Politics, p. 87; also ch. v.

upon to assemble a Cabinet of his own, so confident was he of
the solidarity of the friendship existing between his associates
and himself, that he was persuaded to continue the practice,
finally selected by Washington, of regularly consulting his
Secretaries at inform'al assemblies.[36]

Concerning the composition of his Cabinet and his relations
with that advisory body, two facts are worthy of emphasis:
first, the superior abilities of the men chosen to serve as his
counsellors, and, second, the disinclination of Jefferson to
dominate these subordinates. Whatever may be the truth of
the charge, occasionally made, that energetic Executives are by
nature unable to brook opposition and, hence, are disposed
to choose for associates mediocre submissive men, further
discussion of these two questions ought clearly to disprove the
applicability of such criticism to Jefferson. Notwithstanding
his acceptance of the political custom which required a geographical distribution of appointments, albeit he considered
this requirement to be an obstacle to a perfect selection of
Cabinet officers, [37] his primary concern was to promote the

---

[36] "The Government, although in theory subject to be directed
by the unadvised will of the President, is, and from its origin, has
been a very different thing in practice. The minor business in each
department is done by the head of the department in consultation
with the President alone. But all matters of importance or difficulty are submitted to all the heads of the departments composing
the Cabinet; sometimes by the President separately and successively,
as they happen to call on him; but in the gravest cases, by calling
them together, discussing the subject maturely, and finally taking
the vote, in which the President counts himself as but one. So that
in all important cases, the executive is in fact a directory, which
certainly he might control; but on this there never was an example,
either in the first or present administration.

"I practiced this last method, [informal assembly] because the
harmony was so cordial among us all, that we never failed, by a
contribution of mutual views on the subject, to form an opinion
acceptable to the whole. I think there never was one instance to
the contrary in a case of any consequence. Yet this does in fact
transform the Executive into a Directory, and I hold the other method
to be more Constitutional." Writings (Ford Ed.), IX, 69, 273.

Having entered the Presidency with greater experience in public
office than did Washington, Jefferson did not find it necessary to
consult his Cabinet as frequently as did his predecessor. That he
did inform it of his important policies or measures is known, however. Hinsdale, pp. 46-47.

[37] See ch. iv. "The Cabinet Council of the President should be of
his bosom confidence. Our geographical position has been an im-
pediment to that." Writings (Ford Ed.), VII, 498.

interests of both his country and his party by choosing, as his counsellors, men of known repute and competency.[38] That he faithfully executed this intention is attested to by the presence in his Cabinet of two men who were virtually his equals in ability—Gallatin and Madison. Having been of calibre equal to that of their President, these men probably would have resented any subordination by Jefferson, but, fortunately, his assertion of supremacy was barely discernible; for such was the harmony and the uniformity of their ideas and opinions that a proposal emanating from him, or any one of them, was almost certain of approval by the others.[39] While Jefferson may therefore have considered himself at liberty to ignore the suggestions offered by his Cabinet officers, the occasions in which the opinions of the latter were at variance with his own were infrequent.

LINCOLN

With Washington excluded, Lincoln is perhaps the only one of the other four Presidents under discussion whose conception of the Presidency was formulated almost entirely during his term of office. That Jefferson, Roosevelt, and Wilson had developed definite opinions concerning the Chief Magistracy prior to their inauguration is verified by their writings; and, although their disposition of certain unforeseen contigencies arising during their respective Administrations may appear as modifications, or even as abandonments of their former opinions, their conduct in office, on the whole, reveals an attempt to apply in practice their preconceived theories. To infer, similarly, that the precedential decisions accredited to Lincoln during the Civil War were adopted in accordance with a preinaugural estimate of the Presidency is, moveover,

---

[38] " It is essential to assemble at the outset persons to compose our administration whose talents, integrity, and revolutionary name and principles may inspire the nation at once with unbounded confidence, and impose an awful silence on all maligners of Republicanism." Ibid., p. 464.

[39] " The harmony among us was so perfect that whatever instrument appeared likely to effect the subject, was always used without objection." Writings, V, 533 (1810).

to forget that the National Government had hitherto not experienced an emergency of such proportions. It would seem inadvisable, therefore, to presume that, even from a most careful scrutiny of the conduct of his predecessors, Lincoln would have deduced a new conception of executive power broad enough to have enabled him to meet this emergency as he did. Rather, may it be said that he entered the office with little more than an acute understanding of his obligation to see to the due execution of the laws—in the fulfilment of which he was to let himself be controlled by the necessities of the occasion.

In ascribing to a doctrine of necessity as a sanction for his exercise of any power essential to the performance of that obligation, Lincoln favored an unquestionably improper rule of interpretation; [40] but his original conclusions concerning the nature of the Federal Union and the competency of the Executive to act in defense thereof were, in contrast to those enunciated by Buchanan, constitutionally correct.

The latter, after having denied the right of the States to secede, and apparently having denounced secession as no less than "revolution," had placed himself in a paradoxical position by declaring that, neither under his duty "to take care that the laws be faithfully executed," nor under the statutes authorizing him to employ the militia to suppress insurrection, was the President competent to combat this danger. To support that lamentable deduction, which was largely influenced by the advice of Attorney-General Black, Buchanan advanced an argument to the effect that " this duty [to enforce the laws] cannot by possibility be performed in a State where no judicial authority exists to issue process, and where there is no marshal to execute it, and where, even if there were such an officer, the entire population would constitute one solid combination to resist him." [41] That there were statutes on the records which authorized the use of force to secure the execution of federal laws, he admitted; but, in his opinion, these statutes afforded the President only an auxili-

[40] See ch. iii.
[41] Messages and Papers of the Presidents, VII, 3162, 3165-3167.

ary power with which to aid the federal courts within the States to enforce the laws, and, since the federal judiciary were no longer functioning in the South, he felt himself obliged to conclude that the armed assistance permitted by these acts could not be extended. Nor could this deficiency be remedied by further legislation; for it was his belief that any statute which authorized the President to dispatch troops into the States, other than for the purpose of protecting federal courts or property, in effect enabled him to wage war against the States, and of the invalidity of that procedure he had no doubt. In other words, his final determination was that the National Government was powerless to prevent the dissolution of the Union.[42]

The defects in Buchanan's position were largely repaired by Lincoln in his Inaugural Address. Holding that this was " an indestructible Union of indestructible States " and that each State received its status as such only through membership in that Union, he further maintained that all state laws contesting the existence of that Union were void and that individuals submitting to them would be guilty of rebellion. Consequently, in fulfiling his duty to see to the execution of the laws by employing troops to quell an insurrection, he was not making war on, or coercing, the States, as Buchanan believed, because, under his theory, the States were not in a position to be coerced. He was only attempting to exact obedience from those individuals within the States who were obstructing the process of the federal courts.

It follows from these views that no State upon its own mere motion can lawfully get out of the Union; that resolves and ordinances to that effect are legally void, and that acts of violence within any State or States against the authority of the United States are insurrectionary or revolutionary, according to the circumstances. I therefore consider that in view of the Constitution and the laws the Union is unbroken, and to the extent of my ability I shall take care, as the Constitution itself expressly enjoins upon me, that the laws of the Union be faithfully executed in all the States. . . .[43]

---

[42] Westel W. Willoughby, The American Constitutional System, pp. 70-78.

[43] Ibid., pp. 78-80; Messages and Papers of the Presidents, VII, 3208.

However, this insurrection very shortly assumed the aspects of a formidible war; and Lincoln, after having correctly determined that the Constitution had empowered the National Government, acting through the President, forcibly to suppress all such insurrections, (even though the persons engaged therein be organized as States), was next called upon to decide whether the Federal Government, again acting through the President as Commander-in-Chief, was possessed of all means necessary to combat a domestic conflict which had for its object, not simply the nullification of a federal law, but the destruction of the Union, its Government, and its Constitution. Involving as it did the sufficiency of the national war powers, this issue was to confront him throughout his Administration, and it was his particular handling of this problem that constitutes his chief contribution to the Presidency.

While it is not the writer's purpose to discuss at this moment Lincoln's unprecedented estimate of the war powers of the Executive,[44] nevertheless, it is in accord with the content of this chapter to present two general constitutional questions to which his liberal rules of interpretation gave rise. Immediately upon making two permissible assumptions; namely, that the Government was adequately equipped with all powers necessary for its self-preservation, and that the Executive was the appropriate officer to employ these powers in defense of the Union, Lincoln proceeded to the erroneous conclusion that, in time of emergency, the war powers become vested entirely in the President, and that he is therefore competent to act independently of congressional authorization.[45] Nevertheless, if the power exercised in pursuance of this untenable rule of interpretation was within the " constitutional competency " of Congress to authorize, the procedural defects in the President's action might be remedied by an act of indemnity.

No equally effective relief, however, could be provided to

---

[44] See ch. iii.

[45] For a contemporaneous discussion as to whether the war powers are vested wholly in the Executive, or whether a portion of them is possessed by Congress, see the debate between Senators Summer and Browning, 37th Cong., 2d sess., pp. 2918 ff.

protect him when, in obedience to a second erroneous deduction of more serious import, he undertook to exercise powers not sanctioned by the Constitution. That the President, in endeavoring, under ordinary circumstances, to fulfil his obligation faithfully to execute the laws, was limited to the employment of those powers expressly or impliedly granted by the Constitution, was a proposition that would have commanded his instant acceptance; but, in this grave crisis, he considered the primary duty confronting him to be that of preserving, rather than of observing the Constitution. To reverse the order and to place emphasis upon conformity to law and strict obedience to constitutional limitations, he believed, was to lose sight of the issues at stake; for, unless the Union and the Government could be saved, the Constitution would become a scrap of paper. Convinced that the preservation of the Union for posterity ought to be the sole object of his endeavors, he believed, not only that it was permissible for him to exercise any power necessary to the accomplishment of that object, but that the necessity which prompted his exercise of such powers would of itself afford his conduct a legal justification. To have taken a more limited view of his powers in this emergency would, in his opinion, have been no less than an admission of a " fatal weakness " in Constitutional Government.[46]

The following excerpts from his writings reveal even more clearly Lincoln's estimate of the problem which the Civil War presented to the Executive.

This issue embraces more than the fate of these United States. It presents to the whole family of Man the question whether a constitutional republic, or democracy—a government of the people by the same people, can or cannot maintain its territorial integrity against its own domestic foes . . . It forces us to ask, Is there in all republics this inherent and fatal weakness? [47]

---

[46] For a judicial condemnation of this principle of interpretation, see the case of *Ex parte* Milligan, 71 U. S. 2, in which the Court said that the Constitution was a rule of law equally applicable in time of war as in time of peace, and that the doctrine of necessity can have no place in our federal system for the reason that the powers which the Government can legitimately deduce from the Constitution are adequate to protect it in any emergency.

[47] Messages and Papers of the Presidents, VII, 3224.

I consider that the central idea pervading this struggle is the necessity . . . of proving that popular government is not an absurdity.[48]

No organic law can ever be framed with a provision specifically applicable to every question which may arise in a practical administration. . . . The whole of the laws are being resisted and all will be destroyed if not protected . . . I am to sacrifice one law in order to save the rest . . The Constitution is silent on the emergency. [49]

I understood that my oath to preserve the Constitution to the best of my ability, imposed upon me the duty of preserving, by every indispensable means, that government, that Nation of which that Constitution was the organic law. Was it possible to lose the Nation and yet to preserve the Constitution? . . . I felt that measures, otherwise unconstitutional, might become lawful, by becoming indispensable to the preservation of the Union. Right or wrong, I assumed this ground, and now avow it.[50]

Notwithstanding the illegal character of many of his activities, Lincoln's conduct was to furnish an unmistakable impetus to the expansion of the powers of the Presidency. Apart from serving as a stimulus to a more liberal interpretation of executive power, his untenable principles of constitutional construction were to receive no further application; but the motives which prompted his espousal of these principles were to be given serious consideration by his most prominent successors. Almost certain is it that the reasons which induced Lincoln to exercise the powers of a dictator were not only a desire to acquit himself loyally of his obligation to execute the laws, but a firm conviction in the superior capacities of the Executive for dealing expeditiously with national problems. And by their assumption of a vigorous legislative and political leadership, both Roosevelt and Wilson would seem to have expressed their concurrence in that belief.

Moreover, in order for Lincoln to have been enabled to exercise the powers of a dictator for the duration of the Civil War, at least the passive support of his party and the public was essential. To what extent his personal leadership and patriotic sentiment were responsible for a popular forbearance toward his war-time dictatorship is, of course, difficult to ascertain, but the writer is inclined to believe that great

---

[48] Diary and Letters of John Hay, I, 31; quoted by James G. Randall, Constitutional Problems under Lincoln, pp. 1-2.

[49] Ibid., p. 18.

[50] Henry Raymond, State Papers of Abraham Lincoln, p. 767.

weight ought to be accorded a popular recognition of the dangers involved in any attempt to hinder the Administration in so grave an emergency. At any rate, whether this conclusion is correct or not, it seems to the writer that Lincoln did not mobilize public opinion in his behalf as effectively as did Wilson in the late War.

However, an explanation of Lincoln's slight indecision, and his occasional modification of his plans in deference to the complaints of hostile factions [51] may be obtained from a consideration of the adverse circumstances under which he prosecuted the Civil War. Having been the successful candidate of a newly created fusion party, which had polled only a minority of the votes in a contest in which three other parties had participated, he could scarcely view his election as carrying with it an encouraging popular mandate for a vigorous suppression of the Rebellion. On the contrary, there was not discernible any uniform expression of popular support, such as was evident in the late War, but, rather, the discordant opinions of zealous factional groups, who sought either to impede the execution of administration measures, or to foist upon the President the adoption of policies more stringent than he considered appropriate. While Lincoln properly refused to recognize these factions as representing the true popular sentiment, or as advocating programs beneficial to the Union, and in most instances relied upon his own judgment in formulating his plans, nevertheless, these groups were too dangerous to be ignored. Perceiving the unwisdom of any attempt to dominate them entirely, he displayed considerable skill in his endeavors to placate these opposing factions and to minimize their capacity for limiting his freedom of decision. His success in securing the favorable acceptance of his important measures, particularly his emancipation policy, is to be attributed, therefore, not to any dominant leadership,

---

[51] The best evidence of his yielding to popular pressure is to be found in his constant interference with the movements of the armies and in his frequent dismissals of unsuccessful commanding officers. His consent to the ill-advised and premature attack at Bull Run was doubtless given in obedience to the popular clamor for an immediate victory. See ch. iii.

but to his ability to conciliate his opponents, and to his prudence in staying the execution of his plans until public sentiment had become sympathetic to his proposals.

The representation of several of these popular groups within his own party served to produce a similar, though less effective, obstacle to his political leadership. Speculative as the statement may be, the writer is nevertheless of the opinion that, under normal circumstances, Lincoln's conciliatory, amicable demeanor would have availed him nothing as against the zealots and the influential factional leaders within his party; and that any effort by him to acquire an ascendancy in the field of legislation would have met with defeat. During the period of the Rebellion, however, he experienced little difficulty in dominating his party for the reason that, by anticipating and hastily disposing of suddenly arising war problems, he was able to create a *fait accompli* which, in view of the gravity of the situation, his political associates could not patriotically refuse to support. Party obedience sustained by such pressure methods obviously could not have been voluntary; but it sufficed to enable him successfully to terminate the War.[52]

On the other hand, in dealing with his Cabinet associates, many of whom were prominent representatives of the factions existent within his party, Lincoln was obliged to assert his supremacy in the most tactful manner possible. Had he preferred to select as his Secretaries only his most intimate supporters, the necessity for such delicacy might have been avoided; but, in forming his Cabinet slate, he consented, at a sacrifice of his personal convenience, to observe all the customary rules concerning geographical distribution and party service.[53]

While the calibre and experience of the officers chosen in conformance with these requisites were indeed commendable, the net result of his sacrifice was an unhappy assemblage of men who were the political rivals of each other, who bore no deep affection for their President, and who, by reason of the

---

[52] See chs. iii and iv.   [53] Hinsdale, p. 175.

length of their public services, were disposed to regard him as an incompetent novice. Despite their disinclination to refrain from petty dissensions and their occasional manifestations of unfriendliness to the Executive, Lincoln, nevertheless, seems to have been of the opinion that their presence in his Cabinet would engender party harmony and administrative efficiency; for, unless a particular subordinate proved to be averse to conciliatory cooperation,[54] he made every effort to retain him. However, neither the importuning of his Secretaries not to resign, nor his toleration of their insubordination is to be interpreted as any irresolution on his part; and those leaders in his Cabinet who aspired to dominate their President soon discovered that Lincoln intended to be the supreme executive officer of the Administration.

To Seward, who entertained hopes of becoming the President's chief counsellor, and had accordingly endeavored to have the formation of the foreign and domestic policy of the Nation entrusted to his department, Lincoln tendered the following reply:

Upon your closing propositions [I remark] that if this must be done, [the formation of these policies] I must do it. When a general line of policy is adopted, I apprehend there is no danger of its being changed without good reason or continuing to be a subject of unnecessary debate; still, upon points arising in its progress I wish, and suppose I am entitled to have, the advice of all the Cabinet.[55]

That his Secretaries assembled in Cabinet conference were viewed by him as his subordinates would seem to be further confirmed by the statement attributed to him that "there was only one vote,—and that unanimous—it was the vote of the President."[56] Like many broad general statements, however, this utterance is not to be accepted without qualification; for there is evidence that Lincoln was subject to the influence of his more prominent departmental chiefs, Seward, Stanton, and Chase, and that he was occasionally persuaded by their

---

[54] The resignation of Chase is an example. Ibid., pp. 182-185.

[55] John G. Nicolay and John Hay, Abraham Lincoln: A History, III, 448. When Seward, in anticipation of the failure of his plans, sought to resign, Lincoln curtly informed him that "when the slate breaks again, it will break at the top." Hinsdale, p. 175.

[56] Taft, p. 35.

arguments to modify or abandon his opinions.[57] In fact, though much to the displeasure of his less favored associates,[58] and to the profound concern of the Senate,[59] he manifested, during the later years of his Administration, a disposition to abandon the method of informal Cabinet meetings for that of consultation singly with each one of his Cabinet members, and particularly with those named above. In view of the fact that the personal meeting of his rival Secretaries was likely to be unpleasant, and that the greater number of the problems created by the War pertained to the State, War, and Treasury Departments, his preference of the latter plan of procedure was therefore not unreasonable. However, on the occasions in which he convened his Cabinet to apprise it of his more important policies, the opportunity for discussion was limited generally to the content of his plans; for the time and manner of their execution were matters which he reserved for his own decision.[60]

ROOSEVELT

Of all the Presidents succeeding Lincoln, Roosevelt is the only one to adopt in theory, albeit even he did not fully apply it in practice, the former's singular interpretation of executive power. Indicative of his enthusiastic acceptance of his predecessor's principles of constitutional construction was Roosevelt's emphasis upon liberality of interpretation as the basis for his novel classification of American Presidents into two groups; one of which he designated as the Lincoln school of thought, and the other as the Buchanan school.[61] Lincoln,

---

[57] Hinsdale, pp. 186-187.

[58] Diary of Gideon Welles, I, 53, 57-58, 59, 66-69, 131-133.

[59] Hinsdale, pp. 179-181. Believing that the military reverses sustained by the Union were attributable to the failure of the President to employ the assistance of his Cabinet associates and to his misplaced confidence in several of his Secretaries (who were unpopular in the Senate), ranking Republican members of the Senate sought to impress upon Lincoln the advisability of acting in closer concert with his entire Cabinet. By boldly demanding that these Senators more fully substantiate their contentions, Lincoln forced the withdrawal of their proposal, and thus defeated their attempted interference with his liberty of action.

[60] Diary of Gideon Welles, I, 142-144, 228-229, 432-433, 526; II, 264.

[61] Autobiography, pp. 395-396; Taft, p. 144.

however, having ascribed to the doctrine of necessity during a conflict which threatened the very existence of the Union, a question quite naturally arises as to what possible justification Roosevelt, who served during a period of domestic tranquillity, had for his advocacy of a theory of presidential power which exceeded in scope even that of his predecessor.[62]

To satisfy that inquiry a survey of the conditions prevailing during his Administration is necessary. Although the rise of a new "imperialistic" spirit and the sudden expansion of American foreign interests resulting from the Spanish War were conducive to an increase in the activity of the Executive, it is certain that even the most far-reaching policies which this favorable situation may have tempted Roosevelt to adopt did not necessitate for their defense the origination of a more extensive theory of Presidential power. Nor would Roosevelt have been likely to resort to such a theory had his entire attention been directed to the conduct of foreign affairs. The true incentive for the adoption of his unusual concept of executive authority was the urgency of providing a remedy for domestic problems confronting his Administration. Involving chiefly a maladjustment of the rights of Capital, Labor, and Consumer produced by a rapid industrialization of the country, these problems had been permitted to accumulate until, at the date of his succession to the Presidency, they had become exceedingly vexatious; and the public, in turn, having been disturbed in the enjoyment of its welfare, was impatient at the delay of the Government in extending relief. That its demand for a remedy was justifiable, that the National Government was the proper agency to provide any remedy, and that there ought to be no legal impediments to that accomplishment, the public was convinced; and with these views Roosevelt was in perfect agreement. Moreover, he was led to believe, as had been Lincoln, that the alleviation of these difficulties could be effected more expeditiously by the President; and it was, doubtless, to enable himself to cite a competency for whatever independent action he might adopt

---

[62] Ibid., p. 147.

in pursuance of that belief that he had recourse to an exceptionally broad interpretation of his powers.

The influence of this desire to serve the public upon his theory of the Presidency is evident in the following statement:

> I believed in invoking the National power with absolute freedom for every National need; and I believed that the Constitution should be treated as the greatest document ever devised by the wit of man to aid a people in exercising every power necessary for its own betterment, and not as a straight jacket cunningly fashioned to strangle growth.[63]

Notwithstanding this similarity of the opinion which actuated their conduct, there was a marked distinction between the objects which Lincoln and Roosevelt sought to achieve. Lincoln considered himself competent to exercise any power necessary to the preservation of the Union, whereas Roosevelt believed himself empowered to adopt almost any measure necessary to satisfy what he deemed to be a national need. Moreover, with Lincoln it was also a question of exercising his powers to fulfil his constitutional duty to see to the execution of the laws; with Roosevelt, it was primarily a matter of discharging his obligation to administer to the wants of the people who elected him. As the only officer nationally representative of the American people, he believed, the Executive was peculiarly competent to discover its needs; and having discovered them, he became, in his opinion, subject to a moral duty to utilize fully the powers of his office, political and constitutional, to remedy such popular deficiencies. That equally beneficial results were obtainable from both sources of authority he ably demonstrated; but because of the delay and uncertainty attending his efforts to influence the adoption by Congress of legislation calculated to solve national problems, Roosevelt preferred to attain that end, wherever possible, through direct executive action.

His theory, generally designated as the "residuum of powers" theory,[64] was stated by him as follows:

---

[63] Autobiography, p. 420.

[64] This theory was first asserted by James Wilson in 1785. See Westel W. Willoughby, On the Constitution of the United States, I, 80.

The most important factor in getting the right spirit in my Administration, next to the insistence upon courage, honesty, and a genuine democracy of desire to serve the plain people, was my insistence upon the theory that the executive power was limited only by specific restrictions and prohibitions appearing in the Constitution or imposed by the Congress under its Constitutional powers. My view was that every executive officer, and above all every executive officer in high position, was a steward of the people bound actively and affirmatively to do all he could for the people, and not to content himself with the negative merit of keeping his talents undamaged in a napkin. I declined to adopt the view that what was imperatively necessary for the Nation could not be done by the President unless he could find some specific authorization to do it. My belief was that it was not only his right but his duty to do anything that the needs of the Nation demanded unless such action was forbidden by the Constitution or by the laws. Under this interpretation of executive power I did and caused to be done many things not previously done by the President and the heads of the departments. I did not usurp power, but I did greatly broaden the use of executive power. In other words, I acted for the public welfare, I acted for the common well-being of all our people, whenever and in whatever manner was necessary, unless prevented by direct constitutional or legislative prohibition.[65]

No one was more competent to refute the legal fallacies of this theory of interpretation than the late Chief Justice Taft, and the latter's criticism of his predecessor's statements are accordingly presented below:

The true view of the executive function is, as I conceive it, that the President can exercise no power which cannot be fairly and reasonably traced to some specific grant of power or justly implied and included with such express grant as proper and necessary to its exercise. Such specific grant must be either in the Federal Constitution or in an act of Congress passed in pursuance thereof. There is no undefined residuum of power which he can exercise because it seems to him to be in public interest, and there is nothing in the Neagle case and its definition of a law in the United States, or in other precedents, warranting such an inference. The grants of Executive power are necessarily in general terms in order not to embarrass the Executive within the field of action plainly marked for him, but his jurisdiction must be justified and vindicated by affirmative constitutional or statutory provision, or it does not exist. My judgment is that the view of . . . Mr. Roosevelt, ascribing an undefined residuum of power to the President is an unsafe doctrine, and that it might lead under emergencies to results of an arbitrary character, doing irremediable injustice to private right. The mainspring of such a view is that the Executive is charged with responsibility for the welfare of all the people in a general way, that he is is to play the part of a Universal Providence and set all things right, and that anything that in his judgment will help the people he ought to do, unless he is expressly forbidden not to do it. The wide field

[65] Autobiography, pp. 388-389.

of action that this would give to the Executive one can hardly limit.[66]

Opposed as it is to all accepted principles of constitutional construction, Roosevelt's theory ought to arouse no more than academic interest. While Mr. Roosevelt may have subsequently viewed certain significant measures adopted by him as representative applications of his theory of interpretation, and may have considered the judicial sanction accorded several of these acts as an approval of the correctness of his theory, it is reasonable to predict that had these measures been dependent for their justification upon that theory, they could not have been validated in court.[67] The only measure of his entire Administration that would have perfectly demonstrated the legal difficulties attending a strict observance of his theory was his proposed plan for the settlement of the Anthracite Coal Strike of 1902, but, fortunately for his reputation, this plan was never carried into effect.[68]

Of greater permanence and value than his contribution of an untenable theory of constitutional interpretation was his assumption of legislative leadership. In seeking to influence the passage of beneficial legislation, Roosevelt was not arrogating to himself a power hitherto unexercised by his predecessors; but he was probably the first to assert openly, and as a matter of policy, that the President ought to enter office with the avowed intention of carrying into effect a legislative

---

[66] Our Chief Magistrate and His Powers, pp. 139-140, 144-145. An official denunciation of this theory is to be found in the opinion tendered by Mr. Justice Miller in the Floyd Acceptance Cases, 7 Wall. 666, 685. "The answer which at once suggests itself to one familiar with the structure of our government, in which all power is delegated, and is defined by law, constitution or statutory, is, that to one or both of these sources we must resort in every instance. We have no officers in this government, from the President down to the most subordinate agent, who does not hold office under the law, with prescribed duties and limited authority. And while some of these, as the President, the Legislature, and the Judiciary, exercise powers in some sense left to the more general definitions necessarily incident to fundamental law found in the Constitution, the larger portion of them are the creation of statutory law, with duties and powers prescribed and limited by that law."

[67] Below, pp. 147-148.

[68] Below, pp. 157-158.

program of his own origination.[69] The circumstance which induced him to believe that he could successfully execute that intention was his confidence in the superior ability of the President to mobilize public opinion in behalf of his measures. Recognizing that the citizen body could more readily focus its attention upon a single Executive[70] than upon a host of Congressmen representing varied local interests, and would willingly lend its support to whoever could effectively satisfy its demands, he accordingly undertook, through the utilization of every means calculated to afford him publicity,[71] to acquire a popular sanction for his sponsorship of measures which he believed the people desired or ought to have. Nevertheless, when he failed "to get the people to look at matters in his way," he wisely deferred to the popular will, and avoided the error committed by Wilson of persisting in his advocacy of a proposal even after its rejection by the public.

However, his ascendancy in the field of legislation was predicated, not alone upon his acquisition of popular support, but also upon his effective maintenance of a dominant control of his party; for, without the cooperation of his political associates in Congress, he could not hope to secure the adoption of his proposals. While Roosevelt was determined at the outset to direct the activities of his party,[72] to formulate its program, and to utilize, if necessary, his entire popular strength to reduce recalcitrant political associates to an acceptance of his predominancy, he never entertained any illusions as to the difficulty of his task. That his political associates, in supporting him and his proposals, not only would be fulfilling the promises of their party to the people, but would be insuring its victory at the ensuing election, was

---

[69] Below, p. 171.

[70] "I am going to be President of the United States and not of any section. I don't care that . . . for sections or sectional lines. Half my blood is Southern and I have lived in the West, so that I feel I can represent the whole country." Joseph B. Bishop, Theodore Roosevelt and His Time, I, 443.

[71] Below, pp. 173-177.

[72] "And, moreover, what was far more important, it was necessary to have it understood at the very outset that the Administration was my Administration, and was no one else's but mine." Autobiography, p. 308.

an argument that may have appealed to the younger, more progressive members of his party; but to obtain the coopera- tion of the older leaders of the party machine, Roosevelt fore- saw that he would have to engage in "practical" politics. Nevertheless, in consenting to bargain for the support of the latter group, he let it be known that concessions would not be made on matters of policy; and that "while [he] would try to get on well with the organization, the organization must with equal sincerity strive to do what [he] regarded as essen- tial for the public good." [73]

Although he accepted the fact that the leaders of the party organization were too powerful to be ignored and that their support could be obtained only through compromise or coer- cion, he did not consider himself obligated to make a similar sacrifice to obtain the cooperation of his Cabinet. Believing, therefore, that the allegiance of his intimate advisors ought to be freely given and not founded upon so tenuous an arrange- ment as compromise, Roosevelt was disposed to disregard conventional party practice [74] in forming his Cabinet, and selected his associates on the basis of presonal friendships [75] rather than upon party prominence. While the Cabinet assembled by that method of choice was neither representative of the country as a whole, nor distinguished by a membership of national repute, it at least assured him of the perfect loyalty he desired. His companions in office were men who were thoroughly in agreement with his principles and ideals, and who could be trusted to apply them in performing the duties of their respective departments.

Of the cordial relations and harmony existent between the members of his Cabinet and himself, Roosevelt later wrote:

I do not think I overstate the case when I say that most of the men who did the best work under me felt that ours was a partnership,

---

[73] "My duty was to combine both idealism and efficiency." Ibid., p. 310.

[74] Hinsdale, p. 291. In particular, the rule concerning geographi- cal distribution was relaxed; for at one time during his Administra- tion, there were present in his Cabinet three members from the State of New York. His appointees appear to have represented groups rather than geographical areas.

[75] Ibid., p. 272.

that we all stood on the same level of purpose and service, and that it mattered not what position any one of us held so long as in that position he gave the very best that was in him.[76]

Notwithstanding their close alliance with him, both in friendship and in community of ideas, his Cabinet officers were, nevertheless, not privileged to consider themselves as other than subordinates charged with the execution of a part of the President's program. His consultations with them, more frequently in private than in formal session, were primarily for the purpose of informing himself as to the needs and progress in the work of each department; and although their suggestions concerning the advisability of specific legislative proposals were given consideration by him, on such matters of domestic policy he was also disposed to confer with an "inner circle" of friends designated by him as his "Tennis Cabinet." [77] However, in disposing of problems arising during his conduct of foreign affairs, he was of the opinion that the necessity of secrecy and dispatch precluded any resort to deliberation.[78]

WILSON

In presenting Wilson's conception of the Presidency, the writer is obliged to modify his previously observed mode of treatment for the reason that Wilson's theory of the Chief Magistracy pertained almost exclusively to the political powers of that office. Anticipating that the future trend of presidential development would witness the Executive "becoming more and more a political and less and less an executive officer," and convinced, after a quarter-century of observation, that, by the acceleration of that development, existing defects in our federal system would be remedied, he devoted the greater portion of his time in office to enhancing the powers

---

[76] Autobiography, pp. 385-386.
[77] Ibid., pp. 51-52, 386.
[78] "I determined on the move [sending the fleet on its world cruise] without consulting the Cabinet precisely as I took Panama without consulting the Cabinet. A council of war never fights, and in a crisis, the duty of a leader is to lead and not to take refuge behind the generally timid wisdom of a multitude of counsellors." Bishop, II, 66.

and influence of the President for a more vigorous legislative leadership.

In view, therefore, of the special significance which he attached to the political aspects of his office, the writer has little other option than to limit discussion to that phase of the subject. But perhaps it may be advisable to preface this attempt by a brief consideration of Wilson's interpretation of his constitutional authority.

Neither a hopelessly strict constructionist, as was Buchanan, nor an indefensibly radical constructionist, as was Roosevelt, he observed in practice a principle of interpretation that was both practical and legal. While he was in perfect accord with the statement that the Constitution was a practical document capable of affording the Government adequate powers to meet every contingency, he was intolerant of the view expressed by certain of his predecessors, that a popular demand or necessity could justify the President in relaxing the limitations imposed upon him by organic law.[79] When desirous of adopting a specific measure, the sanction for which could not be reasonably inferred from the second Article of the Constitution, he maintained that the President should first seek a legislative authorization from Congress;[80] but, in subscribing to this laudable view, he was doubtless influenced by a confidence in his ability to induce that body to act favorably upon his requests.

Wilson utilized his election to the Presidency as an opportunity to test the merits of certain conclusions adopted during the course of a prolonged study of the operation of the National Government. Compiling the results of his earlier observations in a treatise entitled " Congressional Government " (1885), he undertook to disclose what, in his opinion, were the major defects discernible in our federal system. The onus of his complaint, as the title suggests, was directed against the legislative branch; and, while the severity of his criticism may have been aggravated by the then prevailing low standard of party ethics and a dearth of spirited leaders,

---

[79] Below, pp. 95, 184.   [80] See ch. iii.

his principal contention was that Congress had proved itself to be uttterly incapable of reflecting public opinion. To give immediate effect to the popular will, he said, there must be a leadership that is " single, responsible, and of the whole "; but, he declared, Congress had completely negatived that possibility by its zealous adherence to the theory of a separation of powers, and by its refusal to cooperate with the Executive. Acting independently, the legislative branch could never offer the electorate more than an example of " patchwork leadership " for the reason that it had become so preoccupied with questions of procedure and organization as to be indifferent to external expressions of opinion. The product of this subordination of popular accountability to the problem of procedural convenience was the objectionable committee system, which not only destroyed all opportunities for free and open debate but subjected members of Congress to the control of irresponsible party chieftains.[81]

Were it not for what he believed to be an inherent weakness in our federal system; namely, the separation of powers theory, he might have reposed greater confidence in the benefits to be secured by an improvement of these lesser defects; but the retention of that theory, in his opinion, constituted an insuperable obstacle to the attainment of that degree of unity and immediate responsibility essential to a successful representative government. While he was not led into the error of

---

[81] For his severest condemnation of the Congressional System, see his early article on " Cabinet Government in the United States," (1879) in Selected Literary and Political Papers of Woodrow Wilson (Harpers), I, 4, 15.

" Congress is a deliberative body in which there is little real deliberation; a legislature which legislates with no real discussion of its business. Our Government is practically carried on by irresponsible committees.

" Only a single glance is necessary to discover how utterly Committee government must fail to give effect to public opinion. In the first place, the exclusion of debate prevents intelligent formation of opinion on the part of the nation at large; in the second place, public opinion, when once formed, finds it impossible to exercise any immediate control over the action of its representatives. There is no one in Congress to speak for the nation. Congress is a conglomeration of inharmonious elements, a collection of men representing each . . . his local interest. . . . There is no guiding or harmonizing power."

believing that these desiderata could be perfectly achieved under any form of government, nevertheless he was convinced that the closest approximation of the result was obtainable under the British parliamentary system; and he always cherished the hope that provision might be made for the assimilation of Cabinet government into our own system. However, he reluctantly admitted that " we cannot have ministerial responsibility in its fullness under the Constitution as it now stands. The most that we can have is distinct legislative responsibility with or without any connection of cooperation or of mutual confidence between the executive and Congress. To have so much would be an immense gain." [82]

In a second treatise, " The Constitutional Government of the United States," written a quarter of a century later (1908), there is a noticeable absence of the pessimism evident in his former volume. This change in attitude, it would appear, was occasioned not by any reform of the defects previously discerned in the legislative branch,[83] but rather by the recent extension of the political powers of the President; for, in the promotion of that development, he foresaw the prospect of an approach to that form of legislative leadership and responsibility characteristic of the British Cabinet system. Indeed, with Congress having definitely forfeited the confidence of the people, and the public already educated to the fact that the responsiveness of the Government to its wishes would depend upon the energy of the Executive, there remained, in his opinion, no serious deterrent to a further expansion of his influence nor to his assumption of the initiative of a Prime Minister.

His assurance that the rapid ascendancy of the Executive would be favorably received was doubtless founded upon the success which attended Roosevelt's efforts to assert a genuinely aggressive leadership. Roosevelt, on the other hand, having

---

[82] " Responsible Government under the Constitution," in Atlantic Monthly, LVII, 563.

[83] The substance of his criticism of Congress remained unchanged, although he ceased to impute a sinister partisan motive to its failure to voice the opinion of the electorate. Constititional Government, pp. 107, 110-111.

been the first of a long line of Presidents to exert a controlling influence in legislation, manifested less confidence in the outcome of his undertaking. Of the correctness of his belief, that the people would acclaim any officer who would give effect to its needs, he was certain; but while he had demonstrated his ability to secure a fulfilment of its wishes, he did not anticipate that the electorate could instinctively "look to the President" for the satisfaction of its demands. Wilson, however, seems to have concluded that his predecessor's Administration definitely produced the latter result; and, accordingly, upon entering office, he was disposed to regard his assumption of leadership not as an experiment, but simply as a matter of fulfilling popular expectations.

There can be no mistaking the fact that we have grown more and more inclined from generation to generation to look to the President as the unifying force in our complex system, the leader both of his party and of the nation.[84]
The President is expected by the nation to be the leader of his party as well as the chief executive officer of the Government, and the country will take no excuses from him. He must play the part and play it successfully, or lose the country's confidence. He must be Prime Minister, as much concerned with the guidance of legislation as with the just and orderly execution of law; and he is the spokesman of the nation in everything, even the most momentus and delicate dealings of the Government with foreign nations.[85]

Having thus acquired a monopoly upon the affections of the people, the President, Wilson believed, need henceforth concern himself only with a judicious manipulation of that asset in order to assume a dominant position in the National Government. However essential the cooperation of Congress and party might be to enable him to effect his leadership, their support would be inevitable as long as he gave the electorate every assurance that its trust had been justly placed.

That part of the Government, which has the most direct access to opinion has the best chance of leadership and mastery; and at present that part is the President.
The President is at liberty both in law and conscience, to be as big a man as he can. His capacity will set the limit; and if Congress be overborne by him, it will be no fault of the makers of the

[84] Constitutional Government, p. 60.
[85] Quoted by Lindsay Rogers, "Presidential Dictatorship in the United States," in Quarterly Review, CCXXXI, 130-131.

Constitution; it will be from no lack of constitutional powers on its part, but only because the President has the nation behind him, and Congress has not. He has no means of compelling Congress except through public opinion.

The rôle of the party leader is forced upon the President by the method of his selection. . . . He can dominate his party by being spokesman for the real sentiment and purpose of the country, by giving direction to opinion, by giving the country at once the information and the statements of policy which will enable it to form its judgment alike of parties and of men. . . . If he lead the nation his party can hardly resist him.[86]

While it is undeniably true that, without the aid of favorable public opinion, the President might not be able to secure obedience to his requests, nevertheless, the wisdom of a complete reliance upon popular support as the sole means of sustaining a party leadership seems open to doubt. Party predominance, though it inevitably involves a use of coercion, would seem to be founded upon something more than an ability to resort to the driving force of public opinion; but, because he had neither the physical impressiveness nor the personal magnetism of Roosevelt, nor his disposition to engage in practical politics, Wilson was unavoidably impelled to have an abounding faith in the potency of popular confidence. To have bargained or offered concessions in return for party support, however, would have been inconsistent with his interpretation of the significance of his election; for, by its very conduct in national campaigns, his party, in his opinion, had obligated itself to support its victorious President in the fulfilment of his program. In other words, he contended that since the people prefer to vote for a man rather than a party, and since the party accedes to that popular preference by endeavoring to produce a " winning " candidate, it cannot do other than regard his victory as a confirmation of the President alone.[87]

---

[86] Constitutional Government, pp. 60, 68-70, 110.

[87] Indicative of Wilson's desire to remove all doubts as to the nationally representative character of the Chief Magistrate and enable him to become more fully the spokesman of the people was his recommendation for legislation establishing a nation-wide Presidential Primary System. Messages and Papers of the Presidents, XVII, 7910; Robert C. Brooks, Political Parties and Electoral Problems, pp. 279-280. " I venture the suggestion that this legislation should provide for the retention of party conventions, but only for

From the quotations inserted in the previous pages it should be obvious that the central idea pervading Wilson's theory of the political ascendancy of the President was the superior accessibility of the latter's office to public opinion. Considered in connection with his resolve to play the part of Prime Minister, his willingness to let the tenure and limits of his hegemony depend upon his retention of popular support would appear to be perfectly consistent with the spirit of responsible Cabinet government; and had he not altered this disposition toward the conclusion of his Administration, perhaps no criticism would be forthcoming. In 1918, however, after having appealed directly to the people in accordance with his principles of relying upon popular approval, Wilson refused to be bound by the unmistakable verdict of the electorate, and persisted in the sponsorship of his peace program. Manifestly, under our present form of government, an adverse popular reception of his policies need not become an occasion for the resignation of an Executive; but it would seem to be especially incumbent upon a professed admirer of the British Parliamentary system to at least defer to the views of the opposition which had been installed. By pursuing an opposite course, Wilson would appear to be subject to the criticism that he aspired to exercise a Prime Minister's prerogative of legislative leadership without wishing to assume the latter's corresponding obligation to defer to the expressed will of the people.

Nevertheless, his conduct in this instance, though it be incompatible with the principles of ministerial responsibility,

---

the purpose of declaring and accepting the verdict of the primaries and formulating the platform of the parties; and I suggest that these conventions should consist not of delegates chosen for this single purpose, but of the nominees for Congress, the nominees for vacant seats in the Senate . . . , the Senators whose terms have not yet closed, the national committees, and the candidates for the Presidency themselves, in order that platforms may be framed by those responsible to the people for carrying them into effect."

Indicative of Wilson's intention to have his own policies become the program of his Administration was his refusal to regard the provisions of the Democratic Party Platform of 1912 concerning a limitation of presidential tenure to a single, six-year term, and opposing a concession to Britain on the Panama tolls question.

was in accord with his obstinacy of character; for by nature he was unable to do other than lead.[88]   As long as he was successful in persuading the people to "look at matters in his way," there could be nothing reprehensible in his attempt to direct public opinion and in his efforts to secure the enactment of remedial legislation, concerning which the public may have hitherto given little or no thought; but there is clearly an element of danger in the attitude manifested by Wilson in 1920; namely, that the President is peculiarly competent to discern the welfare of the Nation, and that his confidence in this conviction, even though the people are temporarily unable to perceive the merits of his policy, justifies his continued insistence upon its adoption.

That his selection of his Cabinet would also be influenced by this disposition or manner of thinking was to be expected. Sensitive to criticisms, and, above all, determined to reserve to himself the task of formulating his administration policies, Wilson could not do otherwise than choose subservient, mediocre men as counsellors.   To have obtained men of prominence and of known competency who would have willingly submitted to complete domination by their President would have been unusual under any circumstances; but, by reason of his inability to make a prudent choice of associates, Wilson denied himself even the possibility of obtaining that advantage. The net result of his selection was a Cabinet of men who were either enthusiastic admirers of the President, or who offered no objection to a diminution of their activities to a mere efficient administration of their respective departments.   Such men he was disposed to procure from the fields of business and the law rather than of politics.[89]

---

[88] Illustrative of his intention to persist in the sponsorship of his own policies, even under adverse circumstances, are the following citations: "No high-spirited man would long remain in office in the business of which he was not permitted to pursue a policy which tallied with his own convictions and principles." Selected Literary and Political Papers of Woodrow Wilson (Harpers), I, 10.   [The President ought to be a] "man who understands his own day and the needs of the country, and who has the personality and the initiative to enforce his views both upon the people and upon Congress." Constitutional Government, p. 65.

[89] Nevertheless, the appointment of Bryan was a purely political

However, in view of the very definite opinions held by him concerning the limited services to be rendered the President by his Cabinet, the type of men selected by him was adequate for his purpose.

> Upon analysis it seems to mean this: the Cabinet is an executive, not a political body. The President cannot himself be the actual executive; he must therefore find, to act in his stead, men of the best legal and business gifts, and depend upon them for the actual administration of the government in all its daily activities . . . looking to them for advice in the actual conduct of the government rather than in the shaping of political policy. They are, in his view, not necessarily political officers at all.[90]

In the writings of a former member of his Cabinet [91] there is contained abundant evidence that the principle expressed in the above statement was applied in practice. Meetings of the President with his Cabinet, though held at regular intervals, were nevertheless of brief duration; and their discussions were limited, either to a presentation of information desired by Wilson, or to an exchange of reports concerning the needs, and the progress in the work, of the respective departments. Except for these assemblies, and occasional interviews with the President, however, his departmental chiefs were permitted to proceed unmolested to the fulfilment of their duties. Only when requesting his Secretaries to assist him in drafting a legislative proposal, or to serve as "liaison officers" between the President and Congress, did Wilson depart from his former opinion and employ his Cabinet for a political purpose.

---

one, and was a reward for his support of the candidacy of Wilson at the Democratic Convention of 1912. See also Ray S. Baker, Woodrow Wilson, Life and Letters, IV, 43 ff., as to Wilson's relations with Burleson.

[90] Constitutional Government, p. 76.

[91] William C. Redfield, With Congress and Cabinet.

CHAPTER II

FOREIGN RELATIONS

Of the numerous duties which have been assigned to the President, perhaps no one of them may be considered as more truly executive in character than his task of conducting the relations of his country with foreign governments. Nor have any provisions of the Constitution proved to be a more fertile source for the extension of his power than those which relate to this subject.[1] To explain the predominance which the President has attained in the business of conducting the foreign affairs of this Nation, one need only refer, however, to the unusual brevity of these constitutional provisions and to the inevitable necessity of according them a liberal construction. Thus, although the Constitution contains neither an express prohibition nor a sanction for his assumption of a power to issue a proclamation of neutrality, or to recognize a new state, the President would in this day view with disfavor any attempt to direct him in the performance of these acts. Furthermore, the disposition of the Chief Magistrate to conclude executive agreements without the consent of the Senate or, similarly, to appoint secret agents, or to take such action as will in effect estop Congress from exercising its discretion in determining the advisability of war, affords an unmistakable indication that his powers have been derived not merely from warranted deductions from the written word of the Constitution but also from the demands of practical expediency.

In seeking a justification for the ascendancy which they have exercised in the administration of foreign affairs, our foremost Executives have consequently been obliged to have recourse to an argument consisting of broad implications. The Constitution being silent on the questions at issue, their first effort has been to introduce historical evidence to prove that, prior to the Convention of 1787, the control of foreign

---

[1] Art. 2, Secs. 1, 2, 3.

affairs had been uniformly adjudged to be an executive function; and to suggest, incidentally, that experience has demonstrated that the executive department of a government is best adapted to assume that control. But, while this "historical" argument has satisfactorily vindicated the President in his exercise of such authority as is necessary and is reasonably inferable from the express provisions of the Constitution, no equally convincing defense has been adduced in support of those acts which have in effect excluded Congress from its exercise of the powers referred to above. However, those Executives who have been guilty of such action may be presumed to have subscribed to the view that, notwithstanding the particular distribution of powers, the framers of the Constitution never intended to deny to the President the employment of those measures of expediency which the head of every state has found necessary for the protection of its interests.

When acting in pursuance of this interpretation, the President is accountable only to the electorate. Since the courts have held non-justiciable disputes concerning the propriety of his committing the Government by his independent decision, the houses of Congress have therefore had to avail themselves of either their own resources or an adverse popular vote, in order successfully to contest the President's assertion of a supremacy in the conduct of foreign affairs. Theoretically, no act of the President can force the hand of Congress, because, as a separate coordinate body, it possesses an indefeasible sanction for the exercise of its constitutional powers; but, when, in practice, the policy of the Executive involves the honor or safety of the Nation, Congress has seldom had any option other than to support him.

Owing to the prevalence of foreign difficulties during the first decade of the existence of the Federal Government, an excellent opportunity was presented for an early pronouncement of the interpretation which the President would place upon his powers with reference to foreign affairs. Although our first Chief Magistrate foresaw at the very outset that the President was to be the conduit for every exchange of negotiations between the Federal Government and foreign nations, nevertheless, his anxiety for the success of the new Nation, and his uncertainty in defining the limits of the participation allotted to Congress, deterred him from acting as confidently and as expeditiously as did his successors in conducting American foreign relations. Hence, many of the pertinent decisions made during his Administration were not wholly the product of his own mind, but were ventured upon only after he had received the mature advice of his counsellors, Hamilton and Jefferson.

Irrespective of the manner in which Washington arrived at his plan of action, his issuance of a proclamation of neutrality and his subsequent recognition of the new French Republic clearly indicated that he considered the task of formulating the foreign policy of his Government to be an executive function. But, in reaching his decision on each occasion, he seems to have been governed by practical motives and intuition rather than by a profound appreciation of his constitutional powers. In short, while he was convinced that the welfare of the Nation demanded its observance of neutrality for the duration of the war on the continent, he was not at all certain that it would be permissible for him to assume the sole responsibility for proclaiming that neutrality to the world.

To remove whatever apprehensions he may have had on this issue, he submitted the following list of questions to his Cabinet:

(1) Shall a proclamation issue for the purpose of preventing interferences of the citizens of the United States in the war between France and Great Britain? Shall it contain a declaration of neutrality or not? What shall it contain?

(2) Shall a minister from the Republic of France be received?

(3) Whether a reasonable interpretation of their obligations to France under the existing treaty of alliance would permit the United States to remain neutral under the present circumstances?

(4) Is it necessary or advisable to call together the two Houses of Congress, with a view to the present posture of European affairs? If it is, what should be the particular object of such a call?[2]

From an examination of these questions it appears that

---

[2] Jared Sparks, Life and Writings of Washington, X, 533.

Washington did intend to issue at least a tentative statement of the attitude which his country would adopt with reference to the existing war in Europe, but was undecided as to whether the President could give to his utterance the finality of a neutrality proclamation, or whether that more momentous decision would require the cooperation of Congress.

When the Cabinet finally consented to his proposal to announce publicly the intention of the United States to remain at peace with the warring nations, Washington was sufficiently encouraged to follow his original inclinations. Choosing a draft of a proclamation prepared for him by his Attorney-General, Randolph,[3] he declared, on April 22, 1793,[4] that it did not comport with the interests of the United States to be other than a spectator in his struggle, and exhorted all loyal citizens, upon pain of prosecution for disobedience, not to embarrass their Government by engaging in any unneutral activities prohibited by the Law of Nations.

In order to arouse popular sentiment against this announcement, and to reveal as sinister the influence exerted upon the President by the chief advocate of neutrality (Hamilton), the party in opposition attacked the proclamation on the grounds that Washington had no express authority to issue it, and, secondly, that it might involve the country in the conflict before Congress could be granted the opportunity of exercising its constitutional power to declare war. Although he employed a more extensive interpretation of executive power than was necessary for his case, Hamilton successfully undertook to vindicate Washington's decision. " The general doctrine of our Constitution then is," he argued, " that the executive power of the nation is vested in the President; subject only to the exceptions and qualifications which are expressed in that instrument." Since the conduct of foreign relations was clearly an executive duty to which the question of neutrality was related, and since no specific provision in the Constitution forbade the issuance of the proclamation, the

---

[3] John H. Latané, American Foreign Policy, p. 81.
[4] Sparks, X, 535-536.

President, in his opinion, had acted within his authority. Furthermore, he added, whatever exercise the President might make of his constitutional powers ought never to be construed as limiting in any way the freedom of Congress to make a similar exercise of its own powers.[5]

On the other hand, Jefferson, in deference to whom the word "neutrality" had been omitted from the proclamation, had originally opposed its issuance largely because he believed it to be more expedient to await the decision of Congress on the matter.

The idea seems to gain credit that the powers combined against France will prohibit supplies even of provisions to that country. Should this be formally notified, I should suppose Congress would be called, because it is a justifiable cause of war, and as the Executive cannot decide the question of war on the affirmative side, neither ought he to do so on the negative side by preventing the competent body from deliberating on the question.[6]

His reasoning in this instance is obviously contrary to the second principle enumerated above by Hamilton, and would also appear to be inconsistent with his later refusal to be bound by the decision of the Federal Courts, a "competent body," on a law which he, himself, believed to be unconstitutional.[7] Moreover, the attitude which he adopted in this issue might also be deemed to be a departure from the context of another of his often-quoted utterances.

The transaction of the business with foreign nations is executive altogether. It belongs then to the head of that department except as to such portions of it as are especially submitted to the Senate. Exceptions are to be construed strictly.[8]

After having issued his proclamation, Washington established what was perhaps a more significant precedent when he undertook to secure the fulfilment of those obligations imposed upon every neutral by the Law of Nations. However, because public opinion in the East, as reflected by grand juries, deprecated the initiation of proceedings without an

---

[5] Quoted by Edwin S. Corwin, The President's Control of Foreign Relations, pp. 11-12.
[6] Jefferson's Writings (Ford Ed.), VII, 250.
[7] Above, p. 21.
[8] Writings (Ford Ed.), V, 162.

express authorization by Congress, prosecutions instituted by the executive department for infractions of these obligations were unproductive. Discerning the practical advantage of complying with the public will, Washington abandoned whatever opinion he may have had of his powers in this matter, and persuaded Congress to enact a bill denominating certain unneutral activities as "crimes against the United States." [9]

Every President who has issued a similar proclamation of neutrality has realized, as fully as did Washington, that he has pledged his country to the observance of a definite rule of conduct and that, if its honor is to be maintained, some one must assume the responsibility of seeing that this pledge is fulfilled. Although Congress has, by a series of Acts, conferred upon the Executive ample authority to secure the enforcement of neutrality, a precedent recently established

---

[9] 1 Stat. L. 381. The verdict of acquital in "Gideon Henfield's Case," tried before the Circuit Court for the District of Pennsylvania, in 1793, led directly to the passage of the Neutrality Act of the following year. The effect of this verdict was to create a doubt in Washington's mind as to whether the inability of the Administration to obtain a conviction would be regarded by its opponents as evidence of the illegality of its position, and it was to remove that possibility that he requested the aid of Congress.

Nevertheless, authoritative judicial opinion of that day, despite the subsequent acknowledgment of the erroneousness of its conclusion, did not consider the additional authorization of Congress as necessary to validate this prosecution. Thus, Supreme Court Justices Wilson and Iredell, sitting with Judge Peters, instructed the jury that: "The participation by the citizens of a neutral State in an attack by one belligerent power upon another is an offense against the law of nations, and may be punished as such by a Neutral State. . . Though there may have been no exercise of the power conferred upon Congress by the Constitution 'to define and punish offenses against the law of nations,' the federal judiciary has jurisdiction of an offense against the law of nations, and may proceed to punish an offender according to the forms of the common law; and it seems that the federal courts have a common law cognizance of offenses against the sovereignty of the United States." Fed. Cas. No. 6360.

In the later case of United States v. Hudson and Godwin, 7 Cranch 32, the Supreme Court emphatically reversed the decision of the lower court and held that: "The Legislative authority of the Union must first make an act a crime, affix a punishment to it, and declare the Court shall have jurisdiction of the offense. . . . The Courts of the United States have no common law jurisdiction in cases against the government of the United States."

would, nevertheless, seem to suggest that, even in the absence of an express sanction, Presidents will follow their predecessor, Washington, in making every effort to perform this manifest duty.

Thus, in order to remove a potential danger to the faithful preservation of his policy of neutrality, Woodrow Wilson, in 1914, seized the radio station at Siasconset, Massachusetts. In taking this action, he was supported by his Attorney-General, who declared:

> If the President is of the opinion that the relations of this country with foreign nations are, or are likely to be, endangered by actions deemed by him inconsistent with a due neutrality, it is his right and duty to protect such relations; and in doing so, in the absence of any statutory restriction, he may act through such executive officer or department as appears best adapted to effectuate the desired end . . . to secure obedience to his proclamation of neutrality.[10]

Incidental to the publication of the neutrality proclamation was the determination of Washington to receive Citizen Genêt, the minister of the new French Republic. In addition to their serving as assurances that the Executive would ascertain the future course of American foreign relations, these two precedents, in themselves, were to constitute traditional foreign policies; the one, as to the conduct which the United

---

[10] 30 Op. Atty.-Gen., 291. See also: Messages and Papers of the Presidents, XVII, 7962. Executive Order, August 5, 1914; ibid., p. 8006. Executive Order, September 5, 1914. In delegating to the Navy Department the control of these stations, Wilson cited for his authority the Act of 1912 (37 Stat. L. 302); but a doubt exists as to whether the terms of this act were intended to apply to this particular situation.

It may be of interest to note herein an analogous exercise of power by the President. With a view to protecting the commercial interests of his country, the Executive, acting through the State Department, assumed the exclusive right to determine whether telegraph companies should be permitted to land cables along our coasts. Although the executive control over the grant of cable landing licenses had not been subjected to judicial inquiry for almost a half century, the courts in the case of United States v. Western Union Telegraph Co., 272 F. 311, 393, declared that, in the absence of an express authorization, the President had no power to refuse a license to a domestic corporation. Whether, independent of statute, he might legally refuse to grant a license to a foreign company was not decided, but the court intimated that he could not. However, a recent act of Congress permits the Executive to continue his control over the grants of these licenses. Leslie B. Tribolet, The International Aspects of Electrical Communications in the Pacific Area, pp. 20, 56.

States will observe ·in the event of a foreign war; the other, as to the tests which this Government will require before according recognition to a new government or state.[11] While the reception of Genêt was also to form the basis of the presumption that the power of recognition resides exclusively with the President, that precedent, strictly construed, merely demonstrated that the Executive, through his power "to receive ambassadors and other public ministers" has in his possession one of the most usual means of granting recognition to a new state.

At this point it is necessary to interrupt the trend of the discussion by presenting those statements of Secretary Jefferson, in which were set forth those rules of procedure which have since governed the exchange of communications between envoys of a foreign state and officers of the Federal Government. In criticizing Genêt for his breaches of diplomatic etiquette, Jefferson said:

> The President being the only channel of communication between this country and foreign nations, it is from him alone that foreign nations or their agents are to learn what is or has been the will of the nation, and whatever he communicates as such they have a right and are bound to consider as the expression of the nation, and no foreign agent can be allowed to question it . . .[12] [Nor is it] the established course for diplomatic characters residing here to have any direct correspondence with him. The Secretary of State is the organ through which their communications should pass.[13]

In view of the disposition of recent Executives, particularly Wilson, to dispense with the agency of the State Department, and personally to direct foreign negotiations, it is of interest to note that Washington appears to have been deterred from initiating this practice by fear of adverse popular criticism.

> You will give me leave to say, likewise, that no third person (were there a disposition for it) shall ever have it in his power to erect a wall between me and the diplomatic corps, that is to say, to prevent necessary communications. Nor has anybody insinuated, that it would be beneath the dignity of a President of the United States occasionally to transact business with a foreign minister. But in

---

[11] However, the credit for enunciating the first American recognition policy belongs to Jefferson. It was his argument in favor of the acknowledgment of the new French Government that influenced Washington to receive Genêt. Writings (Ford Ed.), VII, 285.

[12] Writings, IV, 84, 90.

[13] John B. Moore, Digest of International Law, IV, 686.

what light the public might view the establishment of a precedent for negotiating the business of a department, without any agency of the head of the department, who was appointed for that very purpose, I do not at present pretend to determine. . . .[14]

Similarly, the likelihood that the peaceful status of our relations with France might have been jeopardized by a request for Genêt's recall, caused him to hesitate before exercising that privilege, although he never doubted that this power could be inferred very clearly from his authority to receive foreign representatives. Not until he had received the advice of his Cabinet did he finally proceed to forward a dispatch to Paris requesting the minister's recall. In contrast to the hesitancy of Washington to assume this unavoidable responsibility was the dispatch with which Wilson dismissed von Bernstoff, and severed relations with Germany; a measure which was but a preliminary to a declaration of war.

In addition to the customary mode of receiving an accredited foreign minister, succeeding Executives have devised other forms of procedure for the purpose of expressing their recognition of a new state or government. For example, Jefferson did not await the arrival of the representative of the Napoleonic Government (1804), but successfully entered into official relations with the new French ruler by dispatching a new set of credentials to the American minister resident at Paris.[15] Or the President may instruct his ambassador, as did Wilson in the case of the Revolutionary Government of Russia (March 22, 1917), when he directed Mr. Francis to make an oral declaration of recognition to the officials of the new government.[16] However, in recognizing the succession states of the late War (Poland, Finland, Jugo-Slavia, Czecho-Slovakia, and Armenia), Wilson preferred to follow the plan of having his Secretary of State, Lansing, either issue a public pronouncement of recognition, or communicate a written acknowledgment of the same to the executives of those countries.[17]

---

[14] Sparks, X, 10.
[15] Moore, Digest, I, 122.
[16] Messages and Papers of the Presidents, XVII, 8270.
[17] Clarence Berdahl, "The Power of Recognition," in American Journal of International Law, XIV, 523-524.

Should the Executive desire to give a more democratic character to his decision, he may associate Congress with him in according recognition to a new state; but this act represents only a concession, and is not to be construed as an affirmance that there exists in Congress, either a concurrent power of recognition, or even a right to declare the recognition policy of the United States.[18] In so far as the Senate receives the opportunity to assent to a treaty, or to confirm the appointment whereby the recognition is to be expressed, that body may fairly be said to have participated in the exercise of that power. However, the failure of the Senate to consent or to confirm would not have the effect of nullifying the intent of the Executive to recognize a new state.

Especially, when the recognition of a succession state is calculated to arouse the displeasure of a third nation, the question has often been raised as to whether the President ought to be the sole judge of a matter of such importance to the safety of the country. Clearly, the solemnity of the situation cannot in law diminish the authority of the President; but the recollection that several Executives, Madison, Monroe, and Jackson, were wont to consult Congress prior to recognizing the South American Republics, has encouraged various members of Congress to claim for the legislative branch a right to be consulted and even to contend that it possesses a concurrent power of recognition.

The boldest pretension to an equal power of recognition ever to be made by Congress occurred during the Civil War, when the House supported two resolutions of Henry Winter Davis, Chairman of its Committee on Foreign Affairs, one of which contained the statement that:

Congress has a constitutional right to an authoritative voice in declaring . . . the foreign policy of the United States, as well in the recognition of new Powers as in other matters, and it is the constitutional duty of the President to respect that policy . . .[19]

---

[18] Corwin, p. 82; John M. Mathews, The Conduct of American Foreign Relations, pp. 123, 127.

[19] Edward McPherson, History of the Rebellion, pp. 349, 354; Berdahl, pp. 525-534.

Speaking for Lincoln, Secretary Seward commented upon these resolutions as follows:

> It truly represents the uniform sentiment of the people of the United States in regard to Mexico . . . it is, however, another and distinct question whether the United States would think it necessary or proper to express themselves in the form adopted by the House of Representatives at this time. This is a practical and purely Executive question, and a decision of it constitutionally belongs not to the House . . . , nor even to Congress, but to the President.[20]

Three years previously, however, Lincoln had condescended to solicit the cooperation of Congress in the matter of recognizing the insignificant republics of Haiti and Liberia. In his first Annual Message (December 3, 1861), he declared that:

> If any good reason exists why we should persevere longer in withholding our recognition of the independence and sovereignty of Haiti and Liberia, I am unable to discern it. Unwilling, however, to inaugurate a novel policy in regard to them without the approbation of Congress, I submit for your consideration the expediency of an appropriation for maintaining a chargé d'affaires near each of those new States.[21]

While this incident was cited by Davis in support of his argument, he was in error in believing that the act of appropriation passed by Congress in compliance with the President's request, was equivalent to a recognition of these Republics.[22]

Nothwithstanding the defeat of its principle in 1864, and contrary to its later admission that the power of recognition was wholly executive,[23] the Senate again sought to impose its advice upon President Wilson as to the policy to be observed with respect to Russia and Mexico. While a resolution of Senator King recommending the recognition of the Government of Omsk, Russia, was never reported, a second resolution by Senator Fall, advising the President to revoke his recognition of Carranza,[24] was more favorably received, and there existed a possibility of its being voted upon.

---

[20] McPherson, p. 350.
[21] Messages and Papers of the Presidents, VII, 3248.
[22] Mathews, p. 121 n.
[23] 54th Cong., 2d sess., S. Doc. No. 56 (1897).
[24] Berdahl, p. 538.

Resenting this action as an encroachment upon executive jurisdiction, as well as an attempt to oppose his policy of "watchful waiting" with reference to governmental changes in Mexico, Wilson promptly terminated this motion by an emphatic protest of Senator Fall declaring the unconstitutionality of his procedure.

I should be gravely concerned to see any such resolution pass the Congress. It would constitute a reversal of our constitutional practice, which might lead to very great confusion in regard to the guidance of our foreign affairs. I am convinced that I am supported by every competent constitutional authority in the statement that the initiative in directing the relations of our Government with foreign Governments is assigned by the Constitution to the Executive only. Only one of the Houses of Congress is associated with the President by the Constitution in an advisory capacity, and the advice of the Senate is provided for only when sought by the Executive in regard to explicit agreements with foreign Governments and the appointment of diplomatic representatives who are to speak for this Government at foreign capitals. The only safe course, I am confident, is to adhere to the prescribed method of the Constitution. We might go very far afield if we departed from it.[25]

No greater criticism can be attached to the conduct of Wilson and Lincoln in excluding Congress from a participation in their recognition of foreign states, or in ignoring the will of the legislative branch in such matters, than to the practice observed by former Presidents of securing or deferring to its advice in advance of their final action. Whether the gravity of a particular case will render it expedient for the two political departments of this Government to act in close concert is a question for the Executive alone to decide, and if any President should decide this question too consistently in the negative, as did Wilson, he would subject himself to no greater charge than of exercising an "undemocratic" control over American foreign relations. In taking the view that recognition was exclusively an executive power, Wilson was ably supported by judicial and constitutional authorities.[26]

The fears of Congress that the peace of this Nation ought not to be dependent upon the decision of one official would nevertheless seem to be justified by the premature recognitions

---

[25] New York Times, December 9, 1919.
[26] Willoughby, On the Constitution of the United States, I, 536. Williams v. Suffolk Insurance Co., 13 Peters 415.

of Panama and Czecho-Slovakia.[27] Only the inability of the parent states in either case effectively to protest exempted the United States from being involved in serious disputes.

Just as the President potentially has an unqualified right to express the attitude of his country on foreign occurrences of international significance, so may he be said to be equally free to supervise the progress of its negotiations with other nations.[28] Upon his disposition of the product of these negotiations, however, the Constitution has imposed certain restrictions.[29] As one commentator has stated it, the object of the Convention in establishing these limitations was to avoid the danger of entrusting too much to the decision of one man, without, on the other hand, depriving the Executive of that " secrecy, efficiency, and dispatch " necessary to the successful conduct of foreign affairs.[30] That this aim had been generally achieved ought to become apparent from a review of the practices adopted by the Executives now under discussion; for the latter have demonstrated that our Chief Magistrate, if he so desires, is able not only to preserve perfect secrecy during his intercourse with foreign envoys, but also to evade even the effect of the constitutional provisions grantin the Senate a coaction in such matters.

It is the frequency with which the Senate has been ignored of late that will perhaps distinguish the procedure followed by Washington, Jefferson, and Lincoln from that observed by Roosevelt and Wilson. Whereas the former were not unwilling to associate the Senate with them during the progress of a treaty negotiation, the latter exhibited an aversion to admit-

---

[27] Moore, Digest, III, 55-56. By recognizing and entering into negotiations with Panama, almost at the very instant that it revolted from Colombia, Roosevelt virtually ignored the sovereign right of the parent state to settle its internal disturbances.

When the United States recognized Czecho-Slovakia in 1918, that nation could be distinguished only by a provisional government or committee resident at Washington, and a small contingent of men fighting with the Allies. The Austro-Hungarian Monarchy was at that date in control of the territory which later comprised this succession state.

[28] Mathews, pp. 136-139.
[29] Art. 2, Sec. 2.
[30] John Jay, Federalist (Lodge Edition), p. 404; Corwin, p. 85.

ting the Senate to their proceedings other than for the purpose which the Constitution absolutely requires. Having resolved to employ their powers to the fullest measure, these recent Executives were confronted by a corresponding determination on the part of the Senate to have its prerogatives respected; and the result has been that the Upper House has, on numerous occasions, either refused to consent to a treaty, or has consented with conditions unacceptable to the negotiators. Whether the original responsibility for this obstructive attitude recently displayed by the Senate can be attributed to the uncompromising conduct of Roosevelt and Wilson, or whether it may be said to have been forced upon the legislative body the writer is not prepared to decide.

Unable to orientate himself by reason of the complete absence of guiding precedents, and extremely circumspect, lest, by any act abridging the Senate's powers, he forfeit its cooperation, Washington experimented almost at random in search of the most advisable procedure to adopt with reference to treaty-making. Believing that the framers of the Constitution intended that the Senate should serve as an advisory council to the President in the making of treaties, he first chose to take the Upper House into his confidence at every stage of the negotiation.[31]   Thus, in conferring with a delegation from the Senate as to the most desirable method of consultation, he suggested that:

> In all matters respecting treaties, oral communications seem indispensably necessary, because in these a variety of matters are contained, all of which not only require consideration, but some may undergo much discussion; to do which by written communications would be tedious without being satisfactory . . . The Senate, when this power is exercised, is evidently a council only to the President, however its concurrence may be to his acts.[32]

---

[31] Prior to his first, and last, oral conference with the Senate, he had requested the advice of that body on the necessity of according treaties with Indian tribes the formal ratification which the Constitution requires of those with foreign powers. Admitting that he desired our national procedure to be uniform, he nevertheless hesitated to act until the Senate had expressed its opinion on this question. The Senate, however, concurred with him in the belief that no distinction ought to be made, and that an Indian treaty, like any other treaty, must be submitted to it for its advice and consent. Messages and Papers of the Presidents, I, 53-54.
[32] Sparks, X, 484, 485.

But, while the abortive result of his first attempt to consult the Senate in person [33] convinced both himself and succeeding Executives of the unfeasibility of this plan, this incident did not dissuade Washington from furthering his desire to act in close concert with the Upper House.

What could not be effectively accomplished by oral conferences was to be done by written communications. Accordingly, when about to negotiate a treaty, Washington sometimes apprised the Senate of the terms of the proposed agreement, and expressly requested it to reply whether or not it could consent to the final draft of the treaty in the form presented. Or, as a substitute for this plan, he submitted the names of the negotiators together with a statement of their instructions, and declared that he would accept the Senate's confirmation of his nominees as an indication of its intention to consent to the treaty formulated in pursuance of these instructions. Moreover, not only did he thus assure himself of the support of that body in advance of the drafting of a treaty, but he continued to inform it of the progress of negotiations, and to consult it even after ratifications had been exchanged; particularly on such matters as the advisability of amending the existing treaty, or the interpretation of a treaty stipulation in dispute.[34]

In these practices, Washington was undoubtedly influenced by the advice of his Secretary of State, Thomas Jefferson. The latter took the view that, since the confirmation of the Upper House was necessary before a treaty could be ordained as a " law of the land," the Executive ought to insure to every treaty a successful ratification by informing the Senate of his intent to negotiate, of the purposes of his negotiation, and of any modification of the latter prior to the conclusion of a final agreement.[35] Consequently, when the American

---

[33] Memoirs of John Quincy Adams, VI, 427; quoted by Mathews, pp. 141, 142.

[34] Evidence of these practices will be found in: Ralston Hayden, The Senate and Treaties, chs. ii, iii; Messages and Papers of the Presidents, I, 62, 64, 68, 69, 71-72, 74, 96-97, 107-108, 110-114, 118-119, 127-128, 133, 139-144, 174-175, 181-182.

[35] Below, p. 74.

envoys to Spain were obliged to alter the object of their mission, it was Jefferson who suggested that the Senate ought to be informed of this change because its consent had been given only to the original instructions of our negotiators.[36]

Of the three remaining Executives who are now being considered, Lincoln was the only one who reverted to the early procedure initiated by our first Chief Magistrate.   Concerning the negotiations with Mexico instituted by the preceding Administration, he informed the Senate that he was willing to follow the policy of his predecessor, and would therefore request its advice as to the desirability of a treaty with that nation.[37]   However, when the Senate finally resolved to reply in the negative, the American minister, Corwin, had already drafted a treaty, and rather than appear discourteous to that country, Lincoln appealed to the Senate to reconsider the decision, confessing, nevertheless, "that the action of the Senate is of course conclusive against the acceptance of the treaties on my part."[38]   At an earlier date, he had also sought counsel from the Senate on a matter relating to the interpretation of an existing treaty.[39]

During the Administrations of Roosevelt and Wilson, the Senate had its participation in treaty-making reduced to the opportunity of consenting conditionally to the agreements submitted to it.   While it may have been informed of the list of the negotiators, the Upper House never was permitted to confirm the appointees,[40] and, in fact, received no official knowledge of the negotiations until the final draft of a treaty was transmitted to it for consideration.   To secure a favorable acceptance of their treaties, these Executives were compelled to rely either upon party support in the Senate, or upon their ability to impress their views upon the leaders of its Foreign Relations Committee.

---

[36] Writings (Ford Ed.), V, 442; Messages and Papers of the Presidents, I, 110.   Jefferson's advocacy of this policy does not appear to have been dictated by any principle of strict construction, but was founded rather upon reasons of expediency.
[37] Messages and Papers of the Presidents, VII, 3213, 3261, 3264.
[38] Ibid., pp. 3282-3283.
[39] Ibid., pp. 3268-3269.
[40] Hayden, pp. 37, 60-80, 137-138.

Before entering upon a discussion of this recent procedure, which is perhaps best illustrated by the negotiation of the Versailles Treaty, it may be of interest to note that this method was not unknown to Washington or Jefferson.[41] Discerning the necessity for clothing with secrecy their two most important negotiations, the Jay Treaty and the treaty for the purchase of Louisiana, these two Executives supplied the Senate with a general outline of the advantages to be secured by these agreements, and then proceeded to conclude their treaties without further consulting that body. Only the exceptional loyalty of the majority party to their Executive prevented the Senate from recording its protest against what was then deemed an improper exclusion of that House from the making of treaties.

Wilson entered office fully cognizant of the difficulties confronting the President in his attempts to secure a favorable acceptance of a treaty. In his " Constitutional Government " he had written:

> The President has not the same recourse when blocked by the Senate that he has when opposed by the House. When the House declines his counsel he may appeal to the nation . . .; but the Senate is not so immediately sensitive to opinion and is apt to grow, if anything, more stiff if pressure of that kind is brought to bear upon it . . . But there is another course which the President may follow . . . He may himself be less stiff and offish, may himself act in the true spirit of the Constitution and establish more intimate relations of confidence with the Senate on his own initiative, not carrying his plans to completion and then laying them in final form before the Senate to be accepted or rejected, but keeping himself in confidential communication with the leaders of the Senate while his plans are in course . . ., in order that there may be veritable counsel and a real accommodation of views instead of a final challenge and contest.[42]

But, when granted an opportunity to prove the efficacy of the latter alternative, he not only ignored it but reverted to the very procedure which, in his own opinion, was least calculated to result in success. Informed by the President of his intent to be his own negotiator and of the probable contents of the peace settlement,[43] the Senate received no further

---

[41] Messages and Papers of the Presidents, I, 145-146; 338-340.

[42] Constitutional Government in the United States, pp. 139-140.

[43] Messages and Papers of the Presidents, XVIII, 8423-8425, 8646-8648. The contention of several Senators that the President had

official communications from Wilson until he returned with the signed drafts of the treaty and covenant. Moreover, when Wilson had returned in February, on the very day he landed, he had delivered at Boston the first of a series of addresses designed to align public opinion in favor of the League, and thus created among Senate leaders the impression that they were to be brow-beaten into accepting the treaty.[44] Nor did his subsequent conduct allay their suspicions; for, after having forwarded the treaty to the Senate, he provided it with no further information,[45] but confined his attention to repeated conferences with the Senate Foreign Relations Committee in an effort to convince it of the prime importance of accepting the treaty as it stood.[46] At no time did he manifest any intention of compromising with the Senate, and when it became evident that his persuasive methods were accomplishing nothing, he resorted to his famous " swing around the circle ". Whether this last bit of strategy, if completely executed, could have reduced the Senate to submission is, however, a problem of speculation. Against his better judgment, perhaps, Wilson's relations with the Senate did degenerate into a "challenge and contest."

While the precedents established by Washington in the negotiation of a treaty have not been permanent, finality has nevertheless attached to the settlement of the disputed issue arising out of the Jay Treaty of 1796. The question presented at that date was whether or not the House of Representatives is entitled to deliberate upon the terms of a treaty which requires for its execution a monetary appropriation. Conceiving the passage of an appropriation bill to be an act of

denied that body its " right " to be represented on the peace commission appears ill-founded. Although service on such a mission is not an " office " in the sense that the Senators could be debarred from an appointment to it, their selection has hitherto been dependent solely on the inclination of the Executive and not upon any established right. Clarence Berdahl, " The War Powers of the Executive," in Illinois University Studies, IX, 237-246.

[44] New York Times, February 16, 1919.

[45] Ibid., July 23, 1919; Setember 2, 1919. Senator Lodge complained that of sixty-five requests for papers, only one had been honored.

[46] Ibid., July 24, 1919.

legislation, on which the Constitution had delegated to it an absolute discretion, the House requested Washington to submit for its consideration all papers pertaining to this treaty in order that it might become better informed of the purpose for which money was to be expended. Washington construed this call for papers as an assertion on the part of the House of a share in the effectuation of commercial treaties, and in the following terms denied the request:

> The nature of foreign negotiations requires caution, and their success must often depend upon secrecy; and even when brought to a conclusion a full disclosure of all the measures, demands, or eventual concessions . . . proposed or contemplated would be extremely impolitic; for this might have a pernicious influence on future negotiations, or produce immediate inconveniences, perhaps danger and mischief, in relation to other powers. The necessity of such caution and secrecy was one cogent reason for vesting the power of making treaties in the President, with the advice and consent of the Senate, the principle on which that body was formed confining it to a small number of members. To admit, then, a right in the House . . . to demand and to have as a matter of course all the papers respecting a negotiation with a foreign power would be to establish a dangerous precedent . . . As, therefore, it is perfectly clear to my understanding that the assent of the House . . . is not necessary to the validity of a treaty; as the treaty . . . exhibits in itself all the objects requiring legislative provision, and on these the papers called for can throw no light, and as it is essential to the due administration of the Government that the boundaries fixed by the Constitution between the different departments should be preserved, a just regard to the Constitution and to the duty of my office, . . . forbids a compliance with your request.[47]

The leaders of the House, however, acknowledged that the treaty power was vested exclusively with the President and the Senate [48] and that the necessity of preserving secrecy might well justify a refusal of their request; but they protested against the doctrine asserted by the Administration that the decision of the two aforementioned branches of the Government would be conclusive upon the House when acting in pursuance of the constitutional provision, that "no money shall be drawn from the Treasury but in consequence of appropriations made by law." [49] Washington was therefore in error in so far as he agreed with Hamilton in maintaining

---

[47] Messages and Papers of the Presidents, I, 186-188.
[48] Annals of Congress, 4th Cong., 1st sess., p. 771.
[49] Art. 1, Sec. 9.

that the legitimation of a treaty by the action of the President and Senate would operate to impose a corresponding ministerial duty upon the House to appropriate the funds stipulated in the agreement.

Among those who correctly dissented from this position was Jefferson, who announced that:

> The true theory of our Constitution [is] that when a treaty is made involving matters confided by the Constitution to the three branches of the Legislature jointly, the Representatives are as free as the President and Senate were, to consider whether the national interest requires or forbids their giving the forms and force of law to the articles over which they have a power.[50]

Only the celerity of the Representatives in appropriating in advance the money necessary for the treaty pending with Algiers [51] (1795) prevented the settlement of the Jay Treaty issue one year previously. During the negotiations of the former treaty, Washington had manifested a similar unwillingness to consult the House, an explanation of which may be found in the minutes of a conversation with Jefferson.

> He asked me, if the treaty stipulating a sum and ratified by him with the advice and consent of the Senate, would not be good under the Constitution, and obligatory on the Representatives to furnish the money? I [Jefferson] answered that it certainly would, and that it would be the duty of the Representatives to raise the money; but that they might decline to do what was their duty, and I thought that it might be incautious to commit himself by a ratification with a foreign nation, where he might be left in a lurch in the execution; it was possible too to conceive a treaty which it would not be their duty to provide for. He said that he did not like throwing too much into democratic hands, that if they would not do what the Constitution called for, the Government would be at an end, and must then assume another form . . . I had observed that wherever the agency of either, or both Houses would be requisite subsequent to a treaty to carry it into effect, it would be prudent to consult them previously; if the occasion admitted. That there was the same reason for consulting the House previously, where they were to be called on afterwards, and especially in the case of money, as they held the purse strings and would be jealous of them. However, he desired me to strike out the intimation that the seal would not be put until both Houses should have voted the money.[52]

However, not even Jefferson was to abide by his own recommendation; for, in securing the execution of the treaty for

---

[50] Writings (Ford Ed.), VII, 41.
[51] Hayden, p. 48.
[52] Writings (Ford Ed.), I, 191.

the purchase of Louisiana, he observed the procedure which has since been employed by succeeding Executives. This practice involves the submission to the House of the treaty and related papers, after it has been finally ratified by the President, in order that the Representatives may exercise "their functions as to those conditions which are within the power vested by the Constitution in Congress." [53]

Remaining for consideration are several precedents created by these Executives with reference to the authority of the President on the subject of the ratification and termination of treaties. In advising and consenting to Jay's treaty with Britain, the Senate stipulated, as a condition of its ratification, that negotiations be resumed for the purpose of suspending the operation of Article XII of that treaty. Having been successful in getting England to sign an agreement toward that end, Washington then found it necessary to consult his Cabinet in order to determine whether the latter need be resubmitted to the Senate. Although Hamilton counselled otherwise, Washington adopted the opinion of Randolph, his Secretary of State, and declined to resubmit the treaty.[54] On the other hand, when, as in the case of the treaty with France (1800), the conditions were reversed and the foreign power ratified conditionally, Jefferson did return the treaty to the Senate.[55]

As the sole instrument of communication between the United States and foreign powers, and as the initiator of its foreign policy, the President is the proper officer to announce to the world that his Government no longer desires to be bound by its obligations arising under a treaty with a foreign power. Whether he is competent to assume the initiative in denouncing a treaty, or whether he must first obtain the consent of the Senate, or seek a congressional authorization is a disputed question, however; but, perhaps, the better view is that the same powers which negotiated a treaty, that is, the

---

[53] Messages and Papers of the Presidents, I, 347.
[54] Samuel B. Crandall, Treaties, Their Making and Enforcement, pp. 79-81.
[55] Ibid., p. 86.

President and Senate, ought to concur in the transmission of a notice of termination.[56] On the other hand, even if it be assumed that the President must act in concert with the Senate or Congress, he is by no means subordinate to them in this matter; for clearly the latter cannot legally compel him to terminate a treaty.

That acts of Congress authorizing, or directing the President to denounce an agreement with a foreign power are ineffective as against his decision to adopt a contrary policy was convincingly illustrated during the Administrations of Lincoln and Wilson. Thus, while the Houses of Congress in 1864 were deliberating upon the expediency of denouncing the Rush-Bagot agreement with Britain, Secretary Seward, on his own initiative, notified London authorities of his desire to be released from the terms of that compact. Although his action was approved by a joint resolution signed by Lincoln, Seward subsequently chose to reverse his position and requested Britain to ignore his earlier notice of termination.[57] In contrast with this resolution of 1864, which merely expressed the congressional approbation of an act already performed by the Executive Department, the Jones Merchant Marine Act of 1920 practically ordered the President to terminate "treaty provisions" which "restrict the right of the United States to impose discriminating" customs and tonnage duties. Through the State Department, Wilson let it be known that he would not execute this order for the reasons: (1) that he did not consider it to represent the "exercise of any Constitutional power possessed by the Congress," and (2) that a compliance with this direction "would amount to nothing less than a breach or violation of said treaties." [58]

Reverting now to a statement made at the beginning of this chapter, the writer reiterates that, while a conservative interpretation of the Constitution would seem to demand that the President procure the consent of the Senate for his appointment of foreign envoys and for his treaties, executive

---

[56] Willoughby, I, 585; Mathews, ch. xiii; contra, Taft, pp. 116-117.
[57] Moore, Digest, V, 169-170, 323.
[58] Messages and Papers of the Presidents, XVIII, 8871-8872.

ingenuity has devised methods, whether strictly legal or not, whereby the Upper House can be excluded from its participation in these matters. To debar the Senate, in the initial stage, from its share in his conduct of a negotiation requiring secrecy, the President has repeatedly resorted to the appointment, without confirmation, of what have been variously denominated secret, private, special, or executive agents. In an effort to justify this practice, writers have classified these agents, like treaty negotiators, as personal representatives of the President, and not as public ministers recognized by the Constitution and have denied that there is contained in their missions those attributes of a public office as were defined in United States v. Hartwell.[59] Arguing by implication, one authority adds that this practice is well established in international usage, and would seem to be possessed by the Executive in his capacity as director of our foreign relations; that the preservation of secrecy necessitates the employment of these agents; and, finally, that even Congress has tacitly sanctioned this practice by the appropriation of contingent funds for the expenses of international intercourse.[60] Moreover, unless the Executive abuses this privilege, the Senate has also been disposed to regard these appointments as a well established practice.[61]

Washington instituted this practice in the very first year of our Government by requesting Gouverneur Morris, then at London, to negotiate in a private and unofficial capacity for the resumption of official relations with Britain. By subsequently informing the Senate of his reasons for adopting this course, Washington doubtless escaped any censure for this precedent.[62] During the Civil War, a group of men, bearing the same unofficial status as did Gouverneur Morris, were sent

---

[59] 6 Wallace 385; Willoughby, III, 1513.
[60] Henry Wriston, " Presidential Special Agents in Diplomacy," in American Political Science Review, X, 481-488.
[61] 56th Cong., 2d sess., S. Doc. No. 231.
[62] Messages and Papers of the Presidents, I, 88. Although David Humphreys bore the sealed commission of a ranking envoy when dispatched to negotiate a treaty with Algiers, his selection was made during the recess of the Senate, and here also that body was subsequently informed. Below, p. 130.

abroad by Lincoln for the purpose of pleading the Union cause in Europe.[63]   Having implicated the United States, by their ambitious policies, in many of the international difficulties of their day, Roosevelt and Wilson not infrequently resorted to the use of private agents in order to envelop their negotiations in secrecy.   Thus, under Wilson, a secret mission headed by Ex-Governor John Lind was sent to Mexico, the noted Colonel House was sent to Europe, and a group led by Elihu Root as ambassador extraordinary went to Russia.[64]   It would seem, however, that, when an agent is to be given the rank of a public minister, as in the case of Mr. Root, the justification for his appointment without confirmation must rest on other than legal grounds.

When the secret agents also conclude an agreement that is in turn not submitted to the Senate, the exclusion of that house from a particular negotiation is rendered complete. One of the most notable incidents in which the Executive has sought to accomplish by simple agreement what he had failed to do by treaty was the *modus vivendi* contracted with Santo Domingo by American naval authorities.   The Senate having refused to accept the original " protocol " by which the United States agreed to supervise the financial reconstruction of that country, Roosevelt felt himself obliged to adopt the former expedient in order to carry out a policy which he deemed was necessitated by our observance of the Monroe Doctrine.[65]   Because this event constitutes a practical application of his theory of the Presidency, Roosevelt's own explanation of his conduct may be quoted at length:

The Constitution did not explicitly give me power to bring about a necessary agreement with Santo Domingo. But the Constitution did not forbid my doing what I did. I put the agreement into effect, and I continued its execution for two years before the Senate acted; and I would have continued it until the end of my term, if necessary, without any action of Congress. But it was far preferable that there should be action by Congress, so that we might be proceeding under a treaty which was the law of the land and not merely by a direction of the Chief Executive which would lapse when that par-

---

[63] John W. Foster, The Practice of Diplomacy, pp. 200-201.
[64] Mathews, p. 76 n.; Messages and Papers of the Presidents, XVI, 7885.
[65] Latané, p. 547.

ticular executive left office. I therefore did my best to get the Senate to ratify what I had done . . . Enough Republicans were absent to prevent the securing of a two-thirds vote . . . , and the Senate adjourned without any action at all, and with a feeling of entire self-satisfaction at having left the country in a position of assuming a responsibility and then failing to fulfill it. Apparently the Senators in question felt that in some way they had upheld their dignity. All that they had really done was to shirk their duty. Somebody had to do that duty, and accordingly I did it. I went ahead and administered the proposed treaty anyhow, considering it as a simple agreement on the part of the Executive which would be converted into a treaty whenever the Senate acted.[66]

However, there have been several executive agreements negotiated by the President on his own initiative which do not bear any resemblance to a treaty, and in fact were not intended to be regarded as such. They merely express in concrete form the foreign policy of this Government with reference to a particular international problem, and are binding, though they may be continued by his successors, only upon the Executive who negotiated them. To be included in this group are the Root-Takahira agreement of 1908 and the Lansing-Ishii agreement of 1917. The true status of the latter was defined by Wilson when he declared that it "was not an agreement at all but an understanding." [67] As in

---

[66] Autobiography, pp. 551-552; Joseph B. Bishop, Theodore Roosevelt and his Time, I, 432. One of the most questionable attempts to accomplish by executive act what is believed by authorities to require a treaty was the extradition of one Arguelles by Seward to Spain, a nation with whom we had no reciprocal extradition agreement. Although Lincoln assumed the responsibility for this act of his subordinate, a member of his Cabinet has charged Seward with the entire blame for this illegality. Diary of Gideon Welles, II, 36, 45-46. See also, Willoughby, I, 546; Diplomatic Correspondence, 1864-1865, part 2, pp. 60-61.

In his volume on the Presidency, William H. Taft recalls that the work on the Panama Canal project was in part carried out under the authority of a " modus vivendi " negotiated with Panama by Roosevelt. Upon his discovery that the existing treaty with that country failed to deal adequately with this undertaking, Roosevelt preferred to employ this more tenuous form of agreement, rather than risk delay by negotiating a new treaty. Our Chief Magistrate and His Powers, pp. 111-112.

[67] New York Times, July 11, 1919. Among other agreements effected by an exchange of notes during Wilson's Administration was one with Britain extending the application of existing extradition treaties to new areas, and another with Panama, granting reciprocally to consuls permission to note values of exports given by shippers to customs inspectors. Foreign Relation, 1913, pp. 549, 1068; Crandall, p. 117.

the case of the employment of executive agents, the President's sanction for the negotiation of these agreements is derived by implication from his general powers of control over our foreign relations, and from the broader proposition that the American Chief Magistrate, except where constitutionally restricted, is invested with authority equal to that exercised by foreign executives in the conduct of international relations.[68] However, should a President indulge too often in this practice, he would subject himself to the charge of exerting an undemocratic control over our foreign affairs.

Deducible from his powers as Commander-in-Chief is the authority of the President to enter into provisional military agreements with foreign powers, granting rights of entry to their troops, or obtaining reciprocal rights of " hot pursuit " into their territories, or even securing assistance in disposing of a particular evil. However, the power of the President to conclude such agreements is so well established, that the writer believes it unnecessary to discuss those entered into by Lincoln, Roosevelt and Wilson.[69]

On many occasions, the President has also offered his assistance to American citizens possessing claims against foreign governments, and has concluded agreements for the settlement of these claims, either directly, or indirectly, through the submission of the matter to arbitration. On the other hand, the President has refused to settle in a like manner claims against the United States for the obvious reason, not to mention any other, that he can give our creditors no assurance that Congress will appropriate funds to fulfil their award. In disposing of claims against this Nation, both Wilson and Lincoln recognized their dependence upon the legislative branch.[70]

---

[68] Watts v. United States, I Wash. Terr. 288; quoted by Crandall, pp. 106-107; Mathews, pp. 182-183.

[69] Tucker v. Alexandroff, 183 U. S. 435; Crandall, pp. 103, 106.

[70] Messages and Papers of the Presidents, VII, 3343; Wilson to Lloyd George on the question of the purchase of the German ships, Cong. Record, LIX, 3249 (February 21, 1920); Mathews, p. 178. If, however, the United States is to be the recipient of a sum of money, without becoming obligated thereby, as in the case of the Boxer

With the numerous other executive agreements negotiated in pursuance of an Act of Congress, the writer does not propose to deal; for, in these instances, the President is merely performing his constitutional duty of seeing to the faithful execution of the laws. Although the weight of authority is of the opinion that the President may be empowered by the terms of a treaty to conclude a similar agreement, the Senate, in amending the arbitration treaties of 1905, inclined to the opposite view. In permitting Roosevelt, in accordance with the original terms of these treaties, to negotiate a protocol with a foreign power prior to the submission of a particular dispute to the Hague Court, the Senate would, it argued, have consented to a delegation of the treaty power, but the better opinion is that it would have only authorized the President to execute the terms of the treaties.[71]

A review of the precedents established by our foremost Presidents in their conduct of foreign affairs makes apparent the inaccuracy of the early prophesies that the power of the Executive to receive foreign envoys would remain a mere ceremonial duty. Nevertheless, in assuming the initiative in declaring our foreign policy, the President exercises a power which would seem to be opposed, at least, to the spirit if not

---

Indemnity, an agreement providing for the payment of the money need not be submitted.

[71] John B. Moore, "Treaties and Executive Agreements," in Political Science Quarterly, XX, 385-520. This argument, which the Senate again employed to defend its rejection of similar treaties negotiated by Taft, was criticized by the latter as follows: "There is no difference in principle between the consent of the Senate that an existing issue between us and a foreign nation shall be settled by arbitration and an agreement that future questions of a defined class shall be so settled. If the submission of a question to arbitration is a delegation to the arbitration tribunal of the power vested in the Senate over our foreign relations, then the Senate has no power to consent to arbitration at all . . . But it is said that by delegating to a preliminary tribunal the question whether the issue arising is within the terms of the treaty or not, the Senate is delegating its power. This view is as faulty as the other one. The question whether an issue is arbitrable within the classification of the treaty is a question of the construction of a treaty; and one of the commonest subjects of arbitration is the proper construction of a treaty. Therefore, . . . it is only consenting to arbitrate the construction of the treaty when the event occurs which requires construction." Our Chief Magistrate and His Powers, pp. 107-108.

to the principle of free government; for the safety of the country is thus entrusted to the decision of one man. Nor were our Executives who have distinguished themselves in the formulation of American foreign policy altogether unmindful of the huge responsibilities attending their assumption of this task. The logic governing their conduct, however, has been that, since the Executive alone has access to the only source of accurate information available concerning international conditions, he, better than any group of Congressmen or even interested voters, is capable of discerning the policy most conducive to his country's welfare. Consequently, in order to determine to what extent a recognition of their accountability to the electorate may have tempered their inclination to rely wholly upon their own judgment, one must examine the nature of the foreign policies enunciated by these several Executives, with a view to discovering whether these policies were positive or negative; that is, whether they held the Government to inaction or involved it in foreign difficulties.

That the traditional policies of recognition, neutrality, and isolation proclaimed by Washington were pacific in character requires no demonstration. Although he undertook to prescribe for the new nation a line of policy which, in his opinion, was essential to its future development, and proceeded to act in accordance with this policy, public sentiment to the contrary notwithstanding,[72] in no instance did the application of his foreign policies preclude the popular branch of this Government from subsequently adopting a different position with respect to our relations with other powers.

On the other hand, it has been frequently true of the policies initiated by recent Executives that a thorough execution of them would have imposed upon this Government obligations from which it could not honorably escape. While the interests of the United States were undoubtedly rashly handled by Jefferson when he contemplated marrying his country " to the British fleet and nation " in the event of his

---

[72] Thus, his proclamation of neutrality and his negotiation of the Jay Treaty were vigorously denounced by sections of the press and public.

failure to obtain Louisiana, nevertheless, the danger incurred by this single negotiation appears negligible in comparison with the consequences which might have ensued from the projects contemplated by the late Mr. Roosevelt. His intervention in the Venezuelan financial disturbance, his proffered assistance in the settlement of the Russo-Japanese War, and his subsequent participation in the Algeciras Conference, all presented a single issue; namely, whether it is permissible for a constitutional Executive to indulge in secret diplomacy, and to threaten to use the armed forces of the United States for the support of a foreign nation in distress.

Thus, in order to secure the observance of the Monroe Doctrine and to dissuade Germany, the most aggressive of the European creditors, from enforcing her claims upon Venezuela, Roosevelt is reputed to have informed Herr Holleben, the German envoy at Washington, as follows:

I saw the Ambassador and explained that in view of the presence of the German squadron on the Venezuelan coast, I could not permit longer delay in answering my request for arbitration and that I could not acquiesce in any seizure of Venezuelan territory . . . I then asked him to inform his government that if no notification for arbitration came within a certain specified number of days, I should be obliged to order Dewey to take his fleet to the Venezuelan coast and see that the German forces did not take possession of any territory.[73]

Absolute secrecy veiled this incident, but had it provoked hostilities, Roosevelt in all probability could have rallied public opinion to support what would very likely have been portrayed as a defense of our traditional doctrine.

However, one can only speculate as to whether there would have been an unwillingness on the part of the American people to vindicate their President if his diplomacy had involved the United States in a war in defense of Japan against Europe, or France against Germany. Having never manifested any profound concern in the destinies of these far distant nations, the public might readily have been expected to question the wisdom of taking up arms in their defense. But Roosevelt apparently was not perturbed by this possibility; for his warning to France and Germany not to inter-

---

[73] Bishop, I, 223.

vene in the Russo-Japanese War was even more provocative than his utterances in the Venezuelan crisis.

> As soon as the war broke out, I notified Germany and France in the most polite and discreet fashion that in the event of a combination against Japan to try to do what Russia, Germany, and France did to her in 1894, I should promptly side with Japan . . . to whatever length was necessary on her behalf.[74]

Once he had been successful in his efforts to bring Russia and Japan to an amicable agreement, his services as peacemaker were again requested, on this occasion by Germany, at the conference held at Algeciras in 1904. Although his influence may have sufficed to terminate this European crisis, he was able to effect this result only by favoring the claims of one nation rather more than those of another, and by this choice invited the possible enmity of the defeated party.[75]

In this hemisphere, Roosevelt enunciated the modern corollary to the Monroe Doctrine, his " Big Stick " policy; [76] in pursuance of which both he and his successors, Taft and Wilson, have employed the armed forces of the United States for police duty in the Caribbean area. While a judicial sanction has attached to the President's use of troops, under his authority as Commander-in-Chief, for the purpose of protecting the life and property of our citizens resident abroad, the question presented by these recent incursions into Haiti, Santo Domingo, and Nicaragua was: whether or not the Executive, in the absence of congressional authorization, is empowered to accord a like protection to our claim of a " sphere of interest " in these areas.[77] The popular conception seems to be that if marines are employed, the expedition is a police measure, but if troops of the regular army are

---

[74] Tyler Dennett, Roosevelt and the Russo-Japanese War, p. 2.

[75] Latané, p. 572.

[76] Messages and Papers of the Presidents, XV, 6923.

[77] By virtue of the treaties negotiated with Haiti and Nicaragua (1916) during Wilson's Administration, a definite sanction has been obtained for the employment of such military measures as may in the future become necessary to preserve peace in these areas. See also, Durand v. Hollins, Fed. Cas. No. 4186.

dispatched, the intervention may then assume the aspect of war.[78]

Most clearly illustrative of the new aggressive policy which has been adopted with reference to the Central American Republics was the conduct of Roosevelt in acquiring the Canal Zone. Although an existing treaty (1846) with Colombia permitted the use of troops to preserve the sovereignty of that Republic over the Isthmus, his action resulted in the denial of the right of a parent state to quell its own domestic disturbances. As he later admitted, his intention was to create a situation which the Government could not disregard.

If I had followed traditional conservative methods, I should have submitted a dignified state paper of probably two hundred pages to Congress, and the debate on it would be going on yet; but I took the Canal Zone and let Congress debate, and while the debate goes on, the Canal does too.[79]

What has been said of Roosevelt may also be applied to Wilson. By words, if not by deed, he disclosed his agreement with the views of his predecessor: that the American people in electing their President must signify a willingness to accept whatever disposition he may make of the power to control the foreign policy of his country. In accordance with this view, as it was further expounded by Wilson, the President occupies a position that is essentially paternal. He must serve as the "trustee"[80] rather than as the agent of the people, in the administration of their interests in foreign negotiations too intricate for their comprehension. Expressive of this attitude was his message to Congress requesting its assistance in the settlement of the Panama Tolls dispute:

I ask this of you in support of the foreign policy of the administration. I shall not know how to deal with other matters of even

---

[78] Our Chief Magistrate and His Powers, p. 195. Mr. Taft doubtless undertook to convey only a "popular distinction" rather than his own opinion.

For expressions of congressional disapprobation of these "unauthorized" military expeditions, see Cong. Globe, 42d Cong., 1st sess., part 2, App. 52.

[79] Bishop, I, 308.

[80] Joseph P. Tumulty, Woodrow Wilson as I Knew Him, p. 231.

greater delicacy and nearer consequence if you do not grant it to me in ungrudging measure.[81]

Throughout his term of office he acted in obedience to this opinion, and only a review of the history of American foreign relations during that period is necessary to remove any doubt as to his authorship of our foreign policy. By his failure to secure the acceptance of the Peace Treaty, however, he was made to realize that there are limitations upon the ability of the Executive to commit his country to his own views, and that following earlier analysis made by him of this subject was only partially correct:

> The initiative in foreign affairs, which the President possesses without any restriction whatever, is virtually the power to control them absolutely. The President cannot conclude a treaty with a foreign power without the consent of the Senate, but he may guide every step of diplomacy, and to guide diplomacy is to determine what treaties must be made, if the faith and prestige of the government are to be maintained. He need disclose no step of negotiation until it is complete, and when in any critical matter it is completed the government is virtually committed. Whatever its disinclination, the Senate may feel itself committed also.[82]

Whether or not the practice is in accord with our general conception of representative government, there can be no avoiding the fact that our recent Executives have not infrequently involved the country in negotiations likely to result in war. Moreover, if we are to accept the observations of Professor Pomeroy as correct, "no other influence than a moral one can curb the President's control of foreign relations"; his "acts are political" and his "responsibility is only political." [83]

Unfortunately, in the event of war, the President, through the use of such expedients as a nationalistic press, has rarely been unable to align public opinion in support of his conduct. A popular verdict, independently arrived at, is therefore apt to be of a post-mortem character, effectual perhaps only in dethroning that Executive at the conclusion of his term.[84]

---

[81] Messages and Papers of the Presidents, XVII, 7934.

[82] Constitutional Government in the United States, pp. 77-78.

[83] J. N. Pomeroy, Constitutional Law, p. 565; quoted by Corwin, pp. 130-131.

[84] James W. Garner, American Foreign Policies. Nevertheless, a popular demand for war may force a weaker President, such as McKinley, to adopt a belligerent policy.

CHAPTER III

WAR POWERS

At the conclusion of the preceding chapter, the writer endeavored to examine the extent to which an appreciation of their responsibilities deterred these Executives from embarking on foreign policies which might have endangered our national safety or necessitated for their continued application the dispatch of armed forces on hostile expeditions abroad. In the present chapter will be presented their interpretations of their constitutional powers, as Commander-in-Chief, to employ these military resources not only when their aggressive policies require them, but when foreign irresponsiveness to their amicable negotiations renders inevitable the use of force.

To defend the conduct of our recent Executives who, prior to the adoption of treaties authorizing the same, assented to " non-political " but hostile interventions in the Caribbean in pursuance of the " Big Stick " policy, one must have recourse to those principles in International Law which are deemed to be part of our law.[1] Like other members of the family of nations, the United States can be presumed to be endowed with both the duty and the power to protect American property, life, and interests abroad by the employment of internationally accepted non-belligerent measures of redress; and the very existence of an army and navy ought to afford conclusive evidence of an intent to perform that obligation. With the Constitution silent as to the officer to be charged with according this protection, the President has been, by reason of his position as Commander-in-Chief and conductor of foreign relations, the logical choice of this task, and, in its execution, his discretion has been adjudged to be unlimited.[2] Therefore, unless the censurers of the militant policies of Roosevelt and Wilson refuse to accept these widely held assumptions of executive power, their disapproval must be

---

[1] Mathews, p. 274, quoting the " Paquette Habana," 175 U. S. 700.
[2] Edwin M. Borchard, Diplomatic Protection of Citizens Abroad, p. 452; Durand v. Hollins, Fed. Cas. No. 4160; above, p. 86.

restricted to a criticism of the expediency of involving our nation in situations actually, though not legally, amounting to war, or to charges that the interests fostered by these leaders were not legitimate subjects of national protection. But even in the last instance there can be assembled no authentic precedents denying that " inchoate " interests can be similarly defended.[3]

However, it is a matter of record that, in the majority of instances in which the President has ordered the army and navy into combat with foreign forces, his decision was prompted not by an aggressive policy toward other nations, but by the necessity of protecting American interests against another power. Varying in the degrees of their seriousness, the forms in which this danger may be presented include a malicious insult to our honor, an intentional program of depredations upon the lands or properties of American nationals abroad or on the high seas and a real or impending invasion of our boundaries. Some of these acts may be regarded as the waging of war against this Nation; and on all such occasions the burden of immediate defense must rest upon the President.

With their conclusion sustained by an argument akin to that employed in defense of the Executive's power to protect American claims abroad, authorities are agreed that the competency of the President to deal with acts of war cannot be limited by the absence of express authorizations or a formal declaration of war.[4] To interpret the provisions of the Constitution as denying to the President, in the absence of congressional action, a power to prosecute a war created by the acts of a foreign aggressor, is, they contend, to render this nation unprotected in an emergency and to reject in part the almost mandatory assumption that there is exercisable at all times in any state an " inherent right of self-defense." [5] That the framers of the Constitution had no intention of creating

---

[3] Corwin, pp. 158-160; Mathews, pp. 292-293; Berdahl, p. 53.

[4] William Whiting, War Powers under the Constitution, p. 37; William E. Birkhimer, Military Government and Material Law, (1st ed.) pp. 23-24; cited also by Berdahl, pp. 54-60.

[5] Ibid., p. 59.

so impractical a situation can be reasonably inferred from their decision to change the power of Congress from that of " making " war to that of " declaring " war,[6] thereby indicating that the Executive was to be intrusted, not only with the prosecution of war, but with the adoption of all necessary measures of defense prior to the action of the Legislature. Whether the latter estimate of their intention is correct or not, it at least has the merit of being in accord with present practice; for at the Hague Convention of 1907, the American Delegation declared that for more than a century this Government had " recognized in the President full power to exercise at all times and in all places the right of national self-defense." [7]

Notwithstanding the existence of this convincing argument in support of his conduct, the Executive, when obliged to employ the armed forces for the national defense, can point specifically to the Acts of 1795 and 1807 [8] for a definite authorization of his commands. Strictly construed, these acts empower the President to adopt such measures as are necessary to " repel " an invasion or to suppress an insurrection; but a more practical interpretation of their content would seem to permit him to anticipate such dangers and to eradicate them at their source. Authorities may be cited who are of the opinion that this additional power is recognized in *dicta* contained in the Prize Cases; and, in practice,[9] only one Executive, Jefferson, has considered himself limited, in the absence of a declaration of war, to repelling attacks only as they are made.

Included in the first class of defensive measures undertaken by the Presidents under discussion is the mere dispatch of a force to dispel a threatened danger or to repulse insignificant guerrilla expeditions across our borders. Thus, one year prior to the enactment of the Act of 1795, when the President

---

[6] Madison's Journal (Hunt Ed.), II, 82; quoted by Berdahl p. 61.

[7] Quoted by Berdahl, p. 62.

[8] 1 Stat. L. 424; 2 Stat. L. 443.

[9] 2 Black 665; Mathews, pp. 289; Corwin, pp. 141-142; Berdahl, p. 76.

seemed to lack a clear statutory authorization to employ troops to repel an invasion, Washington ventured to rest the future peace of the country in the discretion of General Anthony Wayne. Although Congress had impliedly sanctioned the punitive expedition against the Northwest Indians in 1794, that body took no action on the report that a British garrison had been established within American territory.[10] Their outpost being situated in the line of the American objective, Washington had to debate whether he would make a determined effort to oust them and invite a possible war, or leave the boundary question to be settled by diplomacy. He seems to have compromised the issue by having Secretary Knox notify Wayne that: " If, therefore, in the course of your operations against the Indian enemy, it should become necessary to dislodge the party at the rapids of the Miami, you are hereby authorized, in the name of the President . . . , to do it." [11] In matters of military concern, Washington seems to have been deterred only by a question as to the expediency of his action and not by considerations of constitutional authority.

However, Jefferson, who persisted in refusing to adopt measures which would prejudice Congress in a free exercise of its own powers, discovered that this theoretically commendable rule of conduct was productive of rather absurd results when applied to the most practical of all problems, war. By adhering to this self-denying interpretation of his powers, he was never able to provide the country with an effective defense, and one clear example of his failure is described in his Congressional Message (1805) reporting the hostile Spanish expeditions across our southern frontier.

They [the Spaniards] authorize the inference that it is their intention to advance on our possessions until they shall be repressed by an opposing force. Considering that Congress alone is constitutionally invested with the power of changing our condition from peace to war, I have thought it is my duty to await their authority for using force in any degree which could be avoided. I have barely instructed the officers stationed in the neighborhood of the aggressions to protect our citizens from violence, to patrol within

---

[10] Messages and Papers of the Presidents, I, 147.
[11] Carl R. Fish, American Diplomacy, p. 83; Berdahl, pp. 62-63.

the borders actually delivered to us, and not to go out of them but when necessary to repel an inroad or to rescue a citizen or his property.[12]

Under this arrangement, until Congress would act, and it refused to act in this case, the restoration of peaceful conditions in the South would depend not on the exertions of American troops but upon the willingness of the Spaniards to cease their attempts to invade. The most that can be said for Jefferson in this matter is that he consistently observed this peculiar rule of interpretation; for he had been censured for his timidity in a similar situation two years previously.[13]

Sharply in contrast with Jefferson's policy of defense was the measure adopted by Wilson to protect the Southwest against the raids of the bandit, Villa. On this occasion, the Executive's power of "repelling an invasion"[14] was extended to include not merely a dispatch of troops to the border, but the sending of a punitive expedition far into Mexican territory for the purpose of permanently disposing of a serious menace. Although American soldiers in pursuit of the bandit became involved in skirmishes with the forces of the Carranza Government, Wilson emphatically informed the press that the expedition, entered upon through an agreement with the *de facto* government of Mexico, was solely a punitive one, aimed only at the elimination of Villa, and was "in no sense intended as an infringement of its sovereignity or an invasion of that republic."[15]

Whether the President can correctly imply, from his duty to defend this Nation from attacks persistently made upon its inhabitants and their property, an additional power to arm merchant vessels, has never been satisfactorily settled. Dictated as it is by the manifest intention of a belligerent to disregard the rights of neutral merchant vessels, the measure has invariably proved to be but a preliminary to our entry into actual war. Therefore, in questioning the power of the President to arm merchantmen, his opponents have not con-

[12] Messages and Papers of the Presidents, I, 377.
[13] Below, p. 95.
[14] Corwin, p. 163.
[15] New York Times, March 26, 1916.

sidered that the expedient is intended to be purely defensive, but have urged their objection on the ground that it is in fact tantamount to a waging of war and consequently must be preceded by a congressional declaration.[16]

But Wilson had already placed our relations with Germany in a precarious condition by his dismissal of von Bernstoff, and, pending subsequent developments, he was determined to afford American shippers the utmost protection within his power. Nevertheless, to satisfy a desire to have an additional legal and a popular sanction attach to his conduct, he requested Congress to authorize the arming of the merchant marine:

> I feel that I ought . . . to obtain from you a full and immediate assurance of the authority that I may need at any moment to exercise. No doubt I already possess that authority without special warrant of law by the plain implication of my constitutional duties and powers, but I prefer not to act upon implication. I wish to feel that the authority and power of Congress are behind me.[17]

Notwithstanding the successful efforts of eleven Senators to prevent the passage of the necessary legislation, Wilson was satisfied that he had a majority supporting his measure, and, supplementing this expression of confidence with a legal defense derived from a modernized interpretation of an obsolete (and perhaps inapplicable) statute of 1819, he proceeded to execute his policy of armed neutrality. Owing to improved methods of naval warfare, the arming of merchant vessels was destined from the start to assume an offensive aspect because safety could be effected only by firing upon submarines at sight and discerning later, if possible, their hostile intent. The inadequacy of the measure was recognized even by Wilson in a later address, in which he declared that

---

[16] This was the opinion held by Jefferson, Writings (Ford Ed.), VII, 221. In opposing Wilson's request, Senator Stone declared that not even Congress was competent to authorize the President to arm these vessels at his discretion, because in so doing the Legislature would divest itself of the constitutional power to choose whether or not this country should enter into a war. 64th Cong., 2d sess., pp. 4637-4878.

[17] Messages and Papers of the Presidents, XVII, 8211.

it was "certain to draw us into the war without either the rights or the effectiveness of belligerents." [18]

Since the Act of 1819 was believed to have been directed only against pirates, and since its vague terms might reasonably be construed to have precluded the use of this expedient against a nation with whom the United States was not officially at war, Wilson could obtain little support from this source.[19] A more substantial sanction might be implied from the fact that, since the President, as Commander-in-Chief, is empowered to employ the navy to protect American shippers, he can choose the alternative of according this aid through the means of an armed merchant marine. Moreover, the declaration of war, coming within less than a fortnight after his order, may be interpreted to have the retroactive effect of confirming the propriety of his measure and of merging the "imperfect" state of war created by his action into a full status of belligerency.[20]

Although the reprisals undertaken by Wilson to avenge Mexican insults to our national honor at Tampico differ in character from his arming of merchantmen, nevertheless, the procedure observed by him to obtain a sanction of his conduct in these two instances is identical. Circumstances having necessitated his order for the occupation of Vera Cruz before he was able to consult Congress, he appeared before that body on the day succeeding this event and asked " approval " of his policy.

No doubt I could do what is necessary . . . to enforce respect for our Government without recourse to the Congress, and yet not exceed my constitutional powers as President; but I do not wish to act in a matter possibly of so grave consequence except in close conference and cooperation with both the Senate and House. I therefore come to ask your approval that I should use the armed forces . . . to obtain . . . the fullest recognition of the rights and dignity of the United States.[21]

---

[18] Ibid., p. 8228.

[19] New York Times Current History Magazine, VI, 55-56; Berdahl, p. 67; 3 Stat. L. 510.

[20] Mathews, pp. 296, 298; citing Bas v. Tingy, 4 Dallas 37.

[21] Messages and Papers of the Presidents, XVII, 793. Congress did approve. 38 Stat. L. 770. Mathews, pp. 278-279. Since a reprisal not only may be regarded as an act of war by the party

In view of the fact that the President, through his control of foreign negotiatiqns, may, in his discretion, produce a situation necessitating our entry into war, and that he is already possessed of an implied authority to adopt the measures employed, Wilson is deserving of special commendation for his willingness to seek a popular sanction for his conduct in these two instances.

On the other hand, when a nation declares war against the United States, or displays an intention to begin a campaign of hostilities amounting to a creation of a status of belligerency, there may not remain sufficient time for Congress to act with a formal recognition of this situation and to authorize the mobilization of additional resources for the national defense. The best of practical reasons would therefore seem to require the President to engage the enemy with all the means at his command and to defend his country both at home and abroad until the legislative department is in a position to act. And if it be possible to dispose of the danger entirely by vigorous strategic manoeuvres, short of an invasion and occupation of enemy territory, there ought to be no legal difficulties to constrain him.[22] By adopting a hopelessly conservative view of his powers during the Tripolitan War, Jefferson merely nullified the efforts of American naval officers, prolonged hostilities, and accomplished nothing. To Congress, he summarized his conduct as follows:

Tripoli, . . . had come forward with demands unfounded either in right or in compact, and had permitted itself to denounce war on our failure to comply before a given day. The style of the demand admitted but one answer. I sent a small squadron of frigates into the Mediterranean, with assurances to that power of our sincere desire to remain in peace, but with orders to protect our commerce against the threatened attack. The measure was seasonable and

against whom it is directed but may provoke a declaration of war by the latter, there is, perhaps, a theoretical justification for the opinion held by Jefferson that Congress alone ought to authorize that measure. That the Constitution expressly vests that power only in Congress, as he believed, would appear to represent the view of the minority. Writings (Ford Ed.), VII, 628.

[22] See above, p. 89, for a list of authorities supporting this contention. However, among these, Mathews and Berdahl concede that the opinions of those dissenting from this view are well founded in theory. For the latter view, see Willoughby, III, 1559-1560.

salutary. The Bey had already declared war. His cruisers were out. . . . One of the Tripolitan cruisers . . . engaged the small schooner, Enterprise, commanded by Lieutenant Sterrett . . . [and] was captured after a heavy slaughter of her men, without the loss of a single one on our part. . . . Unauthorized by the Constitution, without the sanction of Congress, to go beyond the line of defence, the vessel being disabled from committing further hostilities, was liberated with its crew. The Legislature will doubtless consider whether, by authorizing measures of offense also, they will place our force on an equal footing with that of its adversaries.[23]

As has been intimated, one of the primary sources of support for the premise previously stated has been the judicial estimation of the significance of the proclamations of blockade issued by Lincoln in 1861. Although, by the rules of International Law, a blockade is construed as an incident of war and its proclamation as a recognition of that status, it is clear that Lincoln viewed the blockade wholly as a measure of defense necessitated by the gravity of the situation, the adoption of which was moreover incumbent upon him in the absence of a Congress in session.[24] That he did not intend this measure to have the consequences attributed to it by the Law of Nations would seem to be indicated by the fact that the subsequent policy of the political departments, Executive

---

[23] Messages and Papers of the Presidents, I, 314-315. Disclaiming to accord a host of wretched pirates the honor of declaring war on them, Congress did put Jefferson at ease by granting him an additional military authority. John B. McMaster, History of the People of the United States, III, 201. For Hamilton's criticism of Jefferson's interpretation of his powers, see Corwin, pp. 133-135.

[24] Messages and Papers of the Presidents, VII, 3225, 3216. The Supreme Court as a body admitted that the uniform approval of these executive Proclamations, Congress having subsequently sanctioned Lincoln's conduct, would operate to permit the beginning of the War to be fixed by the dates of these former pronouncements. However, only five members of that tribunal would concede that the President " possesses the power under the Constitution to declare war or recognize its existence within the meaning of the law of the nations, which carries with it belligerent rights and thus change this country from a state of peace to a state of war." They held further that: "Whether the President in fulfilling his duties, as Commander-in-Chief, in suppressing an insurrection, has met with such armed hostile resistance, and a civil war of such alarming proportions as will compel him to accord to them the character of belligerents, is a question to be decided by him. . . . He must determine what degree of force the crisis demands. . . . The President was bound to meet it in the shape it presented itself, without waiting for Congress to baptize it with a name; and no name given to it by him or them could change the fact." Prize Cases, 2 Black 635.

and Legislative, was neither to recognize nor to look with favor on the recognition by a third Power of the Confederacy as a belligerent.

On the other hand, the President's influence in determining the peaceful or belligerent status of this Nation is no less diminshed when, as in the World War, American military measures are preceded by a congressional declaration. While, in theory, the latter, as a coordinate body, is at liberty to make an independent exercise of the important legislative power to declare war, in practice Congress has acted uniformly only in pursuance of executive recommendation.[25] As a result, it is possible for the President, through his control of foreign relations and his influence upon legislation, that is, his privilege of giving Congress information on the " state of the Union," to retain an initiative throughout.[26] Wilson illustrated this situation very convincingly by electing to proclaim our neutrality in 1914, by endeavoring to maintain it through peaceful negotiations, then, reversing his position, by dismissing von Bernstorff, severing relations with Germany, experimenting with armed neutrality, and finally requesting Congress to acknowledge Germany's ruthless submarine policy as constituting war against the United States. Acting immediately upon his appeal,[27] Congress declared war against Germany, and subsequently against Austria-Hungary; but, in accordance with the reasons stated by the Executive, excluded from these declarations the lesser Central Powers.

As a strict constructionist, Jefferson was of the opinion that a declaration of war emanating from Congress ought to represent the independent, uninfluenced decision of that body, and he therefore deprecated the attempt of any Executive to transmit his own bellicose sentiments to a tractable Legisla-

---

[25] Statement by Representative Dill, Cong. Record, 65th Cong., 3d sess., p. 1824. Cited by Berdahl, pp. 93-94.

[26] Simeon Baldwin, " The Share of the President in a Declaration of War," in American Journal of International Law, XII, 1-15.

[27] Messages and Papers of the Presidents, XVII, 8226. Nevertheless, Congress did not follow Wilson in including within its resolutions his statement of America's War Aims. 40 Stat. L. 1, 429; Mathews, p. 311.

ture. He accordingly preferred not to communicate to Congress his opinions on the serious " Leopard-Chesapeake " affair, but sought to adjust this insult alone. To a friend he wrote:

Whether the outrage is a proper cause for war, belonging exclusively to Congress, it is our duty not to commit them by doing anything which would have to be retracted. We may, however, exercise the powers entrusted to us for preventing future insults within our harbors, and claim firmly satisfaction for the past. This will leave Congress free to decide whether war is the most efficacious mode of redress in our case, or whether having taught so many other useful lessons to Europe, we may not add that there are peaceable means of repressing injustice.[28]

Notwithstanding a declaration of war, it is obvious that, before the more significant powers of the President can be put into execution, he must be in possession of the means of prosecuting the conflict. While the Constitution expressly assigns to Congress the duty of raising and supporting armies,[29] that provision has never had the effect of precluding the Executive from exercising a potent influence in this matter. However negligible may have been his legislative leadership in the sphere of domestic reform, he has, in most emergencies, found Congress disposed to heed the military recommendations prepared for him by his Secretaries of the War and Navy Departments. Generally, those Executives who have served in office during times of peace have witnessed the adoption of only a fraction of their military program, whereas Lincoln and Wilson, having had their demands confirmed by the exigencies of war, found the Legislature most obedient to their suggestions.[30]

Similarly, the existence or non-existence of war will determine the amount of discretion which Congress will allot to the President in the mobilization, organization, and choice of per-

---

[28] Writings (Ford Ed), IX, 87. The outrage to which Jefferson referred was the unwarranted attack upon the American frigate, " Chesapeake," by the British frigate, " Leopard." At the date of this altercation the legal status of our relations with England was one of peace.

[29] Art. 1, Sec. 8, Cl. 12, 13, 14.

[30] See in general, Howard White, " Executive Influence in Determining Military Policy in the United States," in University of Illinois Studies, XII, 1-292.

sonnel of the armed forces provided for in successive legislative enactments. In time of peace it has been customary for
Congress to provide in detail the manner in which the armed
forces are to be maintained, permitting the President, however, within the maximum enrollment stipulated, to enlist
men at such intervals and in such divisions as he may
designate. Nevertheless, as long as the volunteer system remained the conventional method of recruiting an armed force,
the President, even in time of an emergency or conflict, witnessed little increase in his control over this task other than
in the form of a relaxation of the limitations on the number
of the men which he might employ, or an occasional permission to devise the organization of an additional military unit.[31]
On the two occasions when conscription was adopted, this situation was substantially modified; but, while its innovation
during the later years of the Civil War [32] resulted in Lincoln's
being accorded an authority to mobilize an unlimited number
of men and being assigned the duty of preparing the draft
quotas for the loyal States, the aggregate control exercised by
him under these early statutes appears insignificant to the
broad discretion allotted Wilson by the terms of the Selective
Draft Act.[33] In accordance with his policy of having Congress authorize only the general object desired, leaving the
President free to select the means by which it might be obtained, Wilson, on his own insistence, acquired the power not
only to enlist practically an unlimited number of men, but to
substitute for the existing method of their organization such
arrangements as he might deem warranted by the circumstances.

   That, legally, armies can be raised and supported only by
congressional authorization has never been controverted; but,
under conditions of extreme necessity, Lincoln proceeded to
increase the army, organize it in an unconventional manner,

---

[31] Washington, however, was authorized to devise the organization
of several newly created military establishments.
[32] 12 Stat. L. 731; 13 Stat. L. 379. A prior Act (12 Stat. L.
697), had granted him a partial discretion in the organization of
troops.
[33] 40 Stat. L. 76. Berdahl, ch. vi.

and purchase naval supplies through private agents, all without a single enactment to justify his conduct. Believing, no doubt, that if he did convene Congress in special session, he could only extract from it after considerable wrangling measures inadequate for his purpose, he chose to act first and to obtain his sanction later.

As long as he preferred to treat this revolt as an ordinary insurrection, he did possess the power, under the Act of 1795, to call out the militia, and, on these grounds, his Proclamation of April 15, 1861, calling for 75,000 militia was valid. However, when he issued a second Proclamation,[34] May 3, 1861, asking for an increase by volunteers of more than 80,000 men in the regular armed forces, he clearly exceeded his authority. Not only was this order illegal, but his method of recruiting these troops through the Treasury Department was repugnant to a former decision which ruled that this task was exclusively within the province of the Secretary of War.[35]

To the Congress, which he had finally convened in July, Lincoln recounted his transgressions, and justified them as follows:

These measures, whether strictly legal or not, were ventured upon under what appeared to be a popular demand and a public necessity, trusting then, as now, Congress would readily ratify them. It is believed that nothing has been done beyond the constitutional competency of Congress.[36]

There was no adequate and effective organization for the public defense. Congress had indefinitely adjourned. There was no time to convene them. It became necessary for me to choose whether, using only the existing means, agencies, and processes which Congress had provided, I should let the Government fall at once into ruin or whether, availing myself of the broader powers conferred by the Constitution in cases of insurrection, I would make an effort to save it . . . for posterity.[37]

I believe that by these and other similar measures taken in that crisis, some of which were without any authority of law, the Government was saved from overthrow. I am not aware that a dollar of the public funds thus confided without authority of law to unofficial persons was either lost or wasted. . . .[38]

[34] Messages and Papers of the Presidents, VII, 3214, 3217.
[35] United States v. Eliason, 16 Peters 302. Berdahl, p. 112n.
[36] Messages and Papers of the Presidents, VII, 3225.
[37] Ibid., p. 3279.
[38] Ibid., p. 3280. What might be cited as an additional instance of his questionable exercise of executive power was his institution

When the military forces of the United States have been made ready for war, the powers of the President, as Commander-in-Chief, become exercisable in their fullest sense. Subject to the provisions of statutes, which establish the procedure by which appointments are to be made and the selections requiring or not requiring the confirmation of the Senate, the President is free to choose his general staff from among the ranking officers eligible, and for the continuation of the war at least, he exercises over these, as well as the entire military personnel, an absolute power of removal.[39] Moreover, although the professional tacticians of his war council have been customarily assigned the task of formulating his military manoeuvres, the Executive is fully competent not only to devise every movement of the armed forces,[40] but to embark them on any expedition which in his estimation is calculated to subdue the enemy. In the area of hostilities he acts free of legal limitations; for, unless he condescend to respect the

of a partial draft by virtue of the discretion conferred upon him by the Militia Act of 1862. Since conscription, prior to its express adoption in 1863, had been unquestionably taboo in this country, Lincoln's interpretation of his powers under the former statute, though legitimately deducible from its vaguely phrased context, was certainly not in accord with the intention of the members of Congress. Nevertheless, all attacks upon the validity of the measure as an unconstitutional delegation of legislative power, or upon the legality of the executive orders of the War Department in connection therewith proved futile, and the entire proceedings under this statute were uniformly sustained in both state and federal courts. James G. Randall, Constitutional Problems under Lincoln, ch. xi.

[39] Although Congress, by the Act of 1866 (14 Stat. L. 90) has provided that in time of peace the President shall dismiss officers only after the latter have been tried by a military tribunal, a doubt, which has been recently fostered by the Myers Case, has existed as to the validity of that statute. That the President's power of removal, even in time of peace, is not seriously restricted, would seem evident from Roosevelt's dismissal of two full companies of negro troops at Brownsville, Texas. The latter had refused to disclose those of their number who had rioted in that city. Messages and Papers of the Presidents, XV, 7329-7347. Also, Willoughby, III, 1527; Berdahl, pp. 128-129.

[40] While there is a dispute as to whether he may take the field in person, the better opinion is that he does possess this authority. No President has ever exercised this power; but Washington did accompany the militia over part of its march to Pittsburgh to quell the Whiskey Rebellion. Only the forecast of a favorable outcome persuaded him to return to the Capital. Messages and Papers of the Presidents, I, 157; Berdahl, pp. 118-120, 135-136.

international laws of war and of humanity, the law to be applied is the law of the invading commander.[41]

An examination of the records of our two great War Presidents, Lincoln and Wilson, reveals the two in sharp disagreement as to the appropriate amount of control to be exercised by the Executive over the operations of American troops in time of war. Probably because of an absence, at that date, of a true appreciation of the value of rigid military efficiency, and because of his inability to resist the pressure directed against him by vain officers seeking promotion, or by partisan groups desirous of immediate victory, Lincoln violated his own maxim of "not swapping horses in the middle of the stream" by appointing no less than six generals to command the Army of the Potomac. During the time in which these men served, he seriously interfered with their freedom of decision by intermittently ordering them to begin an attack or a retreat.[42] Much of this executive interference was attributable, however, to the failure of the eastern armies to advance consistently; for, when he finally discovered a victorious

---

[41] This statement is applicable only to measures which the Executive may adopt to defeat the opposing belligerents. American troops continue to remain subject to the Military Law of the United States, for infractions of which they may be punished by the verdicts of courts-martial. Although Congress has authorized the President to convoke courts-martial at his discretion, nevertheless authorities are to be found who maintain that, notwithstanding this legislative sanction, he is possessed of that power by virtue of his position as Commander-in-Chief. It is for the Executive, however, to determine when these tribunals shall be employed, and to decide, within limits prescribed by statute, upon their organization, their procedure, and the finality of their verdict.

On the other hand, for the redress of wrongs not designated as such by the terms of Military Law, American troops may be tried by military commissions. Unlike courts-martial, these institutions have no status in our municipal law, nor do they apply domestic law. Established by the invading commanding officer to assist him in policing residents of occupied enemy territory, these courts are wholly under his direction. It is he who defines their jurisdiction, fixes the penalties of crimes of which they take cognizance, and specifies the law which they are to apply. While Congress has acknowledged their existence, their status is to be found in the international law of war, and it is that law, as modified by the commanding officer, which they apply. Berdahl, ch. vi.

[42] Messages and Papers of the Presidents, VII, 3301-3302. Herein is contained his order for the general movement of troops after the battle of Manassas.

leader in Grant, he permitted him to devise his own campaign of attack.

Doubtless aware of the serious deficiency of the original volunteer system of the Civil War, with its untrained, politically appointed personnel, and its decentralized command, Wilson successfully avoided the repetition of these evils; first, by securing the immediate adoption of conscription, and secondly, by safeguarding the army against external, nonprofessional influence. Accordingly, after having selected Pershing to command the Expeditionary Forces, he transferred to him and his General Staff the duty of recommending minor appointments and preparing all plans of action. However advantageous to the army this arrangement may have been, for Wilson it produced only the politically injurious Wood-Roosevelt episode. Yet, despite the criticism directed against him by these disappointed patriots, Wilson refused to modify his policy. To his Secretary he confided that:

> I selected General Pershing for this task and I intend to back him up in every recommendation he makes. . . . I do not care a damn for the criticism of the country. It would not be fair to Pershing if I tried to escape what appears to be my responsibility. I do not intend to embarrass General Pershing by forcing his hand. If Pershing does not make good, I will recall him, but it must not be said that I have failed to support him at every turn.[43]

Except for his sponsorship of the unified command, subsequently adopted by the Allied Powers, and his general advice to the commanders of the Atlantic Fleet, Wilson faithfully adhered to his policy of non-interference with the military department. In an address to the junior officers of the Atlantic Squadron, prior to their departure, he outlined to them the nature of their task and instructed them " to do the thing that is audacious to the utmost because that is exactly the thing that the other side does not understand." [44]

For assenting to the dispatch of American troops, in connection with those of our Allies, to points detached from the operations along the Western Front, Wilson was, nevertheless, charged by several Congressmen with usurpation of his powers.

---

[43] Tumulty, pp. 292-293. [44] Ibid., p. 298.

Asserting that a declaration of war had been issued only against Austria and Germany, they maintained that the power of the President was restricted to the use of troops against those two belligerents and did not extend, especially after the establishment of an armistice, to the dispatch of our armed forces to the aid of Italy or Russia.[46] As against these objections it is well established that an armistice does not terminate a status of war and that the President, as Commander-in-Chief, has an absolute discretion to determine the location, objective, and movement of his troops. Or, as one prominent jurist has declared, " it is for the President as Commander-in-Chief to direct the campaigns of the army wherever he may think they should be carried on." [47]

Wilson apparently entertained no doubts as to the validity of his conduct, for, when requested to render an explanation, he offered no defense of his action upon legal grounds, but confined his replies to a description of the circumstances necessitating these expeditions. Disclaiming from the outset any intention of using troops to sustain any existing government not desired by the Russian people, he admitted that American soldiers, later supplanted by volunteers electing to serve in that area, were sent to Siberia to aid a beleaguered ally, the Czechs, to encourage loyal Russians against marauding bands of released German prisoners, and to protect international trade interests. As for the temporary landing in 1919 of a naval force at Trau, on the Adriatic, Secretary Daniels stated that the measure was requested by Italy for the purpose of quieting a group of disorderly Italians engaged in skirmishes with South Slavs over disputed boundaries.[48]

In view of the opinion recently expressed that Congress, by withholding appropriations, may prohibit the departure, in time of peace, of American troops beyond our territorial lim-

---

[46] Quoted in part by Berdahl, pp. 124-125.
[47] Charles E. Hughes, " War Powers under the Constitution," in 65th Cong., 1st sess., S. Doc. No. 105, p. 7; Willoughby, III, 1567-1568.
[48] Messages and Papers of the Presidents, XVIII, 8589-8592. New York Times, August 27, 1919; October 3, 1919; 66th Cong., 1st sess., S. Doc. No. 60.

its, it may be of interest to note the ease with which Roosevelt defeated a threatened exercise of this power. When the announcement of the projected cruise of the fleet around the world was made, eastern financiers, fearing that the Atlantic coast would be left without adequate protection, petitioned Congress to prevent the vessels from sailing. In response to these appeals, a movement was begun to defeat the President's intention by refusing to appropriate the necessary funds; but Roosevelt promptly let it be known that the fleet would sail, that he would defray the expenses of its departure out of existing funds, and that if Congress refused to provide for their return, the vessels would remain in the Pacific. Needless to add, the fleet departed and returned.[49]

Although on the field of battle the Commander-in-Chief is said to have an unrestricted choice of measures designed to subdue the enemy, nevertheless, as a result of the adherence, during the Civil War, to a confusing double status theory, whereby the Confederate States were deemed never to have been out of the Union, but were for certain purposes regarded as belligerents with all the rights of war pertaining thereto, certain military expedients devised by Lincoln, particularly his Emancipation Proclamation,[50] could not be divorced of legal considerations.

Convinced that the abolition of slavery as a domestic institution would require a constitutional amendment,[51] Lincoln concluded that the President, as Commander-in-Chief, was competent to determine whether military necessity rendered it advisable to liberate slaves in those States remaining in revolt against the Federal Government. Nevertheless, until he was assured that the measure could be enforced to the extent of depriving the Confederates of a valuable military resource, he believed that the mere issuance of an Emancipation Proclamation would be akin to a " Pope's bull against the comet." " But," he added, in explaining his hesitancy to the Chicago Delegation who had advised immediate liberation,

---

[49] Autobiography, pp. 597-598.
[50] Messages and Papers of the Presidents, VII, 3358.
[51] Ibid., p. 3389.

"I raise no objections against it on legal or constitutional grounds, for, as Commander-in-Chief of the Army and Navy in time of war I suppose I have a right to take any measure which may best subdue the enemy." [52]

Consequently, when he finally issued that edict, he was careful to apply this war measure only to regions remaining in hostile insurrection against federal authority. In refusing to adopt the suggestion of Secretary Chase that the Proclamation be extended to the conquered sections of Virginia and Lousiana, Lincoln made the following reply:

> The original Proclamation has no constitutional or legal justification except as a military measure. The exemptions were made because the military necessity did not apply to the exempted localities. Nor does that necessity apply to them now any more than it did then. If I take this step must I not do so without the argument of military necessity and so without any argument except the one that I think the measure politically expedient and morally right? Would I not thus give up all footing upon the Constitution or law, would I not thus be in a boundless field of absolution? [53]

What would be the fate of the Proclamation at the conclusion of the war, was a matter on which he declined to speculate. He was satisfied that the measure had achieved its purpose by hastening the defeat of the insurgents, and whether subsequently declared void or not, its retraction was impossible. In any event, by superimposing the Thirteenth Amendment upon the existing situation, he felt that the discrepancies in his Proclamation would be completely rectified.[54]

Assuming that the laws of war do permit a belligerent to deprive enemy civilians of such portion of their private property as is possessed of a military value, one may justify Lincoln's action only in so far as it did in fact accelerate the surrender of the rebel army. That Confederate slaves forcibly liberated by Federal troops acting in pursuance of this Proclamation would remain permanently free may be viewed as an accident of war. Manifestly, Lincoln was in error if he

---

[52] John G. Nicolay and John Hay, Abraham Lincoln, A History, VI, 155-156.

[53] Ibid., pp. 434-435.

[54] John G. Nicolay and John Hay, Complete Works of Abraham Lincoln, II, 397, 695.

believed that the mere utterance, " are and henceforward shall be free " could have the magic effect of legally emancipating every negro in these unconquered regions.[55]

Similar anomalies were present in his administration of the military governments established in the Confederate States prior to the total cessation of hostilities. Although the laws of war commend for his observance certain rules of moderation, the invading Commander-in-Chief, in setting up provisional military governments over the territory occupied during his campaigns against the enemy, rules as an absolute dictator. As long as a military necessity exists to justify his conduct, he may exercise complete legislative, executive, and judicial powers over the areas, and any local governmental institution which continues to function does so only by his grace. Usually, however, when the Commander-in-Chief erects a military government, he does so with no other purpose than to preserve order; for it is not within his province to act on the assumption that the territory thus occupied will be retained by the United States at the conclusion of the war.[56]

---

[55] Randall, chs. xv, xvi.

[56] The fact that, in the ensuing peace negotiations, the treaty-making power annexes the territory thus occupied does not operate, however, to suspend the President's power to govern these areas. Under these modified conditions the " military " governments suffer no physical change; but his authority to administer them is now derived not wholly from his war powers as Commander-in-Chief but from " his constitutional obligation to see that the authority of the United States over the territory is maintained." Similarly, when Congress, in the exercise of its power to provide for the government of territories, stipulates as a preliminary measure that the President shall exercise legislative, executive, and judicial powers over such areas, his original military government may not be altered; but the source of his governing power is now a congressional authorization.

In the case of the Canal Zone, Congress having permitted its statute providing for the government of this area to lapse, an obligation was imposed upon him, by necessity as well as by his duty to see to the execution of the laws, to continue his supervision of this Zone. Taft, pp. 93-94.

It has been suggested that the territorial governments continued by the President in time of peace, though armed force may be necessary to sustain them, might more accurately be described as " executive " governments, for the reason that he no longer rules in his personal capacity as Commander-in-Chief, but as " an agent of the sovereign " United States. His powers having thus been reduced from those of a dictator to those of an administrator, the President is confronted with the problem of determining what local laws of

Lincoln, on the other hand, established military governments within the conquered Southern district to assist the people thereof to resurrect governments of the republican form guaranteed by the Constitution.

Accordingly, when prospects for a successful termination of the revolt became brighter, he announced that if ten per cent of the inhabitants of the conquered States would erect a republican form of government, he would recognize it as such and accord it the protection guaranteed by the Constitution.[57] That the President was competent, during the continuation of the war, to establish military governments, and that he was authorized by Congress to protect republican governments within the States against domestic violence, has been asserted in judicial decisions.[58] Concerning the policy to be observed as to the reconstruction of the South after the war, Lincoln expressed a preference, however, that this task be left to the Executive and that the preliminary civil governments sponsored by him be acknowledged by Congress as republican in form without the imposition of any additional requirements. Nevertheless, he was fully cognizant of the

---

the newly acquired areas are political and must therefore be eliminated, and whether the local regulations which he may issue will conflict with the Constitution and the laws of the United States. In the light of the recent Insular Cases, Jefferson seems to have taken the correct view when, notwithstanding the fact that the local Spanish procedural customs differed from our conceptions of justice, he refused, in the absence of an express congressional authorization, to apply either the Constitution or federal statutes to Louisiana. However, in accordance with the doctrine first established in Cross v. Harrison, 16 How. 164, he erred in continuing to levy Spanish customs duties rather than the American tariff laws on goods imported from abroad. Fleming v. Page, 9 How. 603.

During Roosevelt's Administration, confusion seems to have existed concerning the latter problem. A tariff, levied by Taft as Governor of the Philippines, was voided in the federal courts, whereas, in respect to the purely executive government of Tuctuila (Samoa), the naval commander collected duty on the entry of American goods and the Secretary of the Treasury permitted the Samoan products to enter the United States free. Taft, pp. 97-102; Willoughby, I, chs. xxviii, xxix, xxxi; III, ch. lxxxvi; David Y. Thomas, "Military Government of Newly Acquired Territory in the United States," in Columbia University Studies, XX, 33-38, 325-326; Downes v. Bidwell, 182 U. S. 244.

[57] Messages and Papers of the Presidents, VII, 3414-3416; 3423-3424.

[58] Luther v. Borden, 7 How. 1; Texas v. White, 7 Wall. 700.

fact that the problems of reconstruction and the execution of the guaranty contained in Article IV of the Constitution were legislative functions, and that, much as he might disapprove the expediency of the proposals emanating from Congress, he was bound by its decision to exercise its rightful authority.

With the detailed administration of these war governments, Lincoln had little to do; for the manner of their operation had to be determined largely by local exigencies of which generals in the field were better able to judge. As has been previously stated, in the control of conquered areas the will of the military officer is supreme; but to mitigate against the terrible despotisms rendered possible under this principle, the laws of war have provided that a more temperate rule would be to leave municipal institutions unchanged whenever their modification was not required by military necessity. It was supervision designed to secure such moderation that Lincoln as supreme military commander exercised over his generals in the South. Thus, in writing to a subordinate stationed in Louisiana, he advised that:

> In the existing conditions of things . . . the military must not be thwarted by the civil authority; and I add that on points of difference the commanding general must be judge and master. But I also add that in the exercise of this judgment and control, a purpose scarcely unavowed, to transcend all military necessity to crush out the civil government will not be overlooked.[59]

Having determined upon a policy of encouraging the speedy resurrection of civil government within the revolting States, Lincoln had an express reason for restraining his generals from exercising too arbitrary an authority. To obtain the former object he devised the office of military governor, manned that post with civilians, and ordered them to these southern regions with instructions to assist the loyal population in establishing governments republican in form. But, because it would have been virtually impossible for these civil officers, in view of the unsettled conditions prevailing in these conquered areas, to have fulfilled their task without the

---

[59] Nicolay and Hay, Complete Works of Abraham Lincoln, II, 480, 598, 619-620.

aid of the resident military commander, and because it would have, been manifestly unwise to have within one district two forms of government, each coordinate and independent of the other, Lincoln proposed to have the army officers retain the final authority, on the condition that they adopt no measures calculated to retard the progress of reconstruction. Indicative of his intentions is the following letter to General Banks, district commander at New Orleans.

I have all the while intended you to be master, as well as in regard to military matters of the department, and hence my letters on reconstruction have nearly, if not quite, all been addressed to you. . . . Governor Shepley was appointed to assist the commander of the department and not to thwart him or act independently of him. Instructions have been given directly to him merely to spare you detail labor and not to supersede your authority.[60]

Nevertheless, by concentrating the paramount authority in the military, Lincoln rendered himself partially responsible for whatever discreditable records were made by Union generals in the South. Acting in accordance with the broad discretion allotted to them, these military commanders not only instituted military governments but reorganized in considerable detail the existing municipal institutions of the Confederate States. In addition to their military courts, or commissions, in which criminal offenses were tried, there were established provisional courts which, together with the local civil courts, the jurisdiction of which had been seriously diminished, entertained civil suits. Under the orders of the military commanders, civilians occupying local political offices were repeatedly removed and others appointed, compulsory elections were held, and the qualifications of both the electorate and the candidates defined. Hours of labor, wage rates, financial and trade relations were similarly regulated by military decree.[61]

Supplementing this activity were the numerous appointments and orders issuing from the departments at Washington, particularly from the Treasury Department, which

[60] Ibid., p. 405.
[61] A. H. Carpenter, " Military Government of Southern Territory," in Annual Report, American Historical Association, 1900, I, 481-495.

regulated commercial intercourse with these reconstructed States. Of the numerous other measures emanating from the President himself, the two most important were his origination of the new war office, that of the military governor, and his order establishing the Provisional Court for Louisiana. To occupy the judgeship of that tribunal Lincoln appointed C. A. Peabody, and authorized him to select all the officials to be connected with the court.[62] Although he had been granted a jurisdiction equal to that exercised by the federal courts, Justice Peabody decided that, in obedience to a prior decision of the Supreme Court, he could not obey the President's order to take cognizance of prize cases.[63]

Nor were the States who had remained loyal to the Union immune from at least a partial application of military government to their territorial limits. Probably because their lands were intermittently overrun by the opposing armies, and notwithstanding the allegiance of their governments and their apparent ability to maintain order, the border States of Maryland, Kentucky, and Missouri suffered most from this form of oppression. Here, martial law was readily instituted, either by order of the President or by the general in command, and vigorous measures were taken to prevent both the electorate and the state governments, central or local, from falling under the control of Southern sympathizers.[64]

In the North, however, the suspension of the privilege of the writ of habeas corpus constituted the main direct interference with civil authority. While it is true that, in announcing a nation-wide suspension of the privilege of this writ, Lincoln declared that disloyal citizens would be " subject to martial law and liable to trial . . . by military commission," this threat was never literally applied.[65] Only where disorder was rampant, as in Missouri, southern Ohio, and Indiana, did martial law with its appendage, the military commission, exist in its broader sense; for all that the

---

[62] Messages and Papers of the Presidents, VII, 3323-3324.
[63] Jecker v. Montgomery, 13 How. 498; Carpenter, p. 486.
[64] Ibid., pp. 480-490.
[65] Messages and Papers of the Presidents, VII, 3299-3300; also, 3216, 3218, 3219, 3220, 3240, 3300, 3371, 3422.

President sought by his suspension was not a complete exemption of the military from the jurisdiction of the civil courts, but a permission for the army commanders to detain summarily any suspected person until his ability to obstruct the Government had been destroyed.[66]

Having once assumed the power to suspend the privilege of the writ, Lincoln seems to have permitted his Cabinet officers to compete for the acquisition of the task of policing the Northern States. Although the project seems to have had no relation to the work of his department, Secretary Seward was first to perform the duty of securing the arrest of citizens accused of disloyal practices; and, as was characteristic of much of the administrative activity during this War, the machinery which he devised to accomplish his purpose was neither elaborate nor regular in its operation. Later, in 1862, this task was transferred by executive order [67] to the War Department, where a more permanent organization, with the Judge Advocate General at its head, was established by Stanton. Having apparently acquired the President's habit of disregarding the wishes of the legislature, this official persisted in retaining the procedure which he himself had originated, despite the attempt of Congress to render these military arrests more amenable to judicial process.[68] Notwithstanding the inconsistency and dubious legality of the measures devised to suppress disloyalty during the Civil War, American citizens were subjected to less rigorous penalties than were their descendants during the late War, in which a rule of law was carefully observed. For the alleviation of much of the severity of military interference, the inhabitants of the North were indebted to Lincoln; for by his personal consideration of individual petitions for pardon, many unjust penalties were avoided.[69]

---

[66] Randall, chs. vii, viii.

[67] Messages and Papers of the Presidents, VII, 3302-3305.

[68] William A. Dunning, "Disloyalty in Two Wars," in American Historical Review, XXIV, 627.

[69] During the war he established a commission to supervise the matter of granting paroles and pardons to citizens unjustly detained, and by this expedient large numbers of political prisoners were liberated at specific intervals.

Although contemporary lawyers hastened to prepare briefs in defense of Lincoln's suspension of the privilege of the writ, the great weight of authority, both before and after the Civil War, has been that while the President, in practice, is the officer to suspend the habeas corpus, his action to be legal must be preceded by a legislative sanction.[70] To give the benefit of the doubt [71] to Lincoln's interpretation of his power in this instance would not be unjustifiable; but not the slightest support can be assembled to sustain him in his establishment of martial law and military commissions in areas removed from the scene of hostilities where local courts were clearly able to function. Nevertheless, out of a probable desire not to disconcert the Administration, the Supreme Court refrained from a consideration of this problem during the War; [72] and it was not until the post bellum decision of Ex parte Milligan that a judicial condemnation was attached to Lincoln's conduct.[73]

However, with indifference to the attitude which the courts might subsequently adopt with reference to his conduct, Lincoln was prepared to defend his measures whenever their legality was called in question. To the Congress assembled on July 4, 1861, he delivered his first justification of his power to suspend the privilege of the writ:

Of course, some consideration was given to the question of power and propriety before this matter was acted upon. The whole of the laws which were required to be faithfully executed were being resisted and failing of execution in nearly one-third of the States. Must they be allowed to finally fail of execution, even had it been perfectly clear that by the use of the means necessary to their execution some single law, made in such extreme tenderness of the citizens' liberty that practically it relieves more of the guilty than of the innocent, should to a very limited extent be violated? . . . Are all the laws but one to go unexecuted, and the Government itself go to pieces lest that one be violated? . . . But it was not believed that this question was presented. It was not believed that any law was

---

[70] Ex parte Bollman, 4 Cr. 75; Ex parte Merryman, 17 Fed. Cas. 144; Ex parte Field, 5 Blatchford 63.

[71] Randall, p. 31.

[72] Ex parte Vallandigham, I Wall. 243. In this case the Supreme Court declined to hear an appeal from the sentence of death imposed by a military commission on the ground that the latter was not a court of record of which it could take cognizance.

[73] 4 Wall. 2. Below, p. 122.

violated. . . . Now, it is insisted that Congress, and not the Executive, is vested with this power; but the Constitution itself is silent
as to which or who is to exercise the power; and as the provision
was plainly made for a dangerous emergency, it cannot be believed
that framers of the instrument intended that in every case the
danger should run its course until Congress should be called together,
the very assembling of which might be prevented, as was intended in
this case, by the rebellion.[74]

Again, when the prominent " Copperhead," Vallandigham,
was arrested, tried, and sentenced to death by a military commission in southern Ohio, large delegations of Democrats
protested against the arbitrary and illegal character of such
proceedings. In replying to these petitions for clemency for
this prominent partisan, Lincoln was afforded a second opportunity to defend his later proclamation of martial law:

You ask, in substance, whether I really claim that I may override
all the guaranteed rights of individuals, on the plea of conserving
the public safety—when I choose to say the public safety requires
it. This question, divested of the phraseology calculated to represent
me as struggling for an arbitrary personal prerogative, is either
simply a question *who* shall decide, or an affirmation that *nobody*
shall decide, what the public safety does require in cases of rebellion
or invasion. The Constitution contemplates the question as likely
to occur for decision, but it does not expressly declare who is to
decide it. By necessary implication, when rebellion or invasion
comes, the decision is to be made from time to time; and I think the
man whom, for the time, the people have, under the Constitution,
made the Commander-in-Chief, . . . is the man who holds the power
and bears the responsibility of making it. If he uses the power
justly, the same people will probably justify him; if he abuses it,
he is in their hands to be dealt with by all the modes they have
reserved to themselves in the Constitution.[75]

Yet, thoroughly imbued with a reverence for the guaranteed rights
of individuals, I was slow to adopt the strong measures which by
degrees I have been forced to regard as being within the exceptions
of the Constitution, and as indispensable to the public safety. Nothing is better known to history than that courts of justice are utterly
incompetent to such cases. Civil courts are organized chiefly for
trials of individuals, or, at most, a few individuals acting in concert,
and this in quiet times, and on charges . . . well defined in the law.
. . . Again a jury too frequently has at least one member more ready
to hang the panel than the traitor. And yet, again, he who dis-
suades one man from volunteering, or induces one soldier to desert,

---

[74] Messages and Papers of the Presidents, VII, 3226. As a staunch
exponent of civil liberty, Jefferson was averse to even a temporary
suspension of the writ. Instead, he advocated as a substitute an
endless chain of trials and retrials before civil courts to -restrict
the freedom of a disloyal citizen. Writings (Ford Ed.), V, 46-47.
[75] Henry J. Raymond, State Papers of Abraham Lincoln, p. 395
(Reply to Ohio Democrats).

weakens the Union cause as much as he who kills a Union soldier in battle. . . . By [your] third resolution, the meeting indicates their opinion that military arrests may be constitutional in localities where rebellion actually exists, but that such arrests are unconstitutional in localities where rebellion or invasion does *not* actually exist. . . . Inasmuch as the Constitution itself makes no such distinction, I am unable to believe that there *is* any such distinction. I concede that the class of arrests complained of can be constitutional only when, in cases of rebellion or invasion, the public safety may require them; and I insist that in such cases they are constitutional wherever the public safety does require them; as well in places to which they may prevent the rebellion extending as in those where it may be already prevailing; . . . equally constitutional at all places where they will conduce to public safety, as against the dangers of rebellion or invasion. . . . Must I shoot a simple-minded soldier boy who deserts, while I must not touch the hair of a wily agitator who induces him to desert? . . . I think that in such a case to silence the agitator and save the boy is not only constitutional, but withal a great mercy. If I be wrong on this question of constitutional power, my error lies in believing that certain proceedings are constitutional when, in cases of rebellion or invasion, the public safety requires them, which would not be constitutional when, in the absence of rebellion or invasion, the public safety does not require them; in other words, that the Constitution is not, in its application, in all respects the same, in cases of rebellion or invasion involving the public safety, as it is in time of profound peace and public security.[76]

During the late War, Wilson indulged in no such sensational extensions of his power; yet he was able to exercise a greater restraint upon the liberty of American inhabitants than had his predecessor. Because of the complexity of the administrative organization established to prosecute the struggle, Wilson found it impossible to assist personally in the execution of the usual war-time police regulations; but, instead, adopted the policy of assigning his powers to specialized administrative boards appointed to perform these services. Whereas Lincoln continued, by personal orders, to cause arrests to be made or newspapers to be suppressed,[77] even after the creation of administrative machinery to supervise such matters, Wilson rarely, if ever, injected himself into the performance of a minor duty once it had been allotted to a subordinate commission. Commendable as this method may have been, insofar as it secured a precision and a regularity to the enforcement of restrictions on speech and press, nevertheless,

---

[76] Ibid., pp. 389-391 (Reply to the New York Delegation).
[77] Randall, pp. 164-165.

it precluded the exercise by the President of a corrective influence designed to mitigate the hardships resulting from the over-zealous efforts of subordinate officials.

To secure the conviction of individuals charged with treasonable practices or seditious utterances, Wilson steadfastly refused to utilize other than the ordinary means at hand.[78] Through a well organized Department of Justice, an administrative unit not in existence during the Civil War, prosecutions were begun in federal courts for the commission of a multiplicity of crimes set forth in the significant Espionage Act;[79] and, with the aid of sympathetic judges, another condition not prevalent during the preceding conflict, rather disproportionate penalties were obtained.[80] In this connection, it will be recalled that much of the interference with the liberty of our population was directed particularly against the large number of enemy aliens residing in the United States at the time. While Wilson was able to exhibit an ample legislative sanction for every order which he issued restricting the freedom of these people, it is believed by one authority that this power of the Executive to prescribe a rule of conduct for such aliens need not rest wholly upon statute but may be implied from principles of International Law.[81]

As to the necessity of preventing the disclosure of valuable information, whether relating to the movement of the armed

---

[78] In reply to Senator Overman's letter concerning a bill to have sedition and espionage cases removed to military courts, Wilson declared that he was absolutely opposed to such legislation and thought it not only unconstitutional but uncalled for in view of the existing laws. Messages and Papers of the Presidents, XVIII, 8493.

[79] 40 Stat. L. 217.

[80] Executive clemency, in the degree that it existed during the Lincoln Administration, was not discernible in the recent War. To investigate the problem of recommending pardons for soldiers imprisoned for violations of military laws, Wilson did establish a Clemency Board; but he did not attempt to follow up its work with a grant of amnesty at the conclusion of the conflict. For his attitude toward the movement to secure the pardon of Eugene V. Debs, see Tumulty, p. 505.

Lincoln's proclamations of conditional amnesty are contained in: Messages and Papers of the Presidents, VII, 3416, 3419.

[81] Berdahl, p. 186; Rev. Stat., sec. 4067; 40 Stat. L. 531; also, William F. Willoughby, Government Organization in War Time and After, pp. 316-320.

forces in the field or to the domestic activities of the Government, both Executives assumed the power, as Commander-in-Chief, to censor the press or messages transmitted over the existing lines of communication. While the imposition of any stricture upon the freedom guaranteed by the first amendment was believed a matter ultimately to be determined by Congress, the action of Lincoln and Wilson may be considered as a permanent precedent capable of affording a justification for similar conduct on the part of their successors.[82] However, in contrast to the policy observed during the Civil War, in which Congress " did not pass measures to help the military authorities check the utterances of the press, except to indemnify them for acts done or omitted by orders of the President," [83] the original voluntary press censorship of Wilson was almost immediately superseded by legislative enactments permitting him to adopt even more stringent measures of censorship.

Continuing the comparison of the methods devised by these two Executives to police non-military areas, we find that the organization established by Lincoln's subordinates to enforce war-time censorship was almost negligible. When it was discovered that press correspondents would not adhere to their voluntary pledge not to publish information injurious to their Government, the War department was finally obliged to order army officers, stationed in Northern cities, to arrest editors and seize their papers upon the disclosure of any prohibited news. In this decision Lincoln concurred by personally ordering General Dix at New York to suppress the New York " World " and " Journal of Commerce." [84] To minimize the harshness of this practice, however, he did not hesitate to rescind the orders of his military subordinates whenever their action lacked ample justification.[85] In a later attempt to regulate the distribution of news at its source, by the censor-

---

[82] Berdahl, pp. 193, 202.
[83] Thomas F. Carroll, " Freedom of Speech and Press during the Civil War," in Virginia Law Review, IX, 529.
[84] Messages and Papers of the Presidents, VII, 3438.
[85] Nicolay and Hay, II, 525. He revoked Burnside's order suppressing the " Chicago Times."

ship of telegraphic communications, a definite organization was created; but this was not until 1862, when, in conformity with an act of Congress, that duty was transferred to an agency in the War Department.[86] Prior to that date, both the Secretaries of State and Treasury had unsuccessfully tried their hands at that task. Assisting all three in this enterprise was the Postmaster-General, Blair, who, though acting without statutory authorization, endeavored to deprive disloyal newspapers of the use of the mails.[87]

Wilson was destined to have better success with the " voluntary agreement " method of controlling the press. Acting on the advice of Secretaries Lansing, Baker, and Daniels, he created, by executive order,[88] the Committee on Public Information, nominated its members, financed it out of executive funds until that organ was recognized by Congress, and permitted it to proceed to form its own organization for the regulation of domestic publications and the dissemination of government news. Since it had no legal status, other than the executive order which created it, this committee acknowledged from the start its inability to enforce its decrees, and appealed to the press to support it from patriotic motives alone.[89]

To avoid the possibility of having damaging information distributed through the remaining instruments of communication, Wilson next undertook to regulate the radio, telephone, telegraph, and cable lines located in the United States. Except for the Act of 1912,[90] which gave him the power to take over and operate radio stations on the occasion of a war, Wilson possessed no legislative authorization for his regula-

---

[86] Messages and Papers of the Presidents, VII, 3309-3310; 12 Stat. L. 334.

[87] Carroll, p. 523. Herein is cited his statement in defense of his power to do so. See also James G. Randall, " The Newspaper Problem in its Bearing upon Military Secrecy during the Civil War," in American Historical Review, XXIII, 303-323.

[88] Berdahl, p. 197; Messages and Papers of the Presidents, XVII, 8247.

[89] " The Committee on Public Information is without legal authority or moral right to bring any form of pressure on publications to enforce observance of its requests. . . . Their enforcement is a matter for the press itself." Willoughby, pp. 33, 35-40.

[90] 37 Stat. L. 302; Willoughby, p. 40.

tions concerning these means of communication, and his executive orders [91a] were accordingly declared to be issued in pursuance of his powers as Commander-in-Chief in time of war. By successive executive decrees, every telegraph, telephone, and cable company in American territory was gradually subjected to a government censorship; but when the initial arrangements devised by the War and Navy Departments were found to be inadequate, Congress, by amending the Espionage Act [92] and enacting the Trading with the Enemy Act, gave to the Administration the blanket authority which it needed. Utilizing this additional grant of authority, Wilson proceeded to put executive censorship upon a more permanent basis by establishing the Censorship Board [93] with authority over all existing instruments of electrical communication.

For the regulation of other domestic activities, the control of which may be necessary to the successful prosecution of a war, but which, even by a most liberal interpretation of his authority as Commander-in-Chief, the Executive cannot legally assert, Congress, under its war powers, is fully competent to provide. [94] Thus, although, during the Civil War, Congress exercised this large and almost unlimited residuum of our national war power only to the extent of ordering the seizure of private railroads affected with a military interest, the confiscation of rebel property, and the regulation of trade relations with the Southern States, the populace during the late conflict witnessed the national regulation of intrastate commerce, the purely private use of the means of transportation and communication, the prices of commodities, the hours of labor, industry, and the consumption of fuels and foods. [95] However, since the President is generally charged with the administration of these regulatory measures and the super-

---

[91] Messages and Papers of the Presidents, XVII, 8241, 8254, 8409; XVIII, 8551, 8593.
[92] 40 Stat. L. 553.
[93] Messages and Papers of the Presidents, XVII, 8369.
[94] Stewart v. Kahn, II Wall. 493; United States v. Miller, II Wall. 268.
[95] Berdahl, ch. xiii.

vision of the subordinate agencies created in pursuance thereof, he has an especial interest in the manner in which Congress provides for such war time emergencies.

That the policy of Congress will determine conclusively whether the President will be restricted to the direction of the machinery originated by the legislative body to mobilize and regulate our economic resources, or whether he will obtain a broad legislative sanction to exercise his own discretion as to the employment of means to attain that objective, was illustrated in the two wars under discussion. For various reasons, probably because of a fear of executive despotism, an apprehension readily stimulated by Lincoln's initial illegal measures, because of a general underestimation of the value of a unified command in time of war, and, finally, because of an intense factional strife which was not conducive to a loyal obedience to executive recommendation, Congress, during the Civil War, preferred not to lend its war powers unconditionally to the President in support of his endeavors to terminate that conflict. To assure itself of an influence and share in the prosecution of this War, accordingly, the legislative body not only drafted its measures in such detail as to leave the President little or no discretion in their enforcement, but subjected his activities to the surveillance of the celebrated Joint Committee on the Conduct of the War. Although the injection of such a committee into a war organization could scarcely be received favorably by any President, Lincoln, rather than increase party dissension, determined to endure its operation.[96]

By reason of his consummate legislative leadership and the cooperation accorded him by the members of both parties, who considered it unpatriotic to delay the prosecution of the War by hostile debate upon executive proposals, Wilson readily defeated attempts to establish a similar division of control during the late War. Thus, on the two occasions in which it was suggested that a congressional war committee be created or that the war be conducted thereafter by a " War Cabinet,"

---

[96] Diary of Gideon Welles, I, 262; II, 198, 226.

over which the President was to exert only a partial control,[97] the announcement of his uncompromising opposition [98] to these proposals sufficed to persuade Congress not to deviate from the program recommended by the Executive. The latter deeming it essential to an efficient prosecution of a war that he be granted the same unity of control over domestic mobilization as that possessed by him in the direction of the armed forces, Congress finally responded by authorizing Wilson to regulate the matters previously enumerated, subject to little or no restriction as to the manner of their control or the machinery set up to effect that end. In addition, to permit him freely to solve the confusion of functions resulting from the rapidly created war agencies, Congress, at his insistence, adopted the Overman Act [99] whereby the President was granted, temporarily, the powers of an administrative dictator.

Since a treaty of peace has been the method customarily employed by the United States to conclude a foreign war, Wilson, as the officer in control of our foreign relations, and as Commander-in-Chief, was enabled to assume the initiative in the negotiations intended to achieve that end. It was he, therefore, who secured acceptance of his Fourteen Points as the basis of a peace settlement, and determined in conjunction with the Allies upon the armistice with the Central Powers, and personally assisted in the drafting of the Versailles Treaty. While this arrogation of an absolute discretion over these matters was unwise to the extent that it incited opposition to

---

[97] Berdahl, pp. 170, 173.

[98] New York Times, January 22, 1918. While his public statements contain only a formal attack upon the inexpediency of these measures, his confidential opinion of their purpose is to be found in the following sentences: "I am opposed to the idea of a super cabinet, and regard it as nothing more or less than a renewal of the perpetual effort of the Republicans to force representation in the Administration. Republicans of the finest sort and of the finest capacity are working for and with the Administration on all hands and there is no need whatever for a change at the head of the administering Departments. I am utterly opposed to anything of the sort and will never consent to it." Tumulty, p. 265.

[99] 40 Stat. L. 556.

the treaty in the Senate, nevertheless it cannot be said that he transcended his powers.[100]

However, during the interval between the proclamation of the armistice and the anticipated ratification of the treaty, two peculiar questions were presented to Wilson for decision. With only a remote possibility of hostilities being renewed, but with the prospects for a speedy ratification of the peace treaty most unfavorable, the President was urged to proclaim peace and thereby hasten the removal of the burdens imposed upon the American people by the wartime legislation. Had the German State been eliminated as a result of this War and there remained no Government with whom the United States could negotiate, or had both Governments manifested an intention not to terminate the War by the usual treaty, Wilson might have complied with this request; but in view of the pending Treaty of Versailles, he replied in the negative. " In my judgment I have not the power by proclamation to declare that peace exists," and " I could in no circumstances consent to such a course prior to the ratification of a formal treaty of peace." [101]

In view of the President's unwillingness to proclaim the termination of the War for the purposes of the wartime statutes, Congress, unwilling to have a return to normalcy held in abeyance by the refusal of the Senate to agree to the treaty, undertook to solve the dilemma by a joint resolution repealing the prior declaration of war and declaring peace restored. While the attempt to terminate a foreign war in this manner was unprecedented, and was believed by many to be of no legal effect,[102] nevertheless, in vetoing the resolution, Wilson did not dispute the competency of Congress to adopt that procedure, but questioned only its expediency.[103]

---

[100] New York Times, August 22, 1919; Mathews, pp. 336-337.
[101] New York Times, August 22, 1919; Mathews, pp. 336-337.
[102] Berdahl, ch. xiii; contra, Mathews, pp. 327-336; Willoughby, III, 1565.
[103] Messages and Papers of the Presidents, XVIII, 8848. If Wilson had proclaimed peace, the proclamation would have had effects in terms of the war-time legislation, but could not have settled our international relations with Germany.

A concluding comparison of the two War Presidents, Lincoln and Wilson, reveals, therefore, that, while both have been acclaimed as dictators, they did not follow the same procedure to attain that supremacy. Thus, whereas Lincoln, in conformity with his belief that the doctrine *inter arma silent leges* applied equally to both hostile and non-military areas, and that Congress, mainly, was restrained by constitutional limitations in time of war,[104] considered himself free to adopt any measure calculated to save the Union; Wilson, in obedience to the principles established in the Milligan case, recognized his inability to act locally without legislative sanction. In complimenting Wilson for adhering to a correct interpretation of his war powers, it should be noted, however, that conditions during the late War were most favorable to a retention of a reign of law. Had a combination of all the difficulties opposing Lincoln again been present, there is good reason to believe, speculative as this may be, that Wilson, like his predecessor, might also have yielded to the doctrine of necessity.

---

[104] Randall, p. 514.

CHAPTER IV

FAITHFUL EXECUTION OF THE LAWS

In consonance with the accepted interpretation of the Constitution, whereby that document has been construed to contain an enumeration of powers rather than a general grant of authority, the stipulation expressed therein that " he shall take care that the laws be faithfully executed,"[1] cannot be viewed as providing the Executive with an additional source of power. Rather is that clause to be regarded as imposing upon him a paramount duty, the fulfilment of which can be attained legitimately only by the exercise of those powers expressly granted him and those reasonably implied therefrom. Nevertheless, since the due execution of the laws might be said to represent the ultimate objective to be attained by the President, and since the failure to attain this objective might result in the dissolution of the Government, this clause, especially in an emergency, has [2] not only served as an impetus to the liberal implication of additional powers, but has also been appealed to directly as the justification for the authority employed in the discharge of the obligation set forth therein.

By such process of reasoning and interpretation has the Executive defended his assumption of the position of administrator-in-chief. His incentive for this acquisition being the necessity of faithfully performing this duty, the President has accordingly endeavored: first, to cultivate those of his powers which are capable of affording him a control or supervision over the federal personnel; and second, to convince Congress of the expediency of granting him such additional authority as will enable him to direct both materially and personally the execution of the laws. From this effort there has accrued to him an extensive administrative power, which, if classified, includes a power of direction, effected through the exercise of his powers of appointment and removal, a

---

[1] Art. 2, Sec. 3.
[2] In Re Neagle, 136 U. S. 1; Myers v. United States, 272 U. S. 52; Willoughby, III, 1474.

power of ordinance-making, and lastly, a "power to perform special acts of individual application." [3]

To predetermine the manner in which the duties imposed upon subordinate federal officials are to be performed, the President frequently may need only to exercise his power of appointment; for, by filling these posts with men of the same political affiliation as his own, he prevents discord and assures himself of a personnel pledged to the application of his policies in their execution of the law. But, while the evolution of the party system has made possible this increased effectiveness of the appointing power, it has also rendered its exercise by the President his most onerous duty. Besieged by the numerous petitions of office-seekers, the Chief Magistrate, after the development of political parties, was confronted with the additional problem of determining by what method preference might be given to his political colleagues without disregarding the essential prerequisite of fitness for service. Probably not the most desirable, but at least a partial alleviation of this difficulty has been effected by the procedure whereby the Executive has permitted the members of the Senate to submit a list of candidates for nomination and has reserved for himself the examination of their competency. [4]

Not anticipating the future establishment of political parties, and consequently unable to foresee its effect on the procedure by which appointments were to be made, Washington, on entering office, was guided by his resolution to foster the immediate success of the new Government by filling its offices with men of highest qualifications. In response to numerous requests for appointments, he therefore let it be known that his responsibilities as President would preclude any deference to personal inclinations or friendships [5] in making his selections, and that, in performing this duty, "fitness of character" would be his "primary object." [6] However,

---

[3] Goodnow, pp. 75-77, 89.
[4] John A. Fairlie, The National Administration of the United States, p. 6.
[5] Sparks, X, 6.
[6] Ibid., p. 57.

if an abundance of candidates possessing that attainment were available, he announced his willingness to grant a preference to older [7] men of prominence, and to see to it that positions were equitably distributed among the several States.[8] That mere potential competency for public service might be rendered nugatory by the appointee's political hostility to the Executive apparently was not appreciated by Washington until the dissension created in his Cabinet by such arch-opponents as Jefferson and Hamilton had reached its height; and it was doubtless this occurrence which prompted the modification of policy expressed in the following statement:

> I shall not, whilst I have the honor to administer the government, bring a man into any office of consequence knowingly, whose political tenets are adverse to the measures, which the general government are pursuing; for this, in my opinion, would be a sort of political suicide.[9]

Nevertheless, on questions concerning the limits of the participation accorded the Senate in appointment-making, his initial decision had not been altered. Although of the opinion that the Senate was to serve as a cabinet council to the Executive in concluding treaties, he did not believe that a similar result was intended in the matter of nominations for office; and, in conferring with members of that body as to the most suitable mode of communications between the two branches of the Government, he excluded the latter subject from consideration. Thus, after suggesting that " oral communications " be adopted as the method for the discussion of treaties, he added:

> With respect to nominations, my present ideas are, that, as they point to a single object, unconnected in its nature with any other object, they had best be made by written messages. In this case the acts of the President and the acts of the Senate will stand upon clear, distinct, and responsible ground.
> Independently of this consideration it could be no pleasing thing, I

---

[7] Ibid., p. 24.

[8] Ibid., p. 432. For Jefferson's acceptance of the custom that a " geographical equilibrium " and not talents alone be considered in the making of appointments, see Writings (Ford Ed.), VIII, 2. Also, see Lucy M. Salmon, A History of the Appointing Power of the President, p. 25.

[9] Sparks, XI, 74.

conceive, for the President, on the one hand, to be present and hear the propriety of his nominations questioned, nor for the Senate, on the other hand, to be under the smallest restraint from his presence from the fullest and the freest inquiry into the character of the person nominated . . . For, as the President has a right to nominate without assigning his reasons, so has the Senate a right to dissent without giving theirs.[10]

While this statement seems to have defeated any expectation entertained by the Senate of acquiring a participation in the selection of officers, nevertheless, by recommending a list of nominees, and leaving the President a choice therefrom,

---

[10] Ibid., X, 484-485. Requests for papers revealing the reasons for the nomination of a particular person have generally been refused. An explanation of such refusals is contained in the following statement by Jefferson. " My nominations are sometimes made on my own knowledge of the persons; sometimes on the information of others given either voluntarily or at my own request and in personal confidence. This I could not communicate without a breach of confidence, not, I am sure, under the contemplation of the committee. They are sensible the Constitution has made it my duty to nominate; and has not made it my duty to lay before them the evidences or reasons whereon my nominations are founded; and of the correctness of this opinion the established usage in the intercourse between the Senate and the President is a proof." Writings (Ford Ed.), VIII, 412.

During Cleveland's first Administration, a refusal to comply with a similar request for papers resulted in a serious dispute between the President and the Senate. In considering the confirmation of a successor to a district attorney suspended by Cleveland, the Senate, through its Judiciary Committee and as a body, dispatched two successive requests to the Attorney-General, and on both occasions was informed by that officer that the President had not directed the transmission of the papers desired. Incensed by these refusals, the Senate thereupon passed a resolution condemning the President for conduct " subversive of good administration "; and it was in defense of so serious a charge that Cleveland interposed with the following reply. " Against the transmission of such papers and documents I have interposed my advice and direction. This has not been done, as is suggested in the committee's report, upon the assumption on my part that the Attorney-General or any other head of a Department ' is the servant of the President, and is to give or withhold copies of documents in his office according to the will of the Executive and not otherwise,' but because I regard the papers and documents withheld and addressed to me or intended for my use and action purely unofficial and private, not infrequently confidential, and having reference to the performance of a duty exclusively mine. I consider them in no proper sense as upon the files of the Department, but as deposited there for my convenience, remaining still completely under my control. I suppose if I desired to take them into custody I might do so with entire propriety, and if I saw fit to destroy them no one could complain." Messages and Papers of the Presidents, X, 4962-4963.

an unofficial approach to that result has been attained by the development of the practice of "senatorial courtesy." Washington does not seem to have objected to the introduction of this custom; for, when the Senate, in deference to the representatives of Georgia who disapproved his selection for an office within that State, rejected his nominee for this post, he very politely announced his satisfaction with the decision of that body.[11]

It remained for Jefferson, however, to arouse the fear that considerations of fitness for service might be subordinated to the test of political affiliation, and to forewarn the public of the impending adoption of the principle of rotation in office. While his conduct renders him only partially amenable to the first charge, it would nevertheless be unjust to criticize him even for that transgression without a consideration of the peculiar situation confronting him on his assumption of office. The Federalists having been in power almost from the establishment of the Government, and having, in their defeat, left all governmental posts in possession of their supporters, the first occasion for an upheaval in the distribution of offices was presented; and it was Jefferson's misfortune to preside when this contingency occurred.[12]

Had his own colleagues, the Republicans, been represented in the national personnel in a ratio in any way approximating equality with the Federalists, it would not be unwarranted to presume that he would have retained the same rigid tests of competency as were applied by his predecessor, Washington.

In the interests of good administration, as well as to avoid the accusation that his political associates were motivated, not by any aim of public service, but by a desire to obtain the rewards of public office, Jefferson did make an honest effort to have capacity for service remain the basis for his selections.[13] His original expressions of policy reveal an intention

---

[11] Ibid., I, 50-51. The writer doubts whether Washington discerned the motives which prompted this rejection.

[12] Salmon, p. 33.

[13] As the increasing number of offices imposes a correspondingly greater burden upon him in the selection of incumbents, the President has proved more willing to acknowledge the assistance accorded

to retain in office Federalists of known ability who would loyally support the Administration, and to remove only those members of the defeated party who were guilty of maladministration of their duties or were politically hostile to the President.[14] Occupation by the Republicans of a proportionate number of federal offices was to be accomplished gradually through their appointment either to newly created posts or to posts made vacant by " deaths, resignations, or delinquences." [15]

Unfortunately, like many of his successors, Jefferson was unable to execute these intentions in defiance of the political pressure brought to bear upon him. Harassed by the petitions of his political followers for their long awaited rewards of office, and realizing that the vacancies created by the contingencies enumerated above would be too few to satisfy the demand, he yielded to the extent of making several questionable removals of Federalists in favor of Republicans in both the law enforcement and revenue departments.[16] To justify this slight reversal of policy, he declared that the incoming party had a right to an immediate representation [17] in the national administration, and added further that only by the removal of marshals and attorneys could he counterbalance the influence of the irremovable Federalist judges.[18] However, when a reasonable distribution had been accomplished, he announced his willingness to return to the original tests of selection: " Is he [the candidate] honest? Is he capable? Is he faithful to the Constitution? " [19]

Not only was Jefferson opposed to the principle of rotation in office, but the number of his removals for political reasons

him through the practice of " senatorial courtesy." Jefferson's statement is an early example. " The most valuable source of information we have is that of the members of the Legislature, and it is one to which I have resorted and shall with great freedom." Writings (Ford Ed.), VIII, 6.

[14] Ibid., IX, 118, VIII, 25.
[15] Ibid., p. 176.
[16] Ibid., pp. 67, 69.
[17] Ibid., p. 70.
[18] Ibid., p. 25.
[19] Ibid., p. 70.

is too insignificant to lend credence to the statement that he was guilty of introducing the "spoil system." [20] It was the Tenure of Office Act of 1820,[21] and not Jefferson's conduct, which introduced and sustained this demoralizing practice for more than half a century. During this period, party regularity and party advantage were the controlling standards of selection, and every installation of a new President was generally attended by the eviction from office of the members of the defeated party. Because he permitted this situation to continue unimproved during the Civil War, Lincoln cannot be said to have espoused, as did several of his predecessors, the principle "to the victor belong the spoils." But while he deprecated the unwholesome results of that practice, he seems to have considered it futile to combat a condition which was at that time publicly approved.[22]

On the other hand, civil service reform was well under way when Roosevelt and Wilson entered office; and with the public supporting them in their efforts, these Executives successfully undertook to return as nearly to the standards applied by Washington as existing circumstances would permit. Realizing that the large number of offices to be filled made it physically impossible for them personally to discover the most desirable incumbents, these men accepted the practice of "senatorial courtesy"—Roosevelt without question, in fact, with gratitude; but, in the interests of efficient administration, they did insist that the candidates thus recommended be eminently capable. Or as Roosevelt declared: "They [the Senators] may ordinarily name the man but I shall name the standard and the men have got to come up to it." [23] Nevertheless, these Executives did reserve for their own consideration such number of offices as could be filled without an unreasonable expenditure of their time; and, in making

[20] Salmon, p. 39.
[21] 3 Stat. L. 582. Jefferson was opposed to the enactment of this measure. Writings (Ford Ed.), X, 168.
[22] Salmon, pp. 88, 85-88.
[23] Bishop, I, 236.

these selections, did not hesitate to disregard party lines in order to secure the best man.[24]

While no serious constitutional dispute has arisen as to the procedure by which appointments are to be made, the Executive and the Senate have occasionally disagreed as to the correct interpretation of the provision referring to vacancies.[25] Members of the Senate have preferred to construe this clause strictly, and, accordingly, have insisted that, unless an office first become vacant during a recess of that body, the latter ought not to be denied the opportunity of immediately confirming the new incumbent.[26] On the other hand, the President has consistently ignored that complaint, and has con-

---

[24] Taft, pp. 70-71. The record of Wilson in the late War is evidence for that statement. For an instance in which Roosevelt selected a Democrat, see Bishop, I, 154-155. The presence in the Senate of several " Old Guard " Republicans who did not welcome civil service reform made it difficult for Roosevelt to maintain these ideals without a struggle. Whenever he could mobilize public opinion in support of his selection, he ventured to defy " senatorial courtesy "; but he confessed that this procedure could not be employed in every minor appointment. In threatening to take such action, however, he merely indicated that, although he did not wish the Senate to surrender its independent discretion in the matter of confirming his nominations, he would not respect its decision whenever it was influenced by personal rather than public motives. Bishop, I, 248-249. For Wilson's attitude and the change wrought in it by the force of circumstances, see Ray Stannard Baker, Woodrow Wilson, Life and Letters, IV, 36-54.

[25] Art. 2, Sec. 2.

[26] Willoughby, III, 1509. Washington is said to have adherred to this view. Corwin, p. 55. Because certain Executives have, during the recess of the Senate, sent abroad " private agents " with officially sealed commissions bearing the rank of public minister, Senators have on occasion been misled into believing that a violation of the constitutional provision concerning vacancies has been committed. The latter have asserted that unless diplomatic relations have been instituted with a foreign nation prior to the recess of the Senate, no office of public minister accredited to that state existed, and hence there remained no vacancy to be filled during the ensuing recess. In reply to their contention, others have declared that the office of public minister comes into being with the intention of the President to enter into friendly negotiations with a foreign power, and being thus vacant because of the recency of its existence, the former was competent to fill it. While disputes on this question occurred long after his death, reference therein was nevertheless made to Washington's dispatch, during the recess of 1795, of one David Humphreys under a sealed commission as commissioner plenipotentiary, to negotiate a treaty with Algiers. See Congressional Debates, V, 88; Thomas Hart Benton, Abridgment of the Debates of Congress, V, 85-91; XI, 197-222; Corwin, pp. 50-63.

sidered himself empowered to appoint during recess to any office then vacant, irrespective of the fact that the vacancy originally may have occurred while the Senate was in session.[27]

Through an inadvertence on the part of the Senate in failing to consider the appointments made by the President during a previous recess, it may become possible for the latter to retain a subordinate in office for a considerable period without having his selection confirmed. Thus, a minor position in the internal revenue service having become vacant during the recess of 1902, Roosevelt attempted, in the next two successive sessions of the Senate, to procure the confirmation of a successor to that office. Since the Senate had adjourned without giving any indication as to when it would be disposed to act, Roosevelt thereupon proceeded to appoint W. D. Crum to the unoccupied office under a temporary commission which was to expire at the conclusion of the next session. Although the termination of this third, or special session, of the Senate and the beginning of its regular session were dated to occur at the same hour, he was nevertheless convinced that a " constructive recess " separated the two meetings, and consequently did not hesitate to extend the commission of Crum when the third session ended with the situation still unchanged. The Senate questioned the propriety of his decision, but took no action.[28]

However, the responsibility for a lengthy retention in office of a recess appointee without confirmation belongs to the Executive more frequently than to the Senate. To avoid the possible rejection of a nominee especially desirable to him, the President may commission the former during a recess, and successively renew that commission without ever submitting the name of his candidate to the Senate. In this manner was Robert Smith enabled to serve, without confirmation, as Secretary of the Navy during the second term of Jefferson.[29] Because the Senate would undoubtedly have refused its assent to the appointment of a Secretary of the Treasury in accord

---

[27] Willoughby, III, 1509-1510.
[28] Ibid., pp. 1508-1509.
[29] Henry J. Ford, The Rise and Growth of American Politics, p. 290.

with his plan to remove the Bank Deposits, Jackson was of necessity obliged to observe this procedure to secure the services of Taney for that purpose. The " transfer " of the funds having been accomplished, a rejection was no longer to be feared, and Jackson thereupon submitted the latter's name to the Senate.[30]   Again, in removing Frank S. Myers (the appellant in the recent case of Myers v. United States), Wilson delayed until the recess of the Senate to appoint a successor, and the latter's name was not forwarded to the Senate for confirmation until Harding had entered the Presidency.[31]

Had these Executives never been able to remove incompetents and political opponents from office, it is doubtful whether success would have attended their efforts, herein partially described, to assemble a personnel who could have been relied upon to remain loyal to the service, to their party, and to their President.   Obviously, therefore, in claiming a power which had not clearly been associated with the Chief Magistracy [32] and was certainly not expressed in the Constitution, the President has had as one incentive a desire to procure every means which might facilitate the performance of his duty to see to the faithful execution of the laws.   And, whether or not the President be logically correct in his assumption, that the power of removal is inherently an executive power, essential to an efficient execution of his responsibilities, and fairly inferable from his power of appointment, it may suffice to add that his pretensions have generally received the approbation of the highest federal tribunal.

---

[30] Ibid., p. 290.

[31] Power of the President to Remove Federal Officers, 69th Cong., 2d sess., S. Doc. No. 174, p. 20.   A suggested explanation of Wilson's conduct is that he expressly refrained from securing an assent to the appointment of a successor, in order to encourage the movement to have the validity of Myers' removal judicially reviewed.   In an earlier case, Wallace v. United States, 257 U. S. 541, the Court had ruled that the Senate, in assenting to the appointment of a successor to an officer believed to have been removed contrary to the procedure stipulated in the statute creating the office, would be deemed to have ratified the conduct of the President.

[32] Goodnow, pp. 70-75.

Although no uniformity of opinion exists concerning the exact significance to be accorded to the first precedent recorded on the subject of removals,[33] it may safely be said that the final decision resulting from the debate in the first Congress (on the proposal to establish a Department of Foreign Affairs) provided an affirmative indication that this power would be exercised by the President. Irrespective of the disputed question whether this debate authorizes the inference that the source from which this power is derived is the general grant of executive power contained in Article II, or the power of appointment, or a congressional sanction, this early decision, even conservatively construed, would seem to permit the deduction that the President is competent to remove at pleasure subordinate executive officers in all cases in which the statute creating their positions stipulates appointment jointly with the Senate, but is silent as to the conditions of tenure.

Having confined his removals to the incumbents of offices in the diplomatic, internal revenue, and military services, all of which had been established by enactments containing provisions identical with those enumerated, Washington cannot, if the above premise be accepted, be charged with any unwarranted exercise of power.[34] Moreover, his reputation for non-partisanship averted any disposition on the part of Congress to request any explanation for these displacements.[35]

However, in undertaking gradually to procure a fair share of offices for members of his own party, as well as to nullify the eleventh-hour attempt of John Adams to fill all vacant or newly created positions with Federalists, Jefferson was compelled to make displacements in almost every branch of the federal service; and in so doing he incurred the risk of having his opponents sponsor a judicial inquiry into the validity of some one of his removals. That he should have been the first to experience this occurrence might be attributed,

---

[33] Edwin S. Corwin, The President's Power of Removal, pp. 10 ff.

[34] Carl R. Fish, " Removal of Officials by Presidents," in Annual Report of American Historical Association (1899) I, 69.

[35] Salmon, p. 27. Defalcations in the collection of government funds formed the basis for removals in the customs service.

perhaps, to existent partisan hostility, rather than to any definitely accepted estimate of the limits of the executive power of removal; for no important alteration [36] in the content of statutes establishing offices had yet been made. Whether Washington, under the same conditions which confronted Jefferson, would have considered this power as inapplicable to officers holding for a fixed tenure cannot be ascertained; but, the fact is, he was not presented with an opportunity to decide that question.

While Jefferson issued no statement to the effect that this power did extend to that class of officers, his conduct suggested very clearly that he did entertain that opinion. Thus, in resolving to ignore the "midnight appointments" of Adams as if they had never been made,[37] and to regard his appointees as having never become entitled to their offices, he took no cognizance of the fact that, of the latter, Marbury had been commissioned to occupy a post for which provision had been made for a tenure of five years.[38] When Marbury sought to obtain a writ of mandamus to compel the Secretary to deliver to him the evidence of his right to his office, that is, the signed and sealed commission, the Supreme Court finally ruled that a want of jurisdiction prevented the grant of this remedy; but to reach that conclusion, Chief Justice Marshall evidently considered it necessary to decide the following propositions: first, that since the commission was signed and sealed by the President and Secretary of State, the appointment was complete, and second, that since the officer was to hold for a fixed term, independent of the executive, the appointment was not revocable, but vested in the officer legal rights.[39] Believing that the admission by the Court of its inability to afford the appellant any relief con-

---

[36] An Act of 1789 (1 Stat. L. 87), creating the office of federal marshal, provided that the incumbent should serve for four years and was to be removable at pleasure; whereas the Act of 1801 (2 Stat. L. 107), establishing the office of justice of the peace in the District of Columbia, stipulated for a term of five years, but was silent on the question of removal.

[37] Writings (Ford Ed.), VI, 36.

[38] See n. 36.

[39] Marbury v. Madison, 1 Cranch 137, 161

stituted the only essential question to be decided, an opinion in which both his successors and a subsequent majority of that tribunal [40] concurred, Jefferson adopted the view that these additional pronouncements of the Chief Justice were unnecessary to the determination of the former question, and hence were mere dicta.[41]

Prior to the earliest emergence of the civil service reform movement during the later years of the Civil War, the congressional enactments establishing subordinate executive offices continued to provide that the incumbent should hold at pleasure, or for a fixed term, or for a fixed term of years removable at the pleasure of the President, or removable when the latter shall deem him guilty of the misconduct specified.[42] Since, in none of these statutes can there be found any stipulation rigidly limiting the Executive's power of removal, it was possible for the early Presidents, including even those who might have considered this authority as derivable only from congressional sanction, to interpret these enactments in favor of their continued, undiminished exercise of this power. Aroused by the belief that the ease with which a President could discharge an officer was proving injurious to the national service, Congress has, since the Civil War, endeavored to render such displacements more difficult by one of the two following methods: first, by joining the Senate with him in the removal of a federal officer, and second, by providing that he shall remove the latter for specified causes.[43]

---

[40] Myers v. United States, 272 U. S. 52; Parsons v. United States, 167 U. S. 324.

[41] By reason of his previous political rivalry with John Marshall, Jefferson was also inclined to suspect that the former had uttered these "superfluous" (?) statements concerning the limits of the removal power solely out of a personal desire to censor the President. However, expressing himself in the technical language of the Court, Jefferson held that a commission constituted a deed, and until it was delivered to the appointee, the latter's rights accruing under that instrument did not become operative. Writings (Ford Ed.), IX, 53.

[42] These statutes are enumerated by Mr. Justices Brandeis and McReynolds in their dissenting opinions in the Myers Case, 272 U. S. 52.

[43] The effect of the first limitations would seem to have been lessened by the decision of the Court in Wallace v. United States, 257

Of the Executive presiding during the progress of this movement, only three [44] have protested that such legislation constitutes an illegal encroachment upon an independent, uncontrollable executive power; but, as Mr. Justice Brandeis has indicated, their general declarations of opinion are peculiarly inconsistent with their conduct in ignoring or in signing other measures imposing similar restraints.[45] However, if this contradiction between belief and practice can be explained by the fact that Cleveland and Wilson could not have undertaken to contest the validity of every statute presenting this question, it may be possible to accept the statements of these Executives as accurately representing their interpretation of the limits of the removal power. On the other hand, if greater weight is to be accorded the instances in which they disregarded an attempt by Congress to restrict their exercise of this power, it may become necessary to presume that they have recognized the competency of Congress to control this power, but have erroneously employed a constitutional argument to express their disapproval of the expediency of qualifying their discretion to displace certain classes of executive officers.

Like his predecessor, Cleveland,[46] Wilson confined his objec-

---

U. S. 541. See above, p. 132. Probably as a result of the adverse ruling in the case of Shurtleff v. United States, 189 U. S. 311, in which the Court said that a mere enumeration of causes would not be construed as limiting the power of the President to remove for other non-specified causes, Congress was disposed to increase the stringency of this restriction by expressly stipulating that removals shall be made for causes specified only. For an example, see the provisions of the War Labor Board Measure signed by Wilson. 41 Stat. L. 470.

[44] Johnson, Cleveland, and Wilson.

[45] Thus, in condemning the Tenure of Office Act of 1867, Johnson does not seem to have objected to its application to minor executive officers; Cleveland, in effecting the repeal of a similar Act of 1869, neglected to secure the recision of the Act of 1876 (19 State. L. 80) making postmasters, such as Myers, removable only by the consent of the Senate; and Wilson, in turn, signed without objection the War Labor Board Act. 69th Cong., 2d sess., S. Doc. No. 174, pp. 290, 291, 296.

[46] For a statement by Cleveland indicating his belief that the President possessed an absolute power of removal, see Messages and Papers of the Presidents, X, 4964. In his own volume, " Presidential Problems," one will find a complete account of his dispute with the Senate on this question. Chs. iii, iv.

tions to statutes in which any part of the legislative branch had been granted a share in the exercise of this power. While his removal of the plaintiff, Myers, was in effect a challenge of the validity of the Act of 1876, which joined the Senate with the Executive in the removal of certain postmasters, he issued no statement of his opinions on this subject until he vetoed the first Budget and Accounting Bill.[47] To this veto he affixed the following message:

> It has, I think, always been the accepted construction of the Constitution that the power to appoint officers of this kind carries with it, as an incident, the power to remove. I am convinced that the Congress is without constitutional power to limit the appointing power and its incident, the power of removal derived from the Constitution.
>
> The section referred to not only forbids the Executive to remove these officers, but undertakes to empower the Congress, by a concurrent resolution, to remove an officer appointed by the President with the advice and consent of the Senate.
>
> I can find in the Constitution no warrant for the exercise of this power by the Congress. There is certainly no express authority conferred, and I am unable to see that authority for the exercise of this power is implied in any express grant of power. On the contrary, I think its exercise is clearly negatived by section 2 of Article II.[48]

Judged by the far reaching decision submitted by Chief Justice Taft in the Myers Case, the early assertions of three prominent Executives, Jackson, Cleveland, and Wilson, appear to have been correct when uttered. But, while a majority of five justices concurred in the statement that the executive power of removal is uncontrollable, this decision must be estimated in accordance with the principle of " stare decisis " rather than of " stare dictis." [49] Applied to the issue squarely before it in the appeal of Myers, the opinion

---

[47] This measure had provided for the offices of Comptroller-General and Assistant Comptroller-General, and stipulated that the incumbents of these positions were to be removable prior to the expiration of their terms only by a concurrent resolution. In the second Act (42 Stat. L. 20), which was signed by President Harding, this section was altered to the extent that the removal was to be instituted by a joint congressional resolution, the modification thus permitting the Executive to interpose with a veto. It is reasonable to assume, nevertheless, that this single modification would not have sufficed for Mr. Wilson.

[48] Messages and Papers of the Presidents, XVIII, 8851.

[49] Herman Oliphant, " A Return to Stare Decisis," in the American Law School Review, VI, 215.

of the Court would seem to hold that the participation of Congress in the removal of executive officers, as one method of regulating the President's exercise of this power, is unconstitutional. However, not until the Court designates whether the officers who are by statute made removable in this manner are executive or congressional officers will it be possible to predict with reasonable assurance that a particular stipulation providing for such displacement will, or will not, be invalidated in the future.[50] Even more difficult is it to prophesy the fate of those provisions which restrict the President to removals for only those causes specified. To intimate that Congress remains competent to employ this one method of limiting his exercise of this power would be to ignore the rather positive language of Chief Justice Taft; but the validity of this form of limitation was not before the Court in the Myers Case, and another ruling may be required to settle this matter.[51]

Reference has herein been made to Jackson, as the first of four Presidents to express the belief that the power of removal is uncontrollable. He has earned distinction, not alone from this early estimate of the extent of that power, but from the unprecedented result which he achieved through the exercise of that weapon. Ordinarily, in displacing a federal officer, the Executive is motivated, exclusive of political considerations, by a desire to rid the service of a person who is either incompetent or negligent in the performance of his duties. For the President to refuse to remove an officer under the latter circumstances would be to ignore his responsibility of seeing that the laws are faithfully executed. It remained for Jackson, however, to demonstrate that the power of removal could be exercised not only to facilitate an efficient administration of the laws, but also to enable the President to direct the manner of their enforcement.

While a power of overseeing the activities of subordinate

---

[50] For a presentation of the reasons for classifying the Comptroller-General and Assistant Comptroller-General as congressional officers, see Willoughby, III, 1525-1526.

[51] James Hart, Tenure of Office under the Constitution.

officers is necessarily inferable from his obligation to see to the due execution of the laws, no provision of the Constitution explicitly bestows upon him a power of direction. In fact his possession of this power, independent of statutory grant, was denied in a dictum of United States v. Kendall,[52] in which the Court said:

> The President, in the execution of his duty to see that the laws be faithfully executed, is bound to see that the postmaster-general discharges 'faithfully' the duties assigned to him by law; but this does not authorize the President to direct him how he shall discharge them.

Moreover, by providing, in its enactments establishing the nonpolitical departments of the Government, that the Secretaries thereof shall report their activities directly to the Legislature, Congress had manifested neither an intention to accord this power to the Executive nor a disposition to recognize it as already within his possession. Thus, the Secretary of the Treasury, by the statute which created his department, was requested to report his activities directly to Congress; and, by a subsequent enactment,[53] was ordered to tender the Legislature a statement of his reasons for the exercise, at any future date, of his discretionary power to remove the federal deposits from the National Bank.

In imposing this duty upon that officer, Congress may have intended that he should be free from all external influence in the exercise of his discretion; and though that body did not attempt to indicate the circumstance which would justify a removal of the deposits, it was generally understood that only "upon unexpected emergencies," or for "high and important reasons of state,"[54] would the Treasurer be warranted in transferring these funds. Applying the older view, one would therefore infer that the duty of the Executive to see to the execution of the laws would obligate Jackson to remove the Treasurer only when the latter should choose to ignore the unmistakable existence of such an emergency;

---

[52] 5 Cranch C. C. 163, 172. Cited by Goodnow, p. 79.
[53] 3 State. L. 274.
[54] Life and Letters of Story, II, 156. Cited by Henry C. Mason, The Veto Power, p. 34.

but that the fulfilment of his responsibility as Chief Magistrate neither required nor authorized him to assist or to control that officer in the exercise of this discretion.

For the most part, this conception of a limited executive power of direction was permanently supplanted by the conduct and assertions of Jackson, who declared:

The whole executive power being vested in the President, who is responsible for its exercise, it is a necessary consequence that he should have a right to employ agents of his own choice to aid him in the performance of his duties, and to discharge them when he is no longer willing to be responsible for their acts. . . .

[It was] settled by the Constitution . . . ; that as incident to that power the right of appointing and removing those officers who are to aid him in the execution of the laws, with such restrictions only as the Constitution prescribes, is vested in the President; that the Secretary of the Treasury is one of those officers; that the custody of the public property and money is an Executive function which, in relation to the money, has always been exercised through the Secreary of the Treasury and his subordinates; that in the performance of these duties he is subject to the supervision and control of the President, and in all important measures having relation to them consults the Chief Magistrate and obtains his approval and sanction; that the law establishing the bank did not, as it could not, change the relation between the President and the Secretary—did not release the former from his obligation to see the law faithfully executed nor the latter from the President's supervision and control. . . .

The dangerous tendency of the doctrine which denies to the President the power of supervising, directing, and controlling the Secretary of the Treasury in like manner with other executive officers would soon be manifest in practice were the doctrine to be established. The President is the direct representative of the American people, but the Secretaries are not. If the Secretary of the Treasury be independent of the President in the execution of the laws, then there is no direct responsibility to the people in that important branch of this Government to which is committed the care of the national finances. And it is in the power of the Bank of the United States, or any other corporation . . . , if a Secretary shall be found to accord with them in opinion . . . , to control through him the whole action of the Government (so far as it is exercised by his Department) in defiance of the Chief Magistrate elected by the people, and responsible to them.[55]

---

[55] Messages and Papers of the Presidents, III, 1298-1299, 1304, 1309. But see also a somewhat contradictory statement, ibid., pp. 1386-1387. While there is nothing in Wilson's record to suggest that he denied the existence of a power of direction, nevertheless he expressed his disapproval of the efforts of any Executive to utilize his powers to procure a result directly opposed to the expressed will of Congress. "No one, I take it for granted, is disposed to disallow the principle that the representatives of the people are the proper ultimate authority in all matters of government, and that administration is merely the clerical part of government. Legislation is the

Through this accomplishment Jackson revealed to Congress a fact of which it had hitherto failed to take cognizance; namely, that in conferring a discretionary duty upon an executive officer, and, in the same instance, expressly or tacitly acknowledging the competency of the President to remove that officer, it unavoidably creates an opportunity for the Executive to direct that subordinate in the performance of this duty. However, the older view, enunciated by the Court in United States v. Kendall, continued to be applicable in the case of a ministerial duty; for, while the President could displace the officer in whom such an obligation had been vested, his efforts to prevent the fulfilment of that duty could be defeated successfully by the issuance of the writ of mandamus.[56]

Nevertheless, as the writer has previously indicated, the possession by the Executive of an independent power of appointment and removal has provided him with only a portion of his present administrative authority. For much of the added importance of his responsibility to see to the execution of the laws, the President is indebted to Congress, which has, in turn, by the very necessities of governmental operation, been compelled to confer upon him a power to issue ordinances regulating the application of its legislative enactments.

Divided into large classes, these administrative ordinances issued by the Executive in pursuance of congressional authorization comprise: 1. a collection of orders regulating the performance of duties by minor officers in the various executive departments; and 2. those proclamations which announce the existence of the circumstances to which a statute was intended

---

originating force. It determines what shall be done; and the President, if he cannot or will not stay legislation by the use of his extraordinary power as a branch of the legislature, is plainly bound in duty to render unquestioning obedience to Congress. And if it be his duty to obey, still more is obedience the bounden duty of his subordinates. The power of making laws is in its very nature and essence the power of directing, and that power is given to Congress." Congressional Government, pp. 273-274. See also ch. v.

[56] James Hart, The Ordinance Making Powers of the President, pp. 189-191.

to apply, or supply the details necessary to carry into effect a legislative policy contained in a particular enactment. It is the latter group of ordinances which impose restrictions on private conduct and define the procedure by which rights conferred by statute may be acquired.[57]

Since the majority of ordinances published by the President derive their sanction from congressional authorizations, it necessarily follows that, if the latter be declared *ultra vires,* the ordinances issued in pursuance thereof are also void, and consequently deprive his conduct of any legal justification. Being intended solely to direct federal officials in the execution of their tasks, and being enforceable generally through the exercise of the removal power, the numerous service regulations issued by the Executive affect no rights of which the courts take notice, and, therefore, are not readily the subject of a judicial inquiry into their validity.[58] The legality of the second class of ordinances, which do materially alter or extend rights of private citizens, has, however, been frequently questioned, chiefly on the ground that the enactments upon which these executive orders depend for their sanction are void as unconstitutional delegations of legislative power to the President. But, while the complainants, in cases in which this contention was submitted for decision, have endeavored to prove that the authority conferred by a particular statute was not a duty to ascertain the existence of the circumstances to which the content of that measure was intended to apply,

---

[57] Goodnow, pp. 84-89; Willoughby, III, 1637-1645; Hart, pp. 57-59. For a more complete classification of ordinances, see Hart, ch. iii.

In the ensuing pages the writer shall consider only the extent of such ordinance-making authority as was delegated to these several Executives. Having in previous chapters discussed their independent constitutional powers, he deems it sufficient merely to note herein that there are discernible in the latter certain ordinance characteristics. Thus rights and duties are created and legislative consequences ensue when the President, in the exercise of his powers to control foreign affairs, recognizes a foreign government or state, proclaims neutrality, or promulgates or terminates treaties. Moreover, he produces like results when he issues army and navy regulations having the force of law, grants amnesties, and administers military governments in hostile areas. Hart, ch. ix.

[58] For examples of Civil Service and Consular Regulations issued by Roosevelt and Wilson, see Messages and Papers of the President, XIV, 6703; XVII, 7959.

but a power to legislate further on the subject matter of that enactment, this argument has not been favorably received by the Supreme Court; for that tribunal has declared invalid no delegation of ordinance-making power.[59] This method of attack having proved ineffective, a second alternative open to an individual affected adversely by an executive regulation is to petition the court to declare the ordinance void for want of an authorization to sustain it: In those ordinances which have met this fate, the most common defects producing that result have been either a stipulation denying to a citizen a right clearly granted in the authorizing statute,[60] or a provision imposing a criminal penalty for disobedience of an executive decree.[61]

Little opportunity for litigation of this nature existed during the terms of the earlier Presidents for the reason that the National Government at that period legislated on fewer problems directly affecting the residents of the States; and, secondly, that both Congress and the public were averse to liberal delegations of discretionary authority to the Executive, particularly if the exercise of that authority was to affect private rights. Consequently, excepting the legislation adopted to meet the emergency created by a threatened war on American maritime commerce, statutes enacted during the Administrations of Washington and Jefferson, in general, empowered the President to issue ordinances concerning only the acquisition of materiel essential to the new Government. While several of these measures did grant him a certain amount of discretion in the issuance of regulations necessary to secure the objects therein enumerated, the greater number authorized him to perform only a single act required to effect a desired end.

Thus, concerning the care and expenditure of governmental funds, Washington was empowered, within definite limits or maxima, to contract loans, disburse money for the conduct of

---

[59] Hart, p. 149n.

[60] Campbell v. United States, 107 U. S. 407.

[61] Congress alone can provide that disregard of an executive regulation shall constitute a crime, and this power cannot be delegated. United States v. Eaton, 144 U. S. 677.

foreign affairs, and, in this connection, to employ envoys for foreign service at his own rates of pay, to issue such advance disbursements of salary to collectors of internal revenue as he deemed appropriate, to hire minor agents necessary for certain designated administrative services, and to pay them out of an appropriate sum of a fixed amount.[62]

Slightly greater discretion was conferred in those statutes which authorized him to issue ordinances respecting the procuring of arrangements necessary to the operation and housing of governmental organs. Although, admittedly, no considerable freedom of choice was involved in the performance of a duty to designate or select, within a named State, ports of entry or lighthouse sites, he was also authorized to direct the construction of such houses in accordance with plans prepared by Cabinet officers. Moreover, in connection with the establishment of the mint, he was permitted to designate the buildings to be used for that purpose, to collect the materials needed to prepare them for occupation, and to hire and instruct the artisans necessary to perform the latter task.[63]

Doubtless, because of its inability to anticipate the various methods by which foreign aggressions would be made upon our merchant marine, and to provide protection against the same, Congress consented to transfer to the President the entire responsibility of combating this danger; and it is in

---

[62] 1 Stat. L. 128, 256, 270, 378, 399, 468, 477.

[63] 1 Stat. L. 54, 251, 263, 368, 369, 130, 225, 248. Hart, pp. 72-76. With such delegations of authority the public had no immediate concern; for the ordinances which they permitted affected principally the officers in the employment of the Government. Probably the only minor regulations which Washington was empowered to issue that would have pertained to private citizens were those relating to the grant of licenses to trade with the Indian tribes, or to permissions to trade without licenses in those areas in which the whites were predominant. By the terms of another Act providing for trade with the natives he was also authorized to evict settlers from the land of the former, and to detain for prosecution those who were guilty of infractions of this statute. 1 Stat. L. 137, 329; Hart, pp. 73-74.

the Embargo Acts of 1794 [64] and 1807 [65] that there are to be found the most significant delegations of authority made during the Administrations of Washington and Jefferson.

By the terms of the Act of 1794, Washington was authorized: first, to determine whether there existed a danger to " public safety " sufficient to justify the laying of an embargo; second, to select the class of vessels to which this restriction was to apply; that is, whether it shall pertain to all vessels in American ports, or to American vessels, or to particular foreign vessels; and, third, to decide upon the advisability of revoking the embargo. Subject only to the admonition that his orders establishing an embargo be duly warranted by the requirements of public safety, and that the severity of his regulations concerning the application of this embargo should not exceed the necessities of the existing situation, Washington was thus granted complete power to carry this Act into effect; and whatever ordinances he might have issued in pursuance thereof would have had the force of a law materially restricting the rights of shippers. To secure obedience to his orders he was also given the power to direct and instruct federal officers as to the manner of their enforcement. But, unlike the emergency legislation of the late War, this statute permitted Washington to proclaim an embargo only during the recess of the Legislature; for both this authorization and his ordinances issued under its sanction were to expire automatically fifteen days from the date of the next session of Congress.[66]

---

[64] 1 Stat. L. 372. In conjunction with the enactment of this statute, Congress also empowered Washington to supplement the existing naval force, if he deemed an increase expedient, by an additional ten ships. To effect that result he was permitted to borrow the necessary funds, and to assume complete supervision of the arming and manning of these vessels. This authorization was to be operative, however, only during a recess of the Legislature. Moreover, he was ordered to provide for the storage of such naval equipment, and to sell all surplus materials. 1 Stat. L. 372; Hart, pp. 77-79.

[65] 2 Stat. L. 451. See also, 2 Stat. L. 339, 473, 490, 499, 506.

[66] Although the powers conferred by this Act were not used by Washington, he did undertake to combat the impending dangers by making preparations for calling out the militia to repel attacks within our harbors, and by issuing instructions to collectors in the

During Jefferson's second Administration, Congress adopted even more stringent measures to protect American citizens against attacks in our harbors by foreign vessels. Differing from the Act of 1794 in that they did not leave to the President the determination of whether or not a particular remedy should be applied, nor the selection of the regulations by which that remedy might be effected, these measures made permanent provision for the enforcement of certain restrictions definitely described therein, and delegated to Jefferson the discretion only to issue orders imposing these restrictions upon, or exempting therefrom, any infractors among a named class of persons. Nevertheless, to obtain an efficient execution of these laws, Congress provided for the infliction of a penalty on those who were guilty of disobeying the President's orders; and also authorized him to employ the armed forces, if necessary, to repel the aggressors, and to instruct subordinate officers, particularly marshals and collectors in the various ports, in the performance of the duties assigned to them under the terms of these acts.

However, what was really the most important delegation contained in these measures was the power conferred upon Jefferson, by the Act of 1808, to suspend, during the recess of the Legislature, the Embargo Acts, either wholly or in part, and subject to such qualifications as would not impair the public safety, whenever it should become apparent to him that the foreigner was beginning to desist from his depredations upon our neutral commerce. Whereas Washington was permitted only to revoke his own ordinances establishing an embargo, his successor, Jefferson, was empowered to suspend a duly recorded act of Congress; and, as one authority on this subject has intimated, whatever action Jefferson might have taken in pursuance of this authorization would have been equivalent to "presidential legislation." [67]

---

various Atlantic ports concerning grants of clearances to outgoing vessels. Messages and Papers of the Presidents, I, 144-145.

[67] Hart, p. 86. For proclamations issued in pursuance of this authority, see Messages and Papers of the Presidents, I, 390-392, 410-412.

Having considered it advisable to reserve for future comparison the delegations of authority to the two War-Presidents, Lincoln and Wilson, the writer will proceed immediately to a discussion of the most significant administrative power exercised by Roosevelt. Of the various ordinances issued by that Executive, probably none were productive of greater political dispute, or of more important litigation, than those concerning the enforcement of the federal conservation policies.

With a view to preserving, from spoliation by exploiters, government lands containing valuable forest and mineral resources, Congress had, during the nineties and a decade thereafter, adopted measures designating certain lands as public lands, and authorizing the President, in his discretion, to set apart portions of these lands bearing timber, " whether of commercial value or not," as national reservations. By another statute he was further empowered to revise his orders concerning these reserves, to alter, reduce, or extend their limits, or to restore them to the public domain altogether, particularly when he should be of the opinion that the lands in question were no longer useful as reserves. Moreover, in permitting specific portions of the national domain to be opened up for occupation and purchase, Congress imposed upon the President the responsibility of conducting the sale of such lands, of adopting all measures necessary to effect that end, and, in addition, of issuing orders preventing settlers on these lands from subverting the efforts of the Government to conserve its natural resources.[68]

Sustained by the knowledge that the enjoyment of rights acquired by settlement were conditioned upon obedience to the police regulations of executive officers, Roosevelt manifested little hesitancy in ordering his subordinates to prosecute vigorously all infractors. Indeed, by a frequent resort to the courts it was hoped [69] that the legality of the Executive's measures of enforcement would be definitely established and local opposition to the national conservation policies

[68] 26 Stat. L. 1103; 34 Stat. L. 233.
[69] Autobiography, p. 395.

would be discouraged. Illustrative of the success which accompanied this procedure is the favorable verdict obtained in the case of United States v. Grimaud.[70] Upon being prosecuted for grazing cattle on a forest reserve without a license in defiance of an executive ordinance requiring the same, the defendants in this case demurred to the charges, and petitioned the court to declare the authorizing statute unconstitutional on the ground that it delegated a rule-making power to the Secretary of Agriculture and attached a penal sanction to his orders. The Supreme Court finally held that the power conferred upon the Secretary was not to legislate but to issue local police regulations applicable to the peculiar conditions affecting this reserve, and that Congress, and not this officer, had declared a violation of these administrative orders to be a crime.

In two other instances, although his conduct ultimately received a judicial sanction,[71] Roosevelt aroused the ire of his political opponents by employing the powers granted to him by these statutes to secure a result apparently not intended by these acts, and certainly not approved by Congress. Having failed to convince Congress of the urgency of preventing the acquisition by "monopolies" of public coal lands at ridiculously low prices, he undertook to remedy this situation by issuing a series of proclamations withdrawing these coal lands from public entry and setting them aside as parts of the national forest reserves. That a doubt existed as to the legality of these orders is attested by the refusal of his successor, Taft, to proceed further without an express sanction of Congress.[72] Again, when an attempt was made to obstruct his efforts at conservation by attaching to an appropriation bill a "rider" exempting from withdrawal as reserves a large portion of public lands in the Northwest, Roosevelt, without assuming the responsibility of vetoing a financial

---

[70] 220 U. S. 506. See also, Light v. United States, 220 U. S. 523.

[71] Diamond Coal Co. v. United States, 233 U. S. 236; United States v. Morrison, 240 U. S. 192; United States v. Midwest Oil Co., 236 U. S. 459.

[72] Autobiography, pp. 393, 395-396, 444; Taft, p. 136.

measure, defeated this effort by setting aside all the timber lands in question before the bill was presented to him for signature.[73]

Having already discussed the differences in the procedure observed by the War-Presidents, Lincoln and Wilson, to secure additional authority deemed by them necessary to the prosecution of their respective conflicts, and having presented an estimate of the extent of their control over the rights and properties of the noncombatant American population, the writer considers it sufficient that he concern himself at this point with the legal significance of the congressional delegations of power to these two Executives.

As distinguished from the exceptional grants of discretionary authority conferred upon Wilson in the late War, the ordinance-making powers exercisable by Lincoln were generally limited to the issuance of orders directing subordinate officers in the performance of statutory duties, or to ascertaining the existence of the conditions to which a specific enactment was intended to apply, and proclaiming the operation of that measure upon the same. The Congress of that period having been disposed to provide in detail for the settlement of its war problems, statutes emanating from that body required the addition of little or no amplification; hence, few delegations permitting any important " presidential legislation " were recorded. In certain instances, however, such as in the statute authorizing Lincoln to take over the telegraph and railroad lines,[74] Congress displayed a liberality akin to that manifested so consistently during the late War, and transferred to the President the task of selecting not only the circumstances and time at which this specific measure was to go into effect, but also the means by which it was to be insti-

---

[73] Autobiography, p. 440.
[74] 12 Stat. L. 334, 625. It may be of interest to note that when Wilson assumed control of the railroads in 1917, he cited as his authority for this act, a statute (39 Stat. L. 645) of 1916, which, though capable of being interpreted as permitting the control of this industry, was scarcely intended to produce this result. W. F. Willoughby, p. 173; Hart, p. 64. For a similar act by Lincoln, see above, p. 100.

tuted and enforced. Thus, by the terms of that statute Lincoln was empowered to take over " any or all " of the railroad and telegraph lines, at such times as in his estimation the public safety required, to devise the means whereby the equipment of these organizations might be utilized, operated, and kept in repairs, and to issue regulations for the mobilization and inclusion of their personnel as part of the military forces of the Union.

Whereas the delegation just cited might be considered as an exception, authorizations even more extensive in scope were quite customary during the World War. In obedience to Wilson's insistent demand, that all powers necessary to produce a speedy termination of the War be conferred upon the President and that the grants of such authority be unaccompanied by any serious restrictions as to the manner of its exercise, Congress responded by inserting only a minimum of detail in its emergency measures. Authorizing statutes generally specified only the result to be achieved, or the subject to be regulated, and left almost entirely to the Executive the determination of the manner in which this control was to be asserted as well as the establishment of the administrative machinery by which such control was to be maintained. It ought to be evident, therefore, that a greater part of the war-time reallocations of personnel, reorganization of functions, and creation of new administrative units or boards, were the product of executive invention; and that the determination [75] of the rigor and appropriateness of the restrictions imposed upon the people rested almost wholly in his hands.

That such unprecedented delegations would be attacked as conferring legislative powers upon the Executive was perhaps inevitable; but the courts with surprising dispatch declared the emergency legislation to be free from that objection. On

---

[75] Unless a claimant could prove that an executive order was issued in excess of the authority conferred upon the President by any statutory grant, he could not succeed. Charges that a particular regulation imposed by Wilson was not warranted by the circumstances, or that no emergency existed to justify it were not recognized by the courts, for the reason that they pertained to matters of discretion and were therefore political questions. Dakota Central Telephone v. S. Dakota, 250 U. S. 163.

the basis of the arguments employed by the courts to sustain the validity of congressional action which had been questioned in previous cases, Congress, during the late War, was judged to have provided in detail as far as it could under the circumstances, and to have satisfactorily restricted the content of its authorizing statutes to specific and narrowed subjects, indicating amply the policy to be observed in the regulation of such matters, and leaving to the President the apparently legitimate task of "concretizing these legislative abstractions." [76]

Finally, in addition to his ability to supervise and direct the personnel who administer the law, and his participation in the completion of legislative policies through delegated ordinance-making, the President is empowered to employ the armed forces of the United States when, in his opinion, the use of that expedient is necessary to secure obedience to federal authority. Legislating in pursuance of its constitutional power, to "provide for calling forth the militia to execute the laws of the Union," [77] Congress has, in successive statutes,[78] transferred to the President the duty of dispatching the army to the scene of insurrection against the Federal Government, and has thus bestowed upon him the means whereby he is enabled to fulfil his obligation to see to the faithful execution of the laws. The President's responsibilities have also been increased by the fact that Congress, in its endeavor to fulfil the guaranty stipulated in Article IV, has designated him as the officer to receive and comply with the requests of States for federal aid in domestic disturbances.

Thus, on the occasion of an organized disobedience of federal law, the President, though he be under a duty and fully competent to assume the initiative, may also have to acknowledge that, since the persons engaged therein are likely to be acting in defiance of all law, the State in which such persons reside will presumably manifest an equal interest in

---

[76] Hart, ch. vi.
[77] Art. 1, Sec. 8, Cl. 15.
[78] For the existing law on the subject, see Rev. Stat., secs. 5298-5299.

the restoration of order. Furthermore, the latter, taking a pride in its reputation as a loyal member of the Union, will probably resent an unrequested dispatch of troops into its confines as a reflection upon the competency of its government. Whether, then, he is to avoid the incurrence of such ill-will, and undertake to protect the interests of the National Government only when requested by the State to assist in its own police measures, or whether he should permit himself to be guided by no consideration other than his paramount obligation to see to the due execution of the federal laws, has accordingly been the problem to plague the President in such cases.

No doubt, with the increased prominence of the National Government, the possible incurrence of a State's displeasure has ceased to be a potent deterrent to the President's employment of the army to dispel resistance to federal authority; but the importance of that consideration during the early existence of the Federation cannot be underestimated. To understand its significance at that date is to know the reasons for Washington's hesitancy for three years before forcibly suppressing the Whiskey Rebellion of 1794. Upon the receipt of the information that the farmers of western Pennsylvania had combined to oppose the enforcement of the Revenue Act of 1791,[79] Washington readily foresaw that, unless the new Government succeeded in reducing them to an acceptance of the terms of that law, it would forfeit public confidence and seriously impair its future stability. Yet he refrained from an immediate exercise of the force capable of removing that danger for fear that a military expedition into Pennsylvania would be viewed as a confirmation of the prophesies that the Central Government would become a source of oppression and that the newly created standing army was to be turned against the people. Nevertheless, in endeavoring to overcome this disaffection by less vigorous methods,[80] Washington never lost

---

[79] 1 Stat. L. 199.

[80] These consisted of recommendations to Congress to make a more favorable modification of the terms of this Act, directions to the marshals to institute more vigorous prosecutions of the offenders,

sight of the fact that he had only one alternative, and that was his duty to see that the laws were faithfully executed. More clearly indicative of his estimate of the problem created by this disturbance are the following statements written by Washington prior to his call for the militia in 1794:

> If, after these regulations are in operation, opposition to the due exercise of the collection is still experienced, and peaceable procedure is no longer effectual, the public interest and my duty will make it necessary to enforce the laws respecting this matter; and, however disagreeable this would be to me, it must nevertheless take place.
>
> But if, notwithstanding, opposition is still given to the due execution of the law, I have no hesitation in declaring, if the evidence of it is clear and unequivocal, that I shall, however reluctantly I exercise them, exert all the legal powers with which the executive is invested to check so daring and unwarrantable a spirit. It is my duty to see the laws executed. To permit them to be trampled upon with impunity would be repugnant to it; nor can the government longer remain a passive spectator of the contempt, with which they are treated. Forbearance, under a hope that the inhabitants of that survey would recover from the delirium and folly into which they are plunged, seems to have had no other effect than to increase the disorder.[81]
>
> I have no doubt that the proclamation will undergo many strictures; and, as the effect proposed may not be answered by it, it will be necessary to look forward in time to ulterior arrangements. And here not only the constitution and the laws must strictly govern, but the employing of the regular troops be avoided, if it is possible to effect order without their aid; otherwise there would be a cry at once, 'The cat is let out; we now see for what purpose an army was raised.' Yet, if no other means will effectually answer, and the constitution and the laws will authorize these, they must be used as a dernier resort.[82]

---

and issuance of proclamations exhorting these farmers to desist from their violent conduct upon pain of future punishment. Unfortunately, lack of sufficient evidence rendered convictions difficult and few.

[81] Sparks, X, 259, 292.

[82] Ibid., p. 297. The proclamation referred to in the last citation was the one issued on September 15, 1792, requesting offenders to cease their opposition and informing them of his instructions to the marshals to increase the vigor of their prosecutions. In this instance, as well as in the case of other measures adopted to quell this disorder, Washington refused to act until he had obtained the advice of his Cabinet. Although a unanimous consent to its issuance was obtained, Jefferson gave only a formal approval to that measure. To a friend he wrote, " A proclamation to be issued, and another instance of my being forced to approve what I condemned uniformly from its first conception." Writings (Ford Ed.), VI, 261.

Whether solely on the strength of his obligation to execute the laws Washington considered himself empowered to employ the existing military resources cannot be answered, but the quotation just cited would seem to warrant the inference that he preferred to fortify his conduct by a congressional sanction. Whatever doubts he may have had on this issue were dispelled, without any effort on his part, however, by the passage of the Act of May 2, 1792; [83] and thereafter his primary concern was the determination of the advisability of resorting to the authority conferred by that statute. Two years of observation having convinced him that conciliatory measures had merely tempted these farmers to more violent deeds of opposition, Washington, late in 1794, finally decided to assemble the militia. Nevertheless, to assure himself that this measure was both feasible as well as expedient, he sought a final consultation with his Cabinet. Though Jefferson, in common with Governor Mifflin of Pennsylvania, was apprehensive as to this display of force,[84] the others approved, and a

---

[83] 1 Stat. L. 264. The terms of this Act provided that when an associate justice or district judge shall certify to the President that the execution of the laws is being opposed by " combinations too powerful to be suppressed " by ordinary means, " it shall be lawful " for him to call forth the militia of the State in which such disorders exist. If that State refused, or was unable to muster a force sufficient to suppress the disturbance, he was further authorized, if Congress was not in session, to call forth the militia of as many States as he might deem necessary. However, he might continue the use of the militia for such purposes only " until the expiration of thirty days after the commencement of the ensuing session." In this instance, Mr. Justice James Wilson certified to the President, after Governor Mifflin had refused his requests for aid, that the marshals were unable to combat the existing situation. " Federal Aid in Domestic Disturbances," 57th Cong., 2d sess., S. Doc. No. 209, pp. 33-34.

[84] Jefferson's position was described as follows by John Marshall: " The Secretary of State feared that the militia of the neighboring States would refuse to march; and that, should he be mistaken in this, their compliance with the orders of the executive might be not less fatal than their disobedience. The introduction of a foreign militia into Pennsylvania might greatly increase the discontents prevailing in the state. His apprehensions of a failure in the attempt to restore tranquillity by coercive means were extreme and the tremendous consequences of a failure were strongly depicted. From the highly inflamed state of parties he anticipated a civil war which would pervade the whole union and drench every part of it with the blood of American citizens." Life of Washington, V, 581-582.

call was sent out to Pennsylvania and neighboring States to assemble their respective militia detachments at a given point. Had the insurrectionists heeded the warning contained in the proclamation of August 7, 1794, and disbanded before September first, the necessity of ordering the departure of this military expedition might have been avoided; but, when they ignored this last proposal for an amicable settlement of their contentions, Washington had no option other than to instruct Governor Lee of Virginia, who had been appointed to command the militia, to march to the scene of the disturbance.[85] Fortunately, a mere threat of force proved sufficient; and, before the arrival of the militia at its destination, the insurrection had completely subsided. The supremacy of the National Government having been successfully demonstrated, Washington thereupon undertook to avert any continued resentment by offering a pardon to the offenders.

Directly in contrast with this precedent is the action taken by Cleveland, a century later, in connection with the Chicago Railway Strike. Irrespective of the considerations which induced Washington to hesitate to resort to force to execute the laws, it should be noted that when he did finally order troops into western Pennsylvania, the measure was undertaken in close cooperation with that State. Not only was the Governor of Pennsylvania granted an opportunity to confer with the President, but he was requested to contribute a portion of the militia employed in restoring order. None of these circumstances were reproduced in 1893. On being informed that the carriage of the United States' mails and interstate commerce was being obstructed, Cleveland, unlike Washington, concerned himself solely with the question as to whether or not the ordinary remedies possessed by the Department of Justice would suffice to solve this difficulty, and, upon receipt of reports to the contrary, he did not hesitate to order a detachment of the regular army to Chicago.

[85] This preliminary proclamation of warning was required by the Act of 1792. A fourth, issued on September 25, 1794, announced the departure of the troops. See Messages and Papers of the Presidents. I. 116, 149, 150, 153.

The fact that the State of Illinois might have been competent to deal with all infractions of law and order was considered by him to have no connection with his duty faithfully to execute the laws; and he consequently refused to allow his decisions to be altered by the protests of Governor Altgeld against this unrequested federal intervention.

The disturbances which caused this intervention of the Federal Government had their inception in the strike of the employees of the Pullman Palace Car Company of Chicago. A large number of these workers being members of the American Railway Union, this organization sought to promote the cause of these strikers by ordering fellow-members not to haul trains to which a Pullman coach was attached. Because the railroads that had contracted to carry the United States mails could not profitably haul federal mail cars other than as units of their passenger trains, this scheme was destined to fail; for, in halting the transit of passenger coaches, the strikers unavoidably obstructed the postal service, an instrument of the National Government.

To prevent interference with the governmental function of carrying the mails, to protect federal property, and to secure obedience to the national laws pertaining to interstate commerce, the Department of Justice advised marshals throughout the Southwest to station armed deputies on mail trains and at points where federal property was situated, and to procure warrants for the detention of strikers engaged in obstructionary tactics. Believing, moreover, that tranquillity could be restored more rapidly by attacking the problem at its source in Chicago, the Attorney-General suggested that the local attorneys petition the district court for an injunction [86] restraining strikers from further interfering with the activities of the Government. However, when the court, after having issued an injunction, was forced to acknowledge its inability to enforce its decree, Cleveland elected to dispatch troops to that city.[87]

In two successive letters to Cleveland, Governor Altgeld,

[86] In Re Debs, 158 U. S. 564.
[87] Presidential Problems, pp. 90-91, 100-101.

after having stated that Illinois was perfectly able to protect the interests of all concerned, demanded that the troops be withdrawn, and protested that this unrequested entry was in violation of the principles of local self-government and State Rights. To the first message Cleveland gave the following reply:

> Federal troops were sent to Chicago in strict accordance with the Constitution and the laws of the United States, upon the demand of the Post-Office Department that obstruction of the mails should be removed, and upon the representation of the judicial officers of the United States that process of the Federal Courts could not be executed through the ordinary means, and upon abundant proof that conspiracies existed against commerce between the states. To meet these conditions, which are clearly within the province of Federal authority, the presence of Federal troops in the city of Chicago was deemed not only proper but necessary; and there has been no intention of thereby interfering with the plain duty of the local authorities to preserve the peace of the city.[88]

---

[88] Ibid., pp. 111-113. Preferring to terminate the dispute, Cleveland answered the second message with a curt suggestion to the effect that less talk and more action would be more advantageous to both State and Federal Governments.

Because the action contemplated by Roosevelt to settle the Anthracite Coal Strike of 1902 affords an additional illustration of his unusual interpretation of executive power, the writer has chosen to include herein a discussion of that incident. Since this labor dispute, which was confined to the coal fields of Pennsylvania, was attended by no disorder which could not be suppressed by the State, nor by any attempt to subvert the execution of a federal law, the President was therefore unable to intervene except as an influential private citizen desirous of preventing the industrial stagnation and poverty likely to result from a prolongation of this strike. Although his efforts to get the labor leaders and the coal operators to arbitrate their differences were finally successful, a deadlock between these two groups was for a long time imminent; and in anticipation of a failure, Roosevelt declared that he had adopted the following plan:

"There was no duty whatever laid upon me by the Constitution in this matter, and I had in theory no power to act directly unless the Governor of Pennsylvania or the Legislature, if it were in session, should notify me that Pennsylvania could not keep order, and request me as commander-in-chief of the army of the United States to intervene and keep order. As long as I could avoid interfering, I did so. . . .

"The method of action upon which I had determined in the last resort was to get the Governor of Pennsylvania to ask me to keep order. Then I could put in the army under the command of some first-rate general. I would instruct the general to keep absolute order, taking any steps whatever that were necessary to prevent interference by the strikers or their sympathizers with men who wanted to work. I would also instruct him to dispossess the operators and run the mines as a receiver until such time as the Com-

In conclusion, it may be profitable to enumerate several recent developments which are very likely destined to add to the importance of the President's position as administrator-in-chief. Since a war-time emergency no longer exists, a continued enactment of such unusually broad delegations of authority as were conferred upon the President in the last War is not to be expected; but it is believed that the recollection of the efficient results obtained by the observance of that method in the prosecution of that conflict will induce Congress to leave more to executive discretion in providing for future governmental problems. An indication of that tendency is the Budget and Accounting Act of 1921;[89] by the

---

mission [arbitration board] might make its report, and until I, as President, might issue further orders in view of this report." Autobiography, pp. 505-506, 514.

Concerning the illegality of such procedure, Taft has made the following comment: "Now it is perfectly evident that Mr. Roosevelt thinks he was charged with the duty, not only to suppress disorder in Pennsylvania, but to furnish coal to avoid the coal famine in New York and New England, and he therefore proposed to use the army of the United States to mine the coal which would prevent or relieve the famine. It was his avowed intention to take the coal mines out of the hands of their lawful owners and to mine the coal which belonged to them and sell it in the eastern market, against their objection, without any court proceeding of any kind and without any legal obligation on their part to work the mines at all. It was an advocacy of the higher law and his obligation to execute it which is a little startling in a constitutional republic. It is perfectly evident from his statement that it was not the maintenance of law and order in Pennsylvania and the suppression of insurrection, the only ground upon which he could intervene at all, that actuated him in what he proposed to do. He used the expression that he would 'get' the Governor of Pennsylvania to call troops from him, and then having secured a formal authority for the use of the army to suppress disorder, he proposed to use it for the seizure of private property and its appropriation for the benefit of the people of other states. The benevolence of his purpose no one can deny, but no one who looks at it from the standpoint of a government of law could regard it as anything but lawless. . . .

"I am aware that there are many who believe in government ownership of the sources of public comfort in the interest of the community at large; but it is certainly only the extreme of that school that favor the use of the army, under the President to seize the needed mines without constitutional amendment or legislative and judicial action and without compensation." Our Chief Magistrate and his Powers, pp. 146-147.

[89] 42 Stat. L. 20. This Act provided for the office of Director of the Budget and stipulated that it shall be manned by an expert to be selected by the President alone and to be accountable solely to

terms of which the President has been made " business man-
ager of the government." Finally, the significance of the
Myers Case cannot be overstated; for that decision will doubtless act as a bulwark against any serious reduction in the
President's powers of control and direction of the federal
personnel.

---

him. Subject to the President's approval, this officer can dictate to
all departmental leaders what shall be the amount of the appropriations requested by them for the ensuing year, and has full power to
revise their estimates. It is through this agent that the President
prepares his Budget.

CHAPTER V

LEGISLATIVE LEADERSHIP

In the previous chapters, the writer has undertaken to illustrate, by precedent and personal utterances, the interpretation which selected Presidents have given to their powers derived, either directly or by their own inference, from the written Constitution. In the present chapter he will endeavor to describe the manner in which they have exercised a power acquired as a result of a movement that has developed outside of the Constitution; a power, moreover, which bids fair, at least in popular estimation, to eclipse in importance the executive authority expressly granted by that written document.

While the assumption by the President of legislative leadership may be said to have had its inception during the first Administration, the potency of his influence in this sphere of governmental operations was not conclusively demonstrated until the beginning of the present century. Today, however, the control exerted by the Executive to secure the enactment of remedial legislation has attained such proportions that some students of our federal system are advocating either a return to the form of government intended by the Convention of 1787, or an amendment to the Constitution whereby a legal recognition will be accorded to this important presidential activity. To ignore the present situation, they contend, is to render lip service to the Constitution which created a government operating under the theories of a separation of powers and checks and balances, while we secretly condone a development which has completely destroyed that arrangement by affording the President the legislative initiative of a parliamentary executive without the latter's political responsibility.[1]

The cause of this existing incongruity between theory and

---

[1] Henry C. Black, The Relation of the Executive Power to Legislation, ch. iii; James W. Garner, " Executive Participation in Legislation as a Means of Increasing Legislative Efficiency," in American Political Science Association Proceedings, X, 176-190.

fact is to be sought in an examination of the form of government established in 1787. Thus, in attempting to set up the legislative and executive departments as two separate, independent units of the federal system, with each exercising its power without fear of encroachment by the other, the members of the Convention took no cognizance of the fact that the officer charged with the enforcement of the laws would, by reason of his immediate knowledge of the difficulties attending the performance of this duty, also become interested in the passage of the laws.[2] Nevertheless, it is doubtful whether a subsequent recognition of this consequence would have sufficed to effect a correlation of the Congress and President in the matter of legislation. Rather was this tendency to be expedited by the evolution of political parties, a system which, though recognized now as essential to the normal operation of representative government, was deemed by the founding fathers to be undesirable and unnecessary. Consequently, the cooperation of these two branches has been brought about through the medium of this extra-legal association, the party, the object of which is to prepare a program of legislation for the electorate and to assist its members in obtaining office in order that that program may be brought to fruition. By utilizing his prestige as the country's only national representative, the President in turn has attained the leadership of his party, directed even the formation of its policies, and when in office, has finally brought pressure to bear upon his associates in Congress to procure the adoption of these policies.

Since the framers of the Constitution did not contemplate the formation of political parties, and hence made no provision for their operation within the new Federation, the growth of the political powers of the Executive would not appear to be susceptible of legal restraint; notwithstanding the fact that their exercise has produced a serious alteration in the form of government provided at Philadelphia. By the affirmative words of the document issuing from that Assembly, the Executive was to have a connection with the process of legislation

[2] Woodrow Wilson, Constitutional Government in the United States, p. 40.

to the extent of his duty to assist Congress by informing it
on the state of the Union and suggesting to it the adoption of
such measures as were necessitated by existing conditions.[3]
Secondly, in accordance with the prevailing theory of checks
and balances, he was also accorded a power of veto; but this
privilege, as interpreted by Wilson, was intended to enable
him to defeat any attempts to encroach upon his own jurisdiction or to prevent the passage of "bad laws" rather than
to obtain the enactment of wise measures.[4] Especial effort
was therefore exerted to insure to Congress an untrammeled
discretion and a freedom from external influence in the exercise of its power to legislate for the welfare of the new Nation.

Having been present at this constituent assembly, Washington could scarcely have been misinformed on the position
which his colleagues had expected the President to adopt with
reference to legislation, and in his official conduct he gave
every evidence of an intention to comply with their wishes.
Like many of his successors who hesitated openly to assume a
leadership in the enactment of a legislative policy, he restricted the content of his messages to Congress to a mere
enumeration of the objects meriting its attention. But, since
a disagreement existed, not upon the wisdom of the objects
suggested for its consideration, but upon the choice of the
means whereby these objects could be attained, Congress
found these executive messages advantageous only as a calen-
dar or reminder of the work confronting it during the ensuing session. For the President at that early date to have
phrased his recommendations more specifically, or in the form
of a bill, would have been regarded as an attempt to force the
hand of Congress on a matter constitutionally allotted to it.
Therefore, although he may have been vexed at the failure of
the legislative branch to act immediately upon his suggestions,
Washington uniformly deferred to it in the following manner:
"It rests with the wisdom of Congress to correct . . . this
plan of procedure."[5]

---

[3] Art. 2, Sec. 3.
[4] Art. 1, Sec. 7; Wilson, pp. 59-60.
[5] Messages and Papers of the Presidents, I, 131.

Further indications of his attitude on this subject are to be found in the contents of the following passages from his letters:

> I have brought the subject in my speech at the opening of the present session of Congress before the national legislature. It rests with them to decide what means ought afterwards to be adopted for promoting the success of the great objects, which I have recommended to their attention, . . . [And again] I question much whether the time is yet arrived, the necessity so generally apparent, or the temper of Congress so well framed for the things, as to render such a proposition acceptable. And I doubt still more, whether at any time its coming from the executive would be the most auspicious mode of bringing it forward; as it might be construed into an implication of want of discernment in that body to foresee the utility of, or of abilities to execute or direct a measure of so much importance.[6]

Yet, notwithstanding his own disinclination to initiate any procedure, open or secret, whereby he might be enabled to influence legislation by Congress, Washington permitted the origination of almost every known method now employed to attain that end. Though opposed to the introduction of political parties, and personally above a resort to partisan tactics, he discovered through later experience that only through the assistance of a united party group could a legislative program be effected. In resolving therefore to favor the policies of the Federalist party, he obtained assurance that his recommendations would be speedily adopted by Congress; while the leader of this party profited to an even greater extent by securing the sanction of the first Chief Magistrate for his own policies.

First, as the favored adviser of Washington in all matters pertaining to finance, Hamilton received the opportunity to have his measures inserted in the President's messages and accordingly presented to Congress in the form of an executive recommendation.[7] During the first Administration, this privilege had an exceptional value for the reason that the public, as a reward for his military services, was disposed to exalt the virtues of their first President, and to give a reverent

---

[6] Sparks, X, 81, 216.

[7] In many of the letters of his Cabinet members, written in reply to Washington's requests for advice, are to be found the sources of several of his congressional messages. For example, see Jefferson's Writings (Ford Ed.), V, 207, 406, 415.

approval to his every utterance. Consequently, by shielding his political manoeuvres behind the cloak of the President's reputation, Hamilton not only carried out his program with little interference, but practically deprived his opponents of a means of protest; for the latter feared to risk popular condemnation by an attack which, though directed against the Secretary of the Treasury, would have unavoidably included the President.[8] Thus, proceeding boldly in pursuit of his policies, Hamilton submitted reports to Congress, expounding in detail both the reasons why and the manner in which the financial recommendations contained in the President's messages should be adopted, saw to it that party associates in accord with his opinions were appointed to committees deliberating upon his measures, and finally, when a doubt arose as to the fate of his program, rounded up his political adherents in order to insure a majority vote in favor of his bills. In fact, the conduct of the Federalists in Congress was invariably predetermined by the decisions reached in their secret party meetings at which Hamilton presided.[9]

Had Jefferson remained faithful to the principles of Republicanism, his election in 1800 should have resulted in the renunciation of this Hamiltonian form of executive direction and in the restoration of Congress to the position of independence originally intended for it. During Washington's Admini-

---

[8] In a letter to his colleague, Monroe, Jefferson recognized the invulnerability of Washington's position. Writings (Ford Ed.), VII, 80.

[9] While it was to be expected that the Executive would recommend the adoption of a greater number of measures than the passage of which his Cabinet officers could personally influence, one may correctly state that almost every major proposal advocated by Hamilton and Knox was finally enacted by Congress. Hamilton is to be credited with the passage of legislation providing for the assumption of state debts, the establishment of a National Bank, and the collection of adequate revenues; and Knox, with those enactments creating a necessary means of national defense. Only in its failure to obtain provisions for the adequate organization of the militia and navy did the Administration sustain a defeat. See, in general, Howard White, " Executive Influence in Determining Military Policy in the United States," in Illinois University Studies, XII, 97-149. For accounts of Hamilton's political activity, see, in general, William Maclay, Sketches of Debate in the First Senate of the United States; George Gibbs, Administrations of Washington and Adams, I; Ralph V. Harlow, Legislative Methods in the Period before 1825, pp. 135-147.

stration, when his party constituted a hopeless minority in the legislative branch, and was unable to profit by the use of Hamilton's policies, much less to appreciate their efficacy, Jefferson had vehemently decried the conduct of his former cabinet associate as constituting none other than a nullification of the separation of powers principle, and conducive to the ultimate corruption of the federal system.[10] Consistency would therefore seem to have obligated him, upon his assumption of the Presidency, to demonstrate the desirability of a strict adherence to the spirit of the Constitution. However, he astounded his followers not only by reverting to the methods of Hamilton, but by enhancing their efficacy with certain innovations of his own. What had produced this reversal of position was the belated realization on the part of Jefferson that the doctrine of individualism, preached by him for more than a decade, had taken the form of a boomerang and had sown a spirit of internecine strife within his party, making it incapable of spontaneous, concordant action.[11] Having waited too long for the opportunity when his party could gain the ascendancy in the government and effect his cherished reforms, he proved himself to be too practical a man to forsake the achievement of his ambitions for the mere retention of an unworkable ideal.

Indeed, in order to secure the adoption of his program, Jefferson found it necessary to rely more extensively upon his position as a party leader than did the favored counsellor of Washington. Whereas Washington was able to exert an influence over the members of Congress, even in his official relations with that branch, Jefferson denied himself that advantage; for, having neither the renown of his predecessor nor an inclination for public speaking, he preferred to tender Congress his messages in writing,[12] and thus deprived his

---

[10] Writings (Ford Ed.), VII, 108.
[11] Ibid., VII, 187.
[12] Messages and Papers of the Presidents, I, 313. Jefferson, however, did not reveal this deficiency as the reason for his discontinuance of Washington's practice. Instead, he argued that the practice smacked of Royal England and intimated that its continued observance would inevitably result in the undesirable domination of the Legislature by a vigorous Executive.

recommendations of whatever weight might have accrued from his personal appearance in the legislative halls. Moreover, with existing opinion averse to any change in the composition of executive messages which would permit the President to submit his recommendations in the forms of bills,[13] Jefferson had no other alternative than to resort to partisan tactics in order to give effect to his program.

Thus, there is little distinction to be made between the methods employed by the Federalists and by the Republicans, except that, in the first Administration, the President was neutral and Hamilton was the active leader, whereas Jefferson himself was in command of his party and his Secretary of the Treasury, Gallatin, only second in rank as the watchdog of this Administration.[14] Measures drafted by Jefferson in Cabinet council [15] were transmitted by this subordinate to the legislative committees, the membership of which was likewise arranged in accordance with the Executive's wishes, and received his constant supervision during all stages of the procedure required for their enactment. Conversely, the floor leaders of the two Houses, the most significant innovation of Jeffersonian politics,[16] cooperated with the Executive in maintaining an effective party organization in Congress and in assuring him an immediate acceptance of his important policies. By thus improving upon the procedure of his rival, Hamilton, to the extent of acquiring the invaluable assistance of a Gallatin, requesting former colleagues to run for congressional office in order to obtain aggressive sponsors of his plans within the legislative halls,[16] and increasing the frequency of caucus meetings,[17] Jefferson was able to carry out his program with such rapidity and dispatch as to gain for himself the reputation of a party dictator.[18]

---

[13] Jefferson, therefore, enumerated his suggestions, as did Washington, and manifested a similar willingness to defer to the discretion of Congress.

[14] See Henry Adams, Life of Gallatin.

[15] Writings (Ford Ed.), VIII, 403-412.

[16] Harlow, pp. 176-177. Wilson C. Nicholas, his most loyal floorleader, was secured by personal solicitation: Writings (Ford Ed), IX, 32; VIII, 468-472.

[17] Harlow, pp. 184-191.

[18] While this appellation may be accepted as correctly descriptive

Among the Executives who have succeeded him, however, not one has attained a political leadership that has surpassed in its intensity the control which Jefferson exercised over his associates in Congress. One authority has declared that Hamilton and Jefferson " assumed the direct initiative in party management to an extent which would be intolerable, if openly asserted at the present time." [19] But, in endeavoring to ascertain the cause of the lack of a sustained increase in the political and legislative powers of the President, one must not overlook the fact that two conditions existent during the early administrations were not thereafter duplicated.

For his election to office, today, the Executive is indebted to his party, a self-sustaining organization whose existence exceeds in length of time the life of the incumbent. Consequently, though he is formally recognized, upon election, as the party leader, the President is compelled to deal with several associates who either aspire to party leadership or have in fact been previously designated as the directors of the party machine. On the other hand, Jefferson and Hamilton had the good fortune to be in office when a factional spirit began to develop, and it was largely their efforts and ingenuity which produced our first two parties, Federalist and Republican. Aware that the organization of these two groups could be attributed to their industry, each could nominate himself the leader of his respective party without fear that a single colleague could rightfully contest his claim to that position.

---

of the unusually detailed supervision which Jefferson maintained over the deliberations of his political adherents in Congress, nevertheless, it does not warrant the inference that he achieved a perfect record in having every one of his recommendations ultimately adopted. Like other Executives who have enjoyed two terms in office, he sustained, partly as a result of his own indifference, and partly as a result of circumstances not within his control, a diminution of his influence toward the close of his second Administration. Neither he nor Washington was able to divest the people of their fear of a sizable military establishment, and it was his suggestions pertaining to this item of national affairs which failed of acceptance. In a manner most creditable to him, however, Jefferson acknowledged these defeats as indicative of the inability of any leader to produce a unity of opinion on every public question. See White, pp. 168-170; Writings (Ford Ed.), X, 280.

[19] Alexander Johnson, Cyclopedia of Political Science, I, 769; quoted by Henry J. Ford, The Rise and Growth of American Politics, p. 134.

Secondly, later Executives have been unable to retain within their grasp those instrumentalities originated by Jefferson to facilitate his control of administration measures in the process of enactment. As the two Houses acquired experience in the performance of their duties, they became less inclined to await the guidance of the President, but perfected an independent organization of their own. Whereas Congress formerly relied‐extensively upon the reports of the Cabinet Secretaries for information necessary to the preparation of a measure, it now obtains technical data more readily through its own special‐ized standing committees. Moreover, the selection of the members of these committees and the incumbents of congres‐sional political offices (such as the floor leader) is determined no longer in conformity with the wishes of the Executive, but largely upon the basis of length of service in the legislative halls.[20] The result has thus been that the incoming President, in attempting to influence the adoption of his legislative policies, has to confer with congressional veterans who not only surpass him in length of their public service, but are jealous of this distinction, and hence are likely to resent any consistent direction on his part. That to these obstacles may be attributed the failure of many Executives to establish enviable records during their administrations would therefore seem probable.

Despite these difficulties, every intrepid Executive who has manifested any concern in the advancement of his party's record has sought to ally himself with the two Houses in an effort to procure the fulfilment of its pledges to the electorate. But, if we correctly interpret the following campaign utter‐ance of Lincoln, public opinion, even after sixty-five years of this extra-legal nullification of the separation of powers theory, was not yet prepared to hear the Chief Magistrate openly resolve to further this divergence between principle and prac‐tice.[21] Perhaps, then, for reasons of political expediency, Lincoln declared:

---

[20] Harlow, pp. 88-89.

[21] Even Jefferson complained of a situation which, on the one hand, compelled an enterprising President to indulge in secret agreements

By the Constitution, the Executive may recommend measures which he may think proper, and he may veto those he thinks improper, and it is supposed that he may add to these certain indirect influences to affect the action of Congress. My political education strongly inclines me against a very free use of any of these means by the executive to control the legislation of the country. As a rule, I think it better that Congress should originate as well as perfect its measures without external bias.[22]

Certainly there is no incident in Lincoln's subsequent conduct to indicate that he adhered rigidly to the opinion expressed in this statement. And although there was evidence of an estrangement between the political branches of the Government during the first year of the War, this phenomenon was occasioned, not by any adherence to constitutional theory, but rather by the belief entertained by Lincoln that the national war powers were vested wholly in the Executive. With this interpretation as his justification, he was disposed to solve the issues of the War, whenever possible, by executive order and proclamation rather than by securing authorization from Congress. The Legislature, in turn, despite its resentment against the usurpation of its powers, was too mindful of the disastrous consequences of a deadlock at this critical period to refuse a ratification of Lincoln's conduct.[23]

When compelled to request the assistance of Congress for continuing the prosecution of the War, Lincoln reverted to the methods employed by his predecessors to influence the passage of legislation. Not being well informed, however, on such problems as military mobilization or the funding of the war debt,[24] he was disposed to permit his prominent Secretaries,

---

with his legislative colleagues, and on the other, condemned him for this very conduct. " Our situation is difficult," he wrote, " and whatever we do is liable to the criticism of those who wish to represent it awry. If we recommend measures in public message, it may be said that members are not sent here to obey the mandates of the President or to register the edicts of a sovereign. If we express opinions in conversation, we have then . . . our back-door counsellors. If we say nothing, we have no opinions, no plans, no Cabinet." Writings (Ford Ed.), VIII, 433.

[22] John G. Nicolay and John Hay, Complete Works of Abraham Lincoln, I, 697.

[23] White, p. 213. Congressional Globe, 37th Cong., 1st. sess., pp. 50, 94-97.

[24] James F. Rhodes, History of the United States from the Compromise of 1850, IV, 207-211.

Stanton and Chase, to originate and influence the adoption of measures designed to provide for these difficulties.[25] While he did not suffer these politically ambitious subordinates to foist their programs upon him without an examination of their merits, nevertheless he clearly appreciated their capabilities and, above all, the strength of their following in Congress.[26] But, having once convinced himself as to the desirability of their proposals, he supported his Cabinet officers thoroughly in their efforts to influence their adoption,[27] both by allotting ample publicity to their recommendations in his message and by defending them in conference with congressional leaders.[28]

Should one desire a more convincing proof of Lincoln's departure from the principle asserted in the above-mentioned campaign address, he need only examine his conduct on the subject of Emancipation. Having devoted much of his time to a consideration of this primary issue of the War, he was especially desirous that his plan for the liberation of the negro should not fail of adoption. In his anxiety to avoid that contingency, he resorted to the unconventional procedure of submitting to Congress in a public message his own bill for the compensated emancipation of slaves, and accompanied it with the request that his measure be enacted *without alteration.* Nevertheless, when he took this action, he seems to have been fully aware of the possibility of its provoking a storm of protest in Congress; for, in a subsequent message, he sought to avert any untoward result with the following explanation:

I do not forget the gravity which would characterize a paper addressed to the Congress by the Chief Magistrate, nor do I forget that some of you are my seniors, nor that many of you have more experience than I in the conduct of public affairs. Yet I trust that in view of the great responsibility resting upon me you will perceive no want of respect to yourselves in any undue earnestness I may seem to display.[29]

---

[25] John G. Nicolay and John Hay, Abraham Lincoln, A History, IX, 96, 102.

[26] Diary of Gideon Welles, I, 68-69.

[27] Nicolay and Hay, VI, 232-233; IX, 96, 102.

[28] Ibid., VI, 247.

[29] Messages and Papers of the Presidents, VII, 3342-3343. Among the considerations making for a subservient Congress during his

Since the close of the nineteenth century, the American electorate has witnessed the inauguration of two Executives who have disagreed with their predecessors as to the inadvisability of openly disclosing an intention to assume a legislative leadership. In giving indication, as Governor of New York, that he would seek an ascendancy in this matter, Roosevelt confessed that he would be acting contrary to theory, but he argued that, if an advantage, otherwise unobtainable, would accrue from the President's adoption of this position, then a non-observance of that theory ought no longer to be decried as immoral.

> In theory the Executive has nothing to do with legislation. In practice, as things now are, the Executive is or ought to be peculiarly representative of the people as a whole. As often as not the action of the Executive offers the only means by which the people can get the legislation they demand and ought to have.[30]

Wilson, however, was not willing to concede that, by a more intensive participation in legislation, the President would be adopting a procedure not contemplated by the Constitution. He declared: [For the Executive to take this action] "is not inconsistent with the actual provisions of the Constitution; it is only inconsistent with a very mechanical theory of its meaning and intention. The Constitution has no theories. It is as practical a document as the Magna Carta." [31]

Administration, of which, perhaps, Lincoln's personal magnetism was the least potent, were the loyalty of the Congressmen to the cause of the Union, and their inability to combat effectively what may be described as Lincoln's "strong arm" tactics; that is, his unauthorized activities, his threat of veto, and his exercise of that weapon. Political support obtained by such coercive methods, especially from a party formed by a coalition of discordant factions, obviously could not be enduring; but before the Republican groups in Congress became recalcitrant, the Executive did put through a series of non-military enactments providing for a department of Agriculture, the construction of a Pacific railroad, and a national banking and tax system. However, on the choice of a plan whereby slaves were to be freed, and the South rehabilitated, Congress revolted against presidential domination, and although Lincoln was able, through the exercise of the veto, and his authority as Commander-in-Chief, to delay the rejection of his reconstruction policy, the defeat of that policy was accomplished shortly after his death.

[30] Autobiography, p. 306.
[31] Constitutional Government in the United States, p. 60.

That these Executives wielded an influence in keeping with their ambitions is attested to by the imposing record of constructive legislation enacted during their respective Administrations. Measured by the volume of laws suggested and obtained and by the proficiency with which the latter alleviated the social and political ills of the times, the legislative leadership of Wilson, followed closely by that of Roosevelt, is unsurpassed; but, in according him a primacy in this field of Presidential activity, one ought not to underestimate the significance of Jefferson's achievement. If allowance is made for the fact that, in 1800, the Federal Government was not subjected to any centralizing influence, that, consequently, it legislated upon a smaller number of problems immediately affected with a public interest, and finally, that its legislative machinery was not capable of churning out laws with the rapidity characteristic of the present day, the disparity between the accomplishment of these two Executives is readily explainable; and, when compared on the basis of the success with which they carried out their legislative programs, the leadership of these two Presidents approaches an equality.[32]

Certainly, the founder of the Democratic party deserves especial commendation for his sagacity in devising those political methods whereby the Executive has been enabled to exert a controlling influence in the passage of legislation; for,

---

[32] Roosevelt was the first of our recent Executives to appreciate the necessity of alleviating the social and economic evils existent during the first two decades of the present century; and he is especially to be credited with having aroused the attention of both Congress and the people to the desirability of a complete reform. So numerous, however, were the problems then confronting him that, despite his laudable, though unprofitable, attempt to submit general plans of reform for every difficulty, he was able to secure the adoption of only a fraction of his recommendations. Entering office after much of the preliminary work had been accomplished, Wilson, on the other hand, could more readily devote his efforts to secure the adoption of specific statutes designed to' solve the problems which had failed of settlement during his predecessor's Administration. Their respective legislative records are summarized below:

Roosevelt: Reclamation Act, Federal Employer's Liability Act, Hepburn Act, Elkins Act, Pure Food and Meat Inspection Laws, Aldrich Act.

Wilson: Underwood Tariff Act, Panama Tolls Legislation, Federal Reserve System, Federal Land Bank, Women's Suffrage, Federal Trade Commission Act, Clayton Act, Newlands Act.

in this field of endeavor, he has not been surpassed. But, while these methods, unaltered except for a more open acknowledgment of their use, were employed with hitherto unrecorded frequency by both Roosevelt and Wilson, they discovered that the rigorous leadership necessitated by their increased legislative activity could be sustained with greater consistency by a skillful campaign of " pitiless publicity " designed to mobilize public opinion in behalf of their policies. For exploiting the power of the press, however, these Executives are to be credited, not with an entirely new discovery, but rather with an adroit manipulation of an instrumentality which attained a maturity of development during their Administrations. Their predecessors were not ignorant of the value of popular support, particularly when Congress was not receptive to their recommendations, nor did they neglect to align public sentiment in their favor; but, having in their possession neither the means for the rapid dissemination of news nor a press service of nation-wide circulation, they could mould public opinion only slowly and upon relatively few issues during a four-year period. Roosevelt and Wilson, on the other hand, had these improved facilities at their command, and to the support afforded their leadership by the utilization of the latter, both acknowledged their indebtedness.[33]

Under these altered circumstances, with these Executives both aspiring to assert a dominant influence in the enactment of a constructive program, and prompt to utilize any device which might assist them to attain that influence, one might naturally expect to discern an improvement in the composition of the President's messages to Congress. Like all forerunners of new movements, however, Roosevelt failed, perhaps through inexperience, to prepare his messages as effectively as did Wilson, and hence could not derive from them as great an advantage as did his successor. In the first place, his messages to Congress were painfully long, many of them exceeding 30,000 words in length; secondy, his recommenda-

---

[33] Autobiography, p. 385; Constitutional Government in the United States, p. 110, quoted above, p. 50.

tions per message were too numerous and not adequately specific; [34] and; finally, the importance of his proposals was frequently obscured by the injection of lengthy discourses upon the moral rectitude of the Executive's activities, or upon subjects not susceptible of legislation by the Federal Government. While it was entirely permissible for him to employ these messages for the dual purpose of attracting popular support to his policies and of acquainting Congress with his demands, nevertheless, it was inexpedient to invite too often the attention of that body to addresses which were designed primarily for popular consumption—especially when the result desired might have been obtained just as effectively by a statement issued directly from the White House to the press. Because of these defects in the construction of his messages, Congress was unable to appreciate the significance of his innumerable requests, and, partly for this reason, responded very slowly to the enactment of his measures. Nor did his messages adequately focus public attention upon one issue at a time.

By resolving to revive Washington's practice of delivering his messages in person, Wilson automatically avoided the incurrence of many of these errors. Brevity, being imperatively essential to the delivery of an oral message, deprived him of any option other than to submit his recommendations in a most compact form. In apparent recognition of this problem he successfully endeavored to compose his messages in accordance with the definite plan of limiting the content

---

[34] Advised by an admirer that his presentation of administrative measures lacked sufficient clarity to make them readily understood by Congress, Roosevelt countered with the following conventional argument: "Are you aware also," he replied, "of the extreme unwisdom of my irritating Congress by fixing the details of a bill, concerning which they are very sensitive, instead of laying down a general policy?" Bishop, I, 233.

While the validity of his statement is partially sustained by the unfavorable reception of Lincoln's detailed recommendations on Emancipation (above, p. 170), nevertheless, Wilson successfully demonstrated that the composition of the Executive's messages might be improved upon without his risking the loss of congressional support. This advancement he effected by subsequently elucidating in greater detail the recommendations outlined in his formal messages.

of each to the presentation and advocacy of one or, at best, a few of the numerous measures comprising his legislative program. If, during the interval between his previous message and the date selected for his next address to Congress, the latter had taken action looking toward the eventual adoption of the recommendations proposed in the former utterance, he would then proceed to urge upon the legislative branch the advisability of enacting an additional portion of his legislative policy. Whereas Roosevelt confused both Congress and the public by attempting to enlist its attention immediately to his entire legislative program, as expounded in a vague message or two, Wilson, by proceeding in this more methodical fashion, enabled his legislative associates to direct their undivided attention to single items of his platform, and accordingly escaped many of the delays produced by congested calendars. Wilson's method also helped him in crystallizing and mobilizing public opinion in support of his proposals.

Although this failure of Roosevelt to utilize the executive message as advantageously as did Wilson contributed in a small measure to his inability to obtain an equally notable record of legislation, the less favorable political conditions which attended his Administration doubtless afford the most convincing explanation for this difference in achievement. In entering office, in 1913, on the occasion of the third presidential victory won by the Democratic party since Lincoln's inauguration, Wilson was accompanied by a large number of political associates who had also been granted their first opportunity to become members of Congress. Of only mediocre ability,[35] inexperienced at their task, yet eager to establish a record that would invite a more frequent election of their party, these men may be said to have welcomed Wilson's assumption of leadership. Had his congressional colleagues been similarly disposed to accept his guidance, Roosevelt might not have been surpassed by Wilson in the amount of legislation procured; for though inclined to be

[35] Black, pp. 34-35; Charles R. Lingley, Since the Civil War, p. 583.

less methodical and consistent than his successor in the control of his party, he was endowed, more fortunately than Wilson, with those attributes which make for a popular political leader. But his endeavor to inject a progressive spirit into his party was undertaken at a time when there were numbered among his colleagues in office many veteran Republican Congressmen, who not only possessed confirmed opinions as to the legislative problems of the day, but were ranking members in their party organization, and hence in a position to resent the direction of a young Executive brought into power by an unexpected contingency. This group of men constituted a permanent source of opposition to his leadership, and their support, given infrequently to his recommendations, was extracted only by compromise or pressure.

That Roosevelt had premonitions of alienating the support of such men is evidenced by one of his conclusions reached early in his political life. As Governor of New York he complained: " It has always been my luck in politics, and I suppose it always will be, to offend some wing of the party— generally the machine, but sometimes the independents." [36] But, since no aggressive leader, Wilson no less than Roosevelt, has proved himself able to avoid making a host of enemies, the latter need not have construed his difficulties to be the result of some personal peculiarity of his own. The distinction, however, between the resistance encountered by Wilson and by Roosevelt was that the former's opponents, being less numerous and less influential politically, were more easily suppressed, and did not really become effective until the close of his Administration; whereas, the " Old Guard Republicans," who opposed Roosevelt from the start, though constituting only a faction in the party, were nevertheless in control of Congress, and, being too adroit to be outgeneraled consistently by their Executive, were quite successful both in delaying, and in partially defeating, his recommendations.[37]

Concerning his relations with this group, the leaders of

---

[36] Francis E. Leupp, The Man Roosevelt, p. 22.
[37] Autobiography, pp. 382-383.

whom were Senators Aldrich and Hale, and Speaker Cannon, Roosevelt later wrote:

> I made a resolute effort to get on with all three and with their followers, and I have no question that they made an equally resolute effort to get on with me. We succeeded in working together, although with increasing friction, for some years, I pushing forward and they hanging back. Gradually, however, I was forced to abandon the effort to persuade them to come my way, and then I achieved results only by appealing over the heads of the Senate and House leaders to the people, who were the masters of both of us.[38]

Both Executives having had, then, to associate with Congresses of different composition, and not being possessed of identical capacities for political leadership, the methods selected by them to effect the adoption of their respective programs quite naturally presented certain corresponding dissimilarities. It will be recalled, however, that Wilson entered office with the definite intention of leading his party after the manner of a British Prime Minister; and, in view of his characteristic tenacity of purpose, one may safely presume that whether or not conditions in 1913 had been favorable to this endeavor, he should not have altered his decision. Roosevelt, on the other hand, being a more practical politician than his successor, let his course be determined by the type of Congressmen with whom he had to deal. Where party loyalty did not suffice to gain him support, he sought through the medium of his magnetic personality to acquire the friendship of his recalcitrant political associates; and when that expedient failed he resorted to political bargaining. Frequent conferences, many of them purely fraternal in their origin, were had with congressional leaders. At these conferences Roosevelt exchanged views with the legislators, and, in turn, received from them invaluable suggestions as to legislative needs hitherto unknown to him.[39]

Not having Roosevelt's faculty for developing a leadership sustained wholly by personal attachment, Wilson manifested less inclination to engage in conference with members of Congress, but preferred to receive their opinions in writing.

---

[38] Ibid, pp. 382-383. [39] Ibid., pp. 383-384, 428.

When, at the request of Congressmen seeking a respite from his dictatorship by way of compromise, he did consent to an open consultation, the occasions were utilized by him, not for the purpose of trading suggestions as to the context of a legislative proposal, but rather to convince his associates of the extreme necessity of unified leadership, of the expediency of acknowledging their Executive as their chief, and of the danger of dissension.

This noticeable distinction in the procedures adopted by these Executives to align Congressmen in support of their recommendations was productive of a further difference, though one of degree only; namely, in the extent to which they assûmed the task of drafting their own legislative proposals in the form of bills. As has been noted, the records of previous administrations contain instances in which Cabinet officers have presented in committee rooms the completed drafts of the legislative proposals of their Chief Magistrate; but doubtless because of a fear that Congress would resent too strongly this usurpation of its duties, that practice was not frequently resorted to. The device having been employed to advantage, however, it was a foregone conclusion that Roosevelt and Wilson, who aspired to an unprecedented leadership in legislation, would not permit it to lapse into desuetude. But, while the intensive control asserted by Roosevelt rendered almost inevitable a proportionate increase in the use of this practice, he did not signally depart from the older view that a reliance upon this device was neither expedient nor necessary to procure the adoption of a program. With his capacity for developing and retaining the loyalty of large numbers of Congressmen, he apparently did not feel the need of deviating from the dependable procedure of outlining his measures in conference with his favorites, and trusting to them, under the supervision of his Cabinet officers or himself, to draft these recommendations into bills and to argue for their adoption in open session. Moreover, Roosevelt frankly admitted that several of the important measures accredited to his Administration had their origin in the minds of Congressmen by whose names these bills are commonly known. It was these men, he confessed, who first brought to his attention the demand for the legislation in question, and it was their drafts which he approved and supported.[40]

In pursuance of his experiment, which was to engraft as much of the Cabinet system as our form of government would accommodate, Wilson was less interested in following past procedure than in being permitted to assume the rôle of Prime Minister, with the latter's privilege of recommending and drafting all major legislative proposals. In fact, as a result of his disinclination for oral discussion with his legislative associates, whereby the latter might be enabled to have their own suggestions incorporated into the text of·his recommendations, or to influence a modification of his program, the importance to Congress of retaining the privilege of drafting all legislative proposals had lost its significance. Since his legislative suggestions were unusually specific and were generally accompanied by a notice that the President would accept no bill which did not contain the essential principles outlined in the suggestions, little discretion was left to Congress, once it voted to enact his measure, other than to put it into the form of a final draft. Under these conditions, it mattered little whether a favored Congressman introduced an executive recommendation in Congress, and first had it drafted within that body; or whether he carried from the White House the President's initial draft of his own proposal; or whether a Cabinet Secretary introduced the same in a congressional committee room.[41] In accordance with his plans Wilson chose to employ the two last-mentioned alternatives most frequently, and endeavored to insure the eventual

---

[40] Charles G. Washburn, Theodore Roosevelt, The Logic of His Career, p. 383; Autobiography, ch. xi.

[41] One critic of the Wilson Administration is of the opinion that, in the absence of any prior training in the task of drafting its own proposals, the Executive Department was unprepared to assume that function, and that as a result of this unwise decision on the part of Wilson, Congress was frequently delayed by the necessity of recasting the inaccurately drawn bills of his associates. Lindsay Rogers, "Presidential Dictatorship in the United States," in Quarterly Review, CCXXXI, 133.

adoption of these recommendations by the most rigid surveillance ever recorded; dispatching his Secretaries continuously both to committee rooms and to the halls adjoining the legislative chambers in an effort to curb a momentary indisposition to adopt his proposals. But, just as executive leadership was asserted more rigorously and sustained more openly during Wilson's Administration than at any other period, so was there recorded a proportionate increase in the number of protests voiced by Congressmen; and it is to be noted that their complaints reveal less a personal abhorrence of Presidential dictatorship than a fear of an impending subversion of congressional prerogative.[42]

Thus, the normal procedure, as outlined in the preceding pages, whereby the Executive acquires a participation in the function of legislation, is through the exercise of his powers of personal persuasion. By striving simultaneously to lead his party and to guide public opinion, to assume the initiative in formulating his party's program, and to instruct the electorate in the excellence of its program, and to instruct the efforts are productive, mobilizes the support capable of assuring his recommendations a hearing; and, with the confidence acquired from that source, he seeks subsequently to secure action on these proposals by convincing Congress, in the manner already described, of the desirability of their adoption. However, when this more pacific expedient proves futile as against a recalcitrant Congress, the Executive may muster into service certain aggressive devices, which, though of dubious efficacy, do frequently suffice to procure the enactment of his program.

Of these aggressive legislative weapons possessed by the Executive, perhaps the least dangerous is his threat to convene a dilatory Congress in extra session unless it accedes to his demands. Especially, if there are prospects of a warm summer, Congressmen may be readily induced to adopt his recommendations rather than to forfeit a much desired vacation. Lincoln obtained a speedy ratification of his questionable

---

[42] Black, pp. 37, 39-40; quoting Senator Works (California) and Representative Slayden (Texas).

military orders by this artifice,[43] and Roosevelt, by a similar
" ultimatum," called a halt to the Senate's delay in ratifying
the Cuban reciprocity tariff agreement.[44]

However, if the opposition of Congress cannot be readily
dispelled, the Executive may appeal over its head directly to
the people in an effort to obtain a reaffirmation of their support; and, if successful, he is enabled to back up his own
recommendation with a mandate which the legislative body
cannot ignore. In the absence of any means for the rapid
distribution of news during the earlier administrations, such
appeals could not be executed expeditiously, and hence were
attempted infrequently, generally only once, during the four-
year term of an Executive. Prominent examples of popular
appeals issued by the older Presidents were those uttered by
Jackson and Lincoln; the former, on the eve of his candidacy
for reelection in order to obtain a public approval of his conduct in the National Bank dispute; the latter, at a similar
time, through his protest [45] against the Wade-Davis Bill,
in an effort to ascertain whether the electorate would support
the executive or congressional reconstruction policy.

When Roosevelt and Wilson entered office, the power of the
press as a medium for the more rapid moulding of public
opinion had increased several fold, and it was their accurate
appreciation of the potency of this weapon which prompted
them to appeal more frequently to the electorate.[46] That
Wilson, more than any other, should repose great confidence
in the value of this expedient was to be expected, for it was
his belief that the abilty of the Executive to dominate Congress is dependent almost wholly upon his success in guiding
" opinion." [47] In signally failing to secure a favorable
response to his appeal for a Democratic election in 1918,
and by his attempt to align popular sentiment against the

[43] White, p. 212.
[44] Bishop, I, 189.
[45] Messages and Papers of the Presidents, VII, 3423-3424.
[46] See an article by J. Fred Essary, " President, Congress, and
Press Correspondents," in American Political Science Review, XXII,
902.
[47] Above, p. 51.

senatorial opponents of the Covenant, he demonstrated the limitations of his favorite method. Yet, on the other hand, his prior pronouncements, one condemning the unwholesome influence of the tariff lobby, and the other criticising those " willful " men who had defeated his armed merchantmen measure, were both effective in removing obstacles to his leadership.[48]

To Wilson the inadequate results obtained from these appeals may have been a disappointment; to others, they merely substantiated a long held conclusion that this expedient is exceedingly dangerous and is to be employed only as a last resort. Unless an Executive be willing to jeopardize his chances of securing the adoption of his remaining recommendations, it is inadvisable to risk an appeal on a single issue; for though he may be successful in his attempt, his conduct is likely to rekindle even more intensely a spirit of resentment in Congress and to confirm it in its resolve to combat his leadership. Moreover, if the public fail to honor his petition, as it did Wilson's in 1918, the President has thus by his own hand prematurely terminated his ascendancy. Unfortunately, the high degree of subserviency demanded of Congress by our recent executive leaders renders inevitable their employment of pressure methods; for no one of them is endowed with sufficient personal magnetism, or superiority of intellect, to induce capable congressional leaders to become voluntarily his mere ratifying agents. An harmonious cooperation between Executive and Legislature in which the former aspires to the rôle of an uncompromising leader is unusually tenuous; and, when congressional leaders subsequently rebel against the abridgment of their freedom of discretion, the President has no alternative other than to revert to certain threats of coercion in order to achieve the acceptance of his program.

---

[48] His appeals on minor issues, such as his letters to the Governors of States requesting them to assist in procuring the ratification of the Nineteenth Amendment, and his public announcements indirectly appealing to the constituents of a district to support or defeat the candidacy of certain Democrats running for congressional office, were similarly productive of varying results, inducing compliance in some instances and inviting opposition in others.

What has been said concerning the uncertain efficacy of an appeal to the people may also be applied to the use of the threat of a veto. Nevertheless, by voicing his threat in such manner as would persuade Congress to believe that an immediate submission to his demands will not subject it to public disapproval, the Executive has on several occasions exercised this expedient without subsequent injury. Thus, soon after Lincoln casually let it be known that he contemplated vetoing the Confiscation Bill, Congress hastened to revise that measure to meet his objections. Before that had been accomplished, however, he favored that body by signing the original bill, but attached to his signature a statement of his dissatisfaction with the measure.[49] Expressing his threat in a similarly indirect fashion, though in words highly contentious in character, Wilson also successfully terminated opposition to his Selective Draft proposal by informing Congress, through Chairman Dent, that he refused to "yield an inch of any essential parts of the programme for raising an army by conscription."[50] Roosevelt, however, took the singularly inappropriate step of issuing a general warning in his message to Congress that he would be "obliged hereafter, in accordance with the policy stated in a recent message, to veto any water power bill which does not provide" for the benefits he had suggested.[51] Uttered at a time when his relations with Congress were anything but amicable, this threat could scarcely have been a palliative, and merely incited his opponents to combat his leadership with greater zeal.

Failing, even by the use of these coercive expedients, to obtain the adoption of measures which he considers eminently desirable, the President may choose to act alone; and, at the

---

[49] Messages and Papers of the Presidents, VII, 3286; Works of Charles Sumner, VII, 183.

[50] Charles Seymour, Woodrow Wilson and the World War, p. 126.

[51] Messages and Papers of the Presidents, XV, 7347. Concerning the Tawney Amendment to the Sundry Civil Bill which reduced the President's power to employ unofficial unsalaried experts, Roosevelt announced to Congress, "If I did not believe the Tawney amendment to be unconstitutional I would veto the Sundry Civil Bill which contained it, and that if I were remaining in office I would refuse to obey it." Autobiography, p. 455.

risk of having his conduct condemned as illegal, may endeavor to procure by independent executive order those benefits which Congress has declined to authorize by legislation. To Wilson, who not only reposed great confidence in his ability to extract from the Legislature any authorization necessary to his Administration, and who desired to preserve his record free from illegality, this procedure was indefensible and he condemned it in no uncertain terms:

> There are illegitimate means by which the President may influence the action of Congress. . . . He may also overbear Congress by arbitrary acts which ignore the laws or virtually override them. He may even substitute his own orders for acts of Congress which he wants but cannot get. Such things are not only deeply immoral, but they are destructive of the fundamental understandings of constitutional government.[52]

Those Executives whose conduct renders them amenable to this criticism are perhaps Jackson and Lincoln; but Roosevelt, though his orders were issued under the circumstances described above, enjoyed the good fortune of having the Supreme Court subsequently sanction them as valid.[53]

When popular sympathy with the Executive's program begins to wane, and Congress is encouraged to contest his leadership; or, when his party support in Congress is decimated by a disastrous biennial election, neither his personal influence nor the exercise of these coercive measures is likely to be conducive to the adoption of his recommendations. Nevertheless, even under these adverse conditions the President may retain a participation in legislation, though it be only a defensive one, by preventing the enactment of measures at variance with his own policies, or the subversion of that which he has already accomplished. For this purpose he is excellently equipped with the veto, the only legislative power expressly granted to the Executive by the Constitution, and, in the utilization of this negative, he has the knowledge that

---

[52] Constitutional Government in the United States, p. 71. It will be recalled, however, that Wilson proceeded to order the arming of merchant vessels after Congress had refused to authorize this measure. Above, p. 92.

[53] Autobiography, pp. 393, 440, 443. United States v. Grimaud, 220 U. S. 506.

only in the extreme absence of party support in Congress can it be overridden.

While authorities now classify the veto as a legislative power and set forth no criticism against its use for the objects enumerated above,[54] it is certain that the framers of the Constitution contemplated no such development when they allotted this privilege to the Executive. In conferring this power upon him, the majority of the Convention probably conceived that they did not thereby accord him any participation in the legislative process but merely a check upon the exercise of this function by that branch of the government in which it was vested. For, according to the principle of the separation of power as then held, there could be only one department endowed with the legislative power, and that body was Congress. Exercised as they anticipated, the veto power would be employed by the President only to thwart any attempt on the part of Congress to legislate itself into a position of superiority over the other two branches of government and, perhaps as Hamilton and others suggested,[55] to prevent the enactment of laws so manifestly inimicable to the national welfare that the President would be guilty of dereliction of duty in signing them. In either contingency, the Executive was expected to give every presumption in favor of the validity and expediency of a decision of Congress, and in no instance was he to permit his personal opinions as to expediency, or his ambition, to control his exercise of his negative.

That contemporary opinion did entertain the hope that the veto would be employed in this manner is substantiated by the following statements of Jefferson:

The negative of the President is the shield provided by the Constitution against the invasions by the Legislature: (1) of the right of the Executive, (2) of the Judiciary, (3) of the States and State

---

[54] Howard Lee McBain, The Living Constitution, p. 170; Taft, p. 14.

[55] Federalist (Hamilton), p. 547; Ford, pp. 178-179. Those who foresaw that the vesting of the President with a veto was equivalent to a grant of legislative power to that officer, and who therefore opposed the arrangement on the ground that it was inconsistent with a true separation of powers, were in the minority. See Jonathan Elliott, Debates on the Adoption of the Federal Constitution, II, 472.

Legislatures. . . . If ,the pro and con for and against a bill hang so even as to balance the President's judgment; a just respect for the wisdom of the Legislature would naturally decide the balance in favor of their opinion. It is chiefly for cases when they are clearly misled by error, ambition, or interest, that the Constitution has placed a check in the negative of the President.[56]

Having consistently evinced a desire to regulate his conduct in accordance with the opinions of the Constituent Assembly, of which he had been a member, Washington could be expected not to deviate from the principles enumerated by Jefferson concerning the proper exercise of the veto power. That he was in agreement with his Cabinet adviser on this issue is confirmed, in fact, by the following correspondence:

You do me no more than justice when you suppose, that, from motives of respect to the legislature (and I might add from my interpretation of the constitution), I give my signature to many bills, with which my judgment is at variance. . . . From the nature of the constitution I must approve all parts of a bill, or reject it in toto. To do the latter can only be justified upon the clear and obvious ground of propriety; and I never had such confidence in my own faculty of judging, as to be ever tenacious of the opinions I may have imbibed in doubtful cases.[57]

So faithfully did Washington adhere to the context of that letter that only two vetoes [58] were interposed by him during his eight years in office, and these were registered so late in his Administration that prophesies were made that the power would lapse into desuetude. The first congressional measure to receive a veto, like many others during the early years of the Government's existence, was exercised on purely legal grounds; that is, because the provisions of the vetoed measure contravened a stipulation of the Constitution. His objections being well taken, few protests were heard against his decision; indeed, many expressed jubilation at witnessing the veto finally exercised.[59] In the second instance, however, Washington assumed the responsibility of interposing his own judgment for that of Congress and vetoed a bill to reduce

---

[56] Writings (Ford Ed), V, 289; VII, 560.
[57] Sparks, X, 371-372.
[58] Messages and Papers of the Presidents, I, 116, 203; Mason, p. 142.
[59] Jefferson's Writings, IX, 115. (1792)

the army on the grounds that it was poorly drawn and detrimental to national safety.

While it is denied that Washington ever acted from personal motives, or that he was furthering his own policy in rejecting this military measure,[60] nevertheless, in view of his previous attempts to have Congress provide for an adequate national defense, this second veto, on its face, would seem to have been issued to prevent the undoing of what had already been accomplished. Moreover, one student of military legislation has intimated that, had the Cabinet officers succeeding to Hamilton's leadership in Congress not relaxed their close supervision of the drafting of this measure, its objectionable provisions would have been abandoned, and the necessity for this veto obviated.[61]

Nothwithstanding this early intimation that the Executive would employ the veto to defeat legislation which, in his opinion, was clearly inexpedient, it was not until Jackson's election that there was presented any flagrant instance in which the President sought by the exercise of this power to force upon Congress the adoption of his own and no other policy. In vetoing the National Bank Bill of 1832 Jackson dared to negative as both unconstitutional and inexpedient a measure which not only had been sanctioned as lawful by the Supreme Court, but had been enacted with approval by two preceding administrations. Under these circumstances, certainly, a strong presumption existed in favor of both the utility of the measure and the wisdom of Congress in reenacting it.

To justify a veto which was motivated by his personal objections to a National Bank, Jackson was obliged to advance a rather astounding argument, but the intrepidity of this Executive was equal to the occasion. In refutation of the significance of the prior sanction accorded this policy by the Supreme Court, he reiterated the view enunciated by Jefferson that the President and Congress, as coordinate, independent branches of the Government, are not bound by the

---

[60] Mason, pp. 108, 127, 132.   [61] White, p. 118.

decisions of the Judiciary but are at liberty to determine for themselves the constitutionality of every question presented to them:

> The opinion of the judges has no more authority over Congress than the opinion of Congress has over the judges, and on that point the President is independent of both. The authority of the Supreme Court must not, therefore, be permitted to control the Congress or the Executive when acting in their legislative capacities, but to have only such influence as the force of their reasoning may deserve.[62]

Moreover, he argued, even had that tribunal been correct in holding the prior Bank Acts to be valid, it would be within the province of the Legislature and Executive, acting independently, to pass upon the expediency of continuing that financial institution. Since the operation of that Bank was wholly an executive problem, and involved the imposition of an onerous duty upon his Department, he deplored the fact that the President had not been consulted in the enactment of this measure. He declared that, had his counsel been requested, he was confident that he could have submitted a bill which would have avoided this dispute. Not having been granted this opportunity, however, he could participate in the legislative process only through the one remaining alternative constitutionally allotted tc him, the veto.

Aside from his views as to the applicability of judicial decisions to executive conduct, there are contained in his veto message, however, certain assertions which, though considered astounding in his day, are now received with equanimity. Probably the first of the earlier Presidents to advance the now prevalent conception that the veto is a legislative power, Jackson further argued that, since this privilege had been granted him unaccompanied by any directions as to the manner of its exercise, he was obligated to employ that weapon as his best judgment dictated, giving to the pronouncements of Congress a persuasive but not a controlling influence in the formation of his decisions. There was nothing undemocratic in his advocacy of this belief, he contended, because the Executive, as the only national representative of the elec-

---

[62] Messages and Papers of the Presidents, III, 1145.

torate, was equally, if not more competent than the Legislature to discern their wishes on any major issue.[63] In substantiation of this conviction he pointed to the fact that he had made his opposition to the National Bank a party issue in the campaign of 1832, and that he had been vindicated in this position by being reelected a second time.[64] Thus, in achieving this victory over Congress, Jackson was guided by an interpretation of the Presidency which is almost identical with that later popularized by Roosevelt and Wilson.

Of the remaining Executives under discussion, only the vetoes of Roosevelt and Wilson require any comment. Lincoln negatived but three isolated measures during his term in office, and these because they were improperly drawn, or duplicated existing statutes, or were manifestly undesirable.[65] Roosevelt and Wilson, on the other hand, together rejected a total of fifty-six bills; but it should be noted that the greater number of these were pocket vetoes for which no subsequent

[63] Ibid., p. 1139.

[64] The executive and legislative branches continued their dispute even after the latter's attempt to continue the National Bank had been decisively defeated. Having steadfastly refused to acknowledge that its constitutional position had been erroneous, the Senate accordingly went on record as opposing those acts of the President which in its estimation were not only without authorization but subversive of the Constitution. Charges of such gravity might readily have merited the institution of impeachment proceedings, and when issued summarily against a Chief Magistrate without extending him an opportunity to repudiate them, certainly justified Jackson in his endeavor to have a defense of his reputation also included in the Senate records. His long Protest, which was largely a restatement of his interpretation of executive power as hitherto presented in his Veto Message, has been described by one authority as not legally a veto but as having many of the effects of one. Mason, pp. 33, 117.
While no legislative protest of a succeeding Executive is as significant as Jackson's, nevertheless one may include in this classification Lincoln's Proclamation against the Wade-Davis Bill, and Roosevelt's message condemning the Tawney Amendment to the Sundry Civil Appropriation Bill. Mason adds, however, that a "protest is constitutional" only "wherever a veto is constitutional," and for this reason Jackson's Protest would not have the validity which attaches to those issued by his successors; for his was directed, not against a joint resolution of Congress, but a single resolution of the Senate. The writer is not in agreement with this distinction.

[65] Messages and Papers of the Presidents, VI, 3288, 3289, 3471-3472.

messages of explanation were tendered to Congress. While this increase in the number of vetoes is in part attributable to the proportionate increase in the amount of federal legislation (much of which is private legislation, such as pension bills rejected by Cleveland), it may also be explained by the aggressive leadership of these two Executives. Since their very assumption of legislative direction involved an intent to superimpose their will upon Congress, these men evinced not the slightest reticence in being guided by their own opinion as against the collective decision of the members of that body; and hence they rejected not only measures opposed to their program but also lesser bills, the contents of which failed to meet their personal approval. Wilson, in effect, declared [66] that if a bill in his opinion appeared inexpedient, he would accord no presumption in favor of the decision of Congress unless the latter could prove that its proposal bore a mandate from the people expressed at the polls.

Another issue reopened by Wilson's conduct in disposing of certain appropriation bills was the advisability of conferring an item veto upon the President. Prior to the adoption of the Budget Reform, partisans in Congress, by attaching their favored proposals as " riders " to financial measures, sought to secure the adoption of their own measures, the theory being that the President would hesitate to endanger the financial needs of the Government by rejecting an entire appropriation bill merely to secure the eradication from it of an item. While remonstrating against this practice, preceding Executives generally accepted the responsibilty which had been thrust upon them in this manner, and signed

---

[66] Ibid., XVII, 8044. " If the people of this country have made up their minds to limit the number of immigrants by arbitrary tests and so reverse the policy of all the generations of Americans that have gone before them, it is their right to do so. I am their servant and have no license to stand in their way. But I do not believe that they have. I respectfully submit that no one can quote their mandate to that effect. Has any political party ever avowed a policy of restriction in this fundamental matter, gone to the country on it, and been commissioned to control its legislation. . . . I doubt it. Let the platforms of the parties speak out upon this policy and the people pronounce their wish. The matter is too fundamental to be settled otherwise."

these appropriation measures, accompanying their signatures, however, with a plea for the subsequent repeal of these objectionable " riders." An analogous presidential predicament is portrayed by the following statement contained in Roosevelt's message:

I signed [the bill] in hesitation as I believe that because of its form it can and will achieve small results and it is highly undesirable for it to become a law as it appears insincere. But I signed it because I believe the defects can be remedied by the legislation I now ask for; and unless it is gotten I understand that this resolution must be mainly and entirely inoperative.[67]

Dissenting from this view adopted by his predecessors, that the President would be held accountable for the financial difficulties of the Administration if he negatived an appropriation bill when too little time remained to permit its reenactment, Wilson dared to veto three important financial measures,[68] one of them only three days prior to the termination of the congressional session. He was apparently of the conviction that if the President, by reason of indefensible " riders " to appropriation bills, felt himself duty bound to veto them even at such inopportune times, the Legislature itself would become responsible for the ensuing financial embarrassment of the Government. But he foresaw that the very realization of this dilemma would invariably impel Congress to revise such legislation before the date of adjournment. Nevertheless, while this analysis of the situation was correct, Congress in each instance amending the vetoed bills to meet his approval, the risk involved in such procedure would not seem to merit its repetition.

In Wilson's Administration, the seriously disputed question as to the power of the President to sign bills after adjournment was brought closer to settlement than it had been for the past half-century. In resolving to sign eight bills [69] after the disbanding of Congress in the early summer of 1920, he had to

[67] Ibid., XV, 7287. The bill was a joint resolution instructing the Interstate Commerce Commission to make examinations into the subject of alleged discriminations by railroads.

[68] Ibid., XVIII, 8757, 8758, 8845; Black, pp. 112-114.

[69] Cited by Lindsay Rogers, " The Power of the President to Sign Bills after Congress has Adjourned," in Yale Law Journal, XXX, 2n.

support him in this decision only the encouraging opinion of his Attorney-General,[70] and a single precedent established by Lincoln in 1863. In that year Lincoln signed a war measure after the adjournment of Congress, and the validity of his conduct was never officially overruled. Although the House Judiciary Committee [71] submitted a report declaring the measure thus signed to be of no effect, Congress as a body never subscribed to that view, but, in fact, recognized the act as existing law by referring to it as such in passing an additional act to amend its provisions.[72] Consequently, when the force of the original measure was questioned in a case before the Court of Claims in 1883, that tribunal did not consider it necessary to decide whether the Executive is competent to sign bills after adjournment, but sustained the act on the basis of its unquestioned acceptance by the political departments.[73]

There having been no repetition of this precedent until Wilson's Administration, the federal courts were presented with no case in which the power of the President to sign after adjournment was directly attacked. However, in consistently deciding for the President in cases disputing the validity of bills signed during recess, the Supreme Court has uttered dicta which may be regarded as favorable to the former proposition.[74] Nevertheless, prior to the reopening of this question by Wilson, the opinion of the majority, to which no less an authority than Ex-President Taft adhered, seems to have been that the power of the Executive extends only to the signing of bills during recess. Those who support the view taken by Lincoln and Wilson have in turn endeavored to prove, not only that the recognition of such a power in the President is highly beneficial, but that the Constitution neither expressly nor impliedly forbids the signature of measures at such times. While they cannot cite any primary and

---

[70] 32 Op. Atty. Gen. 225.
[71] Cited by Lindsay Rogers, p. 1.
[72] 12 Stat. L. 820; 13 Stat. L. 375; Mason, p. 115.
[73] 18 Ct. Cl. 700.
[74] La Abra Silver Mining Co. v. United States, 175 U. S. 423, 542.

mandatory decision in support of their contention, they can submit cases in which appellate courts in the several States [75] have interpreted provisions in their respective state constitutions, which are identical with clause two, section seven, of Article I of the federal Constitution, as granting to the Governor a power to sign after adjournment. Finally, under the circumstances, this second precedent recorded by Wilson can only serve as an impetus to the position taken by this latter group; for, until the federal courts receive an opportunity to pass upon the validity of the acts signed by that Executive, this issue will remain mooted.

A survey of the legislative activities of the Presidents discussed amply confirms the validity of the complaint that that element of the separation of powers theory which excludes the Executive from the legislative process has been largely nullified in practice. But, while no protest can be entered against the practicability of applying this theory to the extra-this situation, one may impugn the merit of their objection. The fact that even the Executives officiating at the inception of the new Government deemed it beneficial to participate in the enactment of legislation (albeit they acknowledged that their conduct was inconsistent with a true observance of a separation of powers) raises a fairly conclusive presumption against the practicability of applying this theory to the extra-legal relations of the departments. If its retention would have been conducive to a less advantageous condition than is now existent, there seems to be little reason for lamenting its abandonment, or in regarding its nullification as iniquitous. Moreover, by the acceptance of the interpretation advanced by Wilson, that this aspect of the theory of the separation of powers has never been a part of the Constitution, but represents only the speculations of its framers popularized contemporaneously with its adoption, the problem of inconsistency is evaded altogether, and the theory may thereupon be viewed as an historical prophecy which never matured.

---

[75] See James B. Barnett, "The Executive Control of the Legislature," in American Law Review, XLI, 215.

Even conceding the contention of the complainants that this theory has really been incorporated within the Constitution, the writer is unable to entertain their fears that its elimination, by a political development not susceptive to legal restraint, threatens to alter our form of government by destroying the independent position constitutionally allotted to Congress. Obviously, the growth in the political influence of the President is incapable, legally, of affecting the formal position of Congress; for that body can be protected against attempts to usurp the supreme legislative powers expressly conferred upon it by the Constitution. However, in the diminution of its discretion to determine the manner in which that authority may be employed, the Legislature admittedly has suffered adversely from the advent of a rigorous executive leadership. Yet, has the assumption of this privilege by the President been so consistent and so complete as to reduce to a mere formality the apparently undisturbed right of Congress to exercise its legislative powers in its own name? To prove the contrary the writer wishes to emphasize two significant facts: first, that the emergence of presidential leaders has been sporadic, reasonably long periods having separated their terms in office;[76] and second, that of the Executives discussed, not one has successfully sustained his leadership for an interval longer than six years. Thus, not only does Congress not appear to be confronted constantly with the menace of being converted into a ratifying agent for the President; but on the very occasions when this threat has been most vigorously pursued, Congress has before long again demonstrated its ability to repulse the aggression of the Executive.

In the light of this absence of continuity to executive leadership, the writer questions whether his legislative activity has or will become sufficiently permanent to be entitled to official recognition. Therefore, to guarantee at this stage a formal legislative leadership to our future Chief Magistrates

[76] William B. Munro, The Invisible Government, ch. iii.

by any of the reforms [77] recently advocated, would, on the basis of past records, be to accord them a power to which a majority would never voluntarily aspire, and which only a select few, even by their own efforts, are but momentarily able to acquire. The error committed by those who would reduce legislative leadership to a permanent, formal basis is that they are apt to let their conclusions be controlled too completely by the accomplishments of the Presidential Dictator presiding at the date of writing.

---

[77] Concerning the more significant reforms suggested, involving the adoption either in whole or in part of the British Cabinet system, see McBain, pp. 145-149; Taft, pp. 31-33; Francis E. Leupp, "The Cabinet in Congress," in Atlantic Monthly, CXX, 769-778.

CHAPTER VI

CONCLUSION

Having endeavored, whenever possible, to state his conclusions at the termination of each of the preceding chapters, the writer considers it profitable to devote the final pages of his study to a prophecy or forecast as to the future appearance of leaders in the Chief Magistracy. If this prediction is to have a reasonably plausible substantiation, however, it will first become necessary to evaluate the importance of the factors discernible in the past history of the Presidency, and to undertake a survey of the tendencies observed in existing conditions.

Were the writer, for the purpose of avoiding possible criticism of his selection, to add the names of Jackson and Cleveland to the list of our foremost Executives, it would nevertheless remain manifest to an observer that a considerable interval has separated the election of these men to the Presidency. To a very limited extent the law of averages may account for this sharp variation in executive ability; but there are other reasons, founded upon considerations other than mere fortuity, that have been particularly responsible for this cycle, or intermittent rise and decline, in the quality of leadership exhibited by the incumbents of the Chief Magistracy. In the first place, as the writer has previously indicated,[1] the American people have been seemingly averse to the successive election of dominant Executives. Whether or not the latter may have fostered this popular indisposition by their failure to remain consistently in accord with public sentiment, it is none the less a fact that the electorate has been unwilling to sustain our prominent Executives for periods in excess of six years, and has invariably sought relaxation from the driving force of their leadership by subsequently electing one or more mediocrities to that office.

While the writer is of the opinion that this tendency of the

---

[1] Ch. v.

people has been the producing cause of this cycle, a second, though less frequently applicable explanation of its existence may be that the retiring Executive may have so completely solved the problems of his day that his immediate successors are presented with no difficulties in the correction of which they may demonstrate their abilities. Thus, it has been suggested that the inactivity of Harding and Coolidge may be attributed directly to the fact that Wilson had secured the enactment of all the remedial legislation demanded by existing conditions.[2]

To predict, therefore, that the ensuing years will be attended by the continued appearance of eminently successful Executives would be to engage in a worthless speculation. The anticipation of so radical an improvement in the calibre of the men chosen for the Presidency can be predicated only upon the immediate, but exceedingly improbable, cessation of this century-old cycle. Moreover, there being discernible in present conditions nothing to warrant the presumption that no further repetition of this variation will occur, the most that may be reasonably expected is that the interval likely to separate the election of our dominant leaders will be appreciably reduced.

Although the writer is unable to justify even this moderate degree of optimism by any convincing proof, he is induced, nevertheless, to believe that the increasing rapidity in our industrial life will occasion a corresponding acceleration in the accumulation of the economic problems invariably resulting therefrom, and that the urgency of procuring a mitigation of these ever-recurring evils will provide the incentive for the more frequent election of prominent Chief Magistrates. As Mr. Wilson himself pointed out, moreover, the position of a world power assumed by the United States in 1896 will make it impossible in the future to hide the President as a mere domestic officer; and it may fairly be predicted that his leadership in foreign policy will become increasingly important.

---

[2] Kent, p. 381.

Certainly the election of two excellent leaders, Roosevelt and Wilson, with only a single term separating their Administrations—an event not reproduced since the inaugurations of Washington and Jefferson—would seem to mark an auspicious beginning for the present century; and if their predecessor, Cleveland, be also included, the writer is enabled to submit additional supporting evidence to the effect that but similar intervals of four years have interrupted the appearance of three superior Executives during the period of 1884-1920. That the duration of these intervals will hereafter not exceed four years is hardly to be expected; but estimated in accordance with these recent occurrences, the elapse of nine years since the expiration of Wilson's Administration would seem to render the present moment propitious to the advent of a leader. In a large measure, therefore, the future verification of the writer's prophecy will depend upon the success to be achieved by our present Chief Magistrate, Mr. Hoover.

Despite this uncertainty as to the date of his arrival, it may be stated with almost complete assurance that the next predominant Executive, meriting classification with the five Chief Magistrates previously mentioned, will exercise the equivalent, if not a greater, amount of power than that assumed by his predecessors. Nothing is more evident in the history of the Presidency than the steady accumulation of power by that office. Although there have been periods of almost a quarter century in which the Chief Magistracy has been filled by mediocrities, the only significance to be accorded to these occurrences is that during such intervals the resources of that office were temporarily not employed; for, let one occupant of the Presidency exercise an additional power, and the advantage thus acquired is never abandoned. His immediate successors may hesitate, or may not have the courage, to employ this asset; but neither their silence nor their inactivity is to be interpreted as evidence of its final surrender.

Nor ought the prospect of a further expansion of executive power to be viewed with apprehension. The generally accepted view now being that the Constitution is a practical document, capable of application under all circumstances, it would seem to follow that, if an additional power sought to be employed by a future Executive can be reasonably and fairly deduced from the grant of authority contained in that instrument, there can be no well founded legal objection to its exercise. Moreover, in the event that a subsequent Chief Magistrate should be tempted, by reason of an erroneous conception of his responsibilities, or of the limits of his authority, to pursue a course of action subversive of the established rights of the citizen, the courts will doubtless be competent to afford the latter adequate relief. As protection against the alleged dangers envisaged as likely to accrue from further extensions of a President's political influence, no remedy as instantly effective as a judicial restraint exists; but there is every assurance that the pressure of public opinion, coupled with the power of the people to thwart an undemocratic President by adverse biennial elections, and to oust him completely at the expiration of his four-year term, will prove amply sufficient to minimize his opportunity for grave wrong-doing. Though there have been instances in which politically powerful Executives have disregarded the wishes of the electorate in their advocacy of measures deemed by them essential to the national welfare, these manifestations of " benevolent despotism " have been too infrequent and too innocuous to justify any anxiety over their possible recurrence.[3] Accordingly, until more conclusive proof can be assembled to support the forecast that the evils attending the future expansion of the Presidency will outweigh the benefits resulting therefrom, the writer is of the opinion that the further development of executive leadership ought to merit a favorable reception.

---

[3] For the contrary view, see Edward Stanwood, A History of the Presidency (1916), pp. 327-337.

BIBLIOGRAPHY

OFFICIAL SOURCES

American State Papers, Foreign Affairs, vols. 1, 2, 3.
American State Papers, Indian Affairs, vols. 1, 2.
Annals of the Congress of the United States (1789-1909).
Congressional Globe.
Congressional Record.
Diplomatic Correspondence (1861-1865).
Federal Cases.
Foreign Relations (1901-1909).
Messages and Papers of the Presidents (18 vols.).
Opinions of the Attorney-General of the United States.
Statutes at Large of the United States.
Supreme Court Reports.
The Power of the President to Remove Federal Officers, 69th Cong., 2d sess., S. Doc. No. 174.
United States House of Representatives, Reports of Committees, and Executive Documents.
United States Senate, Reports of Committees, and Executive Documents.

UNOFFICIAL COLLECTIONS AND WRITINGS

Diary of Gideon Welles (3 vols.).
Elliott, J., Debates on the Adoption of the Federal Constitution (5 vols.).
Federalist, The.
Journal of William Maclay.
New York Times (1914-1920).
New York Times Current History Magazine (1914-1920).
Selected Literary and Political Papers of Woodrow Wilson (3 vols.).

SECONDARY AND PRIVATE SOURCES

Beck, J. M., The Political Philosophy of George Washington, 76th Cong., 2d sess., H. Doc. No. 611.
Berdahl, C., The War Powers of the Executive.
Birkhimer, W. E., Military Government and Martial Law.
Bishop, J. B., Theodore Roosevelt and His Time (2 vols.).
Black, H. C., The Relation of Excutive Power to Legislation.
Borchard, E. M., Diplomatic Protection of Citizens Abroad.
Bowers, C., Jefferson and Hamilton.
Brooks, R. C., Political Parties and Electoral Problems.
Chambrun, A. de, The Executive Power in the United States.
Cleveland, G., Presidential Problems.
Corwin, E. S., The President's Control of Foreign Relations.
————, The President's Power of Removal.
Crandall, S. B., Treaties, Their Making and Enforcement.
Creel, G., The War, The World, and Wilson.
Dennett, T., Theodore Roosevelt and the Russo-Japanese War.
Dodd, W. F., Woodrow Wilson and His Work.
Dunning, W. A., Essays on the Civil War and Reconstruction.
Fairlie, J. A., The National Administration of the United States.

201

Fish, C. R., American Diplomacy.
Ford, H. J., The Rise and Growth of American Politics.
———, Washington and His Colleagues.
Ford, P. L., The Writings of Thomas Jefferson (12 vols.).
Foster, J. W., The Practice of Diplomacy.
———, A Century of American Diplomacy.
Garner, J. W., American Foreign Policies.
Gibbs, G., The Administrations of Washington and Adams (2 vols.).
Glenn, G., The Army and the Law.
Goodnow, F. J., The Principles of the Administrative Law of the
    United States.
Harlow, R. V., Legislative Methods in the Period Before 1825.
Harrison, B., This Country of Ours.
Hart, J., The Ordinance Making Powers of the President.
———, Tenure of Office under the Constitution.
Hayden, R., The Senate and Treaties (1789-1817).
Hinsdale, M., A History of the President's Cabinet.
Hughes, C. E., War Powers under the Constitution, 65th Cong., 1st
    sess., S. Doc. No. 105.
Kent, F. R., The Democratic Party: A History.
Latané, J. H., American Foreign Policy.
Leupp, F. E., The Man Roosevelt.
Lingley, C. R., Since the Civil War.
Marshall, J., Life of George Washington (vol. 5.).
Mason, H. C., The Veto Power.
Mathews, J. M., The Conduct of American Foreign Relations.
McBain, C., The Living Constitution.
McKinley, A. E., Collected Materials for the Study of the War.
McMaster, J. B., History of the People of the United States (8 vols.).
McPherson, E., The Political History of the United States of
    America during the War of the Rebellion.
Moore, J. B., Digest of International Law (8 vols.).
Nicolay, J. G. and Hay J., Abraham Lincoln; A History (10 vols.).
———, Complete Works of Abraham Lincoln (2 vols.).
Ogg, F. A., National Progress.
Randall, J. G., Constitutional Problems under Lincoln.
Raymond, H., State Papers of Abraham Lincoln.
Redfield, W. C., With Congress and Cabinet.
Rhodes, J. F., History of the United States from the Compromise of
    1850 (8 vols.).
———, The McKinley and Roosevelt Administrations.
Rogers, L., The American Senate.
Roosevelt, T., Autobiography.
Root, E., The Military and Colonial Policy of the United States.
Salmon, L. M., A History of the Appointing Power of the President.
Semour, C., Woodrow Wilson and the World War.
Sparks, J., The Life and Writings of George Washington (12 vols.).
———, The Life of George Washington (abridged. 2 vols.).
Stanwood, E., A History of the Presidency (2 vols.).
Sumner, C., The Works of Charles Sumner (15 vols.).
Taft, W. H., Our Chief Magistrate and His Powers.
Thomas, D. Y., A History of Military Government in Newly Acquired
    Territory of the United States.
Tucker, H. St. G., Limitations on the Treaty Making Power.
Tumulty, J. P., Woodrow Wilson as I Knew Him.

Upton, E., The Military Policy of the United States.
Washburn, C. G., Theodore Roosevelt, The Logic of His Career.
Washington, H. A., The Writings of Thomas Jefferson (9 vols.).
Wheaton, H., Elements of International Law.
White, H., Executive Influence in Determining Military Policy in the United States.
Whiting, W., War Powers under the Constitution of the United States.
Wigmore, J. H., A Source Book of Military Law and War Time Legislation.
Willoughby, W. F., Government Organization in War Time and After.
Willoughby, W. W., The American Constitutional System.
———, On the Constitution of the United States (3 vols.).
Wilson, F. T., Federal Aid in Domestic Disturbances, 57th Cong., 2d sess., S. Doc. No. 209.
Wilson, W., Congressional Government.
———, Constitutional Government in the United States.
Wriston, H. M., Executive Agents in the Foreign Relations of the United States.

SPECIAL ARTICLES

Alger, G. W., "Executive Aggression," in Atlantic Monthly, CII, 577-584.
Baldwin, S., "The Share of the President of the United States in A Declaration of War," in American Journal of International Law, XII, 1-14.
Ballantine, H. W., "Constitutional Limitations on the War Power," in California Law Review, VI, 134-141.
Barnett, J. B., "Executive Control of the Legislature," in American Law Review, XLI, 215-238.
Barrett, J. F., "International Agreements Without the Advice and Consent of the Senate," in Yale Law Journal, XV, 63-82.
Berdahl, C., "The Power of Recognition," in American Journal of International Law, XIV, 519-539.
Carpenter, A. H., "Military Government of Southern Territory," in Annual Report, American Historical Association, 1900, vol. I, 465-498.
Caroll, T. F., "Freedom of Speech and of the Press during the Civil War," in Virginia Law Review, IX, 516-551.
Corwin, E. S., "The Power of Congress to Declare Peace," in Michigan Law Review, XVIII, 669-675.
Dunning, W. A., "The War Power of the President," in the New Republic XI, 76-79.
———, "Disloyalty in Two Wars," in American Historical Review, XXIV, 625-630.
———, "The Constitution of the United States in the Civil War," in Political Science Quarterly, I, 163-198.
Fairlie, J. A., "Administrative Legislation," in Michigan Law Review, XVIII, 181-200.
———, "The President's Cabinet," in American Political Science Review, VII, 28-44.
———, "American War Measures," in Journal of Comparative Legislation and International Law, XVIII, 90-100.
Fish, C. R., "Removal of Officials by Presidents of the United States," in Annual Report, American Historical Association, 1899, vol. 1, 65-86.

Fisher, S. G., "The Suspension of the Habeas Corpus during the War of the Rebellion," in Political Science Quarterly, III, 454-488.

Ford, H. J., "The Growth of Dictatorship," in Atlantic Monthly, CXXI, 623-640.

Garner, J. W., "Le Pouvoir Exécutif en temps de guerre aux Etats-Unis," Revue du Droit Public et de la Science Politique, XXXV, 5-62.

———, "Executive Participation in Legislation as a Means of Increasing Legislative Efficiency," in Proceedings, American Political Science Association, X, 176-190.

Hyde, C. C., "Agreements of the United States Other than Treaties," in Green Bag, XVII, 279-288.

Leupp, F. E., "The Cabinet in Congress," in Atlantic Monthly, CXX, 769-778.

Lieber, G. N., "Executive Regulations," in American Law Review, XXXI, 876-890.

Mason, H. C., "Congressional Demands upon the Executive for Information," in Papers of the American Historical Association, V, 367-375.

Moore, J. B., "Treaties and Executive Agreements," in Political Science Quarterly, XX, 385-420.

O'Donnell, T. J., "Military Censorship and Freedom of the Press," in Virginia Law Review, V, 178-189.

Orth, S. P., "Presidential Leadership," in Yale Review, X, 449-466.

Parton, J., "The Cabinet of George Washington," in Atlantic Monthly, XXXI, 29-44.

Paxson, F. L., "The American War Government, 1917-1918," in American Historical Review, XXVI, 54-76.

Penfield, W. L., "Recognition of a New State—Is It an Executive Function?" in American Law Review, XXXII, 390-408.

Pierson, W. W., "The Committee on the Conduct of the Civil War," in American Historical Review, XXIII, 550-576.

Powell, T. R., "The President's Veto of the Budget Bill," in National Municipal Review, IX, 538-545.

Randall, J. G., "The Newspaper Problem in its Bearing upon Military Secrecy during the Civil War," in American Historical Review, XXIII, 303-323.

Rogers, L., "Presidential Dictatorship in the United States," in Quarterly Review, CCXXXI, 127-148.

———, "President Wilson's Theory of His Office," in Forum, LI, 174-186.

———, "The Power of the President to Sign Bills After Congress has adjourned," in Yale Law Journal, XXX, 1-22.

Thorpe, F. N., "Can the President Appoint Paramount Diplomatic Agents Without the Consent of the Senate?" in American Law Register (N. S.), XXXIII, 257-264.

Willoughby, W. F., "The Correlation of the Organization of Congrees with the Executive," Proceedings, American Political Science Associations, X, 155-167.

Wilson, W., "Responsible Government under the Constitution," in Atlantic Monthly, LVII, 542-553.

Woolsey, T. S., "The Beginnings of War," Proceedings, American Political Science Association, I, 54-58.

Young, J. T., "The Relation of the Executive to the Legislative Power," Proceedings, American Political Science Association, I, 47-55.

INDEX

Budget and Accounting Act, 158.

Cleveland, G., relations with Senate in appointments, 126 n.; opposes Tenure of Office Act, 136 n.; suppresses Chicago Railway Strike, 155-157.

Congress, inability to oppose President's control of foreign relations, 56; participation of, in recognition of foreign governments, 64-65; right to be consulted in negotiation of treaties, 72-73; war powers of, 118-119.

Constitution, threatened alteration of, 160-162.

Cycle, of executive leadership, 196-197.

Emancipation Proclamation, legal aspects of, 104-106.

Habeas Corpus, enforcement of suspension of, under Lincoln, 110-112; judicial criticism of Lincoln's suspension of, 112.

Hamilton, A., defends Washington's neutrality proclamation, 58; legislative leader for Washington, 163-164; opinion of, on use of veto power, 185.

Henfield, case of Gideon, 60 n.

Jackson, A., recess appointments of, 132; establishes power of direction, 139-141; removes Bank Deposits, 139-141; appeals to electorate, 181; use of veto power by, 187-189; opposes principle of judicial review, 188; compared to Roosevelt and Wilson, 188-189; opinion of, on veto power, 189; "Protest" of, 189 n.

Jefferson, T., wide knowledge of government, 20; exponent of many theories, 20; abandons preinaugural theories after election, 20; inconsistently ob-

serves separation of powers theory, 21; refuses to obey decrees of Supreme Court, 21; abuses pardoning power, 22; compared to Jackson and Lincoln, 22 n.; compared to Roosevelt, 23; purchases Louisiana, 23; advocated doctrine of necessity; 24; observes third term tradition, 25; originally favors seven year term, 25-26; desirous of popular support, 27; opinion of, on utility of parties, 28; favors party government, 28; Cabinet relations of, 28-30; alters his theories pertaining to Cabinet, 28-30; opinion of, on President's power to proclaim neutrality, 59; believes Executive spokesman for Nation, 62; favors recognition of France, 62 n.; establishes new mode of recognizing foreign governments, 63; favors close association with Senate in treaty-making, 69-70; negotiates Louisiana Purchase, 71; opinion of, on power of House to deal with financial treaties, 74-75; procedure observed by, in ratifying treaty, 75; endangers national safety, 82; strictly construes his war powers, 89-91, 94; defends frontier against Spaniards, 90-91; defends vessels againt Pirates, 94; refuses to influence Congress to declare war, 96-97; conduct of, in " Leopard-Chesapeake " affair, 96-97; opinion of, as to application of Constitution to acquired territory, 107 n.; geographically distributes appointments, 125 n.; relations with Senate in appointment-making, 126 n.; political appointments of, 127-129; acknowledges " senatorial courtesy," 128 n.; opposes spoils system, 129; recess appointments of, 131; exercises

205

VITA

Norman J. Small was born in Baltimore, Maryland, on August 4, 1907, and received his education in the schools of that city. Graduated from Baltimore City College in 1924, he entered The Johns Hopkins University in the fall of that year, and received the degree of Bachelor of Arts in 1927. He then entered upon a course of graduate study in the Department of Political Science of the same institution, and was graduated with the degree of Doctor of Philosophy in June, 1930. In 1928, in conjunction with his graduate studies, he entered the law school of the University of Maryland, and received the degree of Bachelor of Laws in May, 1932. Since 1928, he has been a reading assistant in the Department of Political Science of The Johns Hopkins University.